THE LAW OF
SEWERS AND DRAINS

EIGHTH EDITION

J. F. Garner
Emeritus Professor of Law,
University of Nottingham

and

S. H. Bailey
Professor of Public Law,
University of Nottingham

Shaw & Sons

Published by
Shaw & Sons Limited
Shaway House
21 Bourne Park
Bourne Road
Crayford
Kent DA1 4BZ

© Shaw & Sons Limited 1995

First Edition	*Published*	June 1950
	Reprinted	March 1954
Second Edition	*Published*	March 1960
Third Edition	*Published*	November 1962
	Reprinted	November 1965
Fourth Edition	*Published*	January 1969
	Reprinted	November 1971
Fifth Edition	*Published*	January 1975
	Reprinted	September 1976
Sixth Edition	*Published*	March 1981
Seventh Edition	*Published*	June 1991
Eighth Edition	*Published*	November 1995

ISBN 0 7219 0583 8

A CIP catalogue record for this book is available from the
British Library

Printed in Great Britain by
Biddles Limited, Guildford

THE LAW OF SEWERS AND DRAINS

"The truth is that the whole of our sanitary legislation is in a state which I hardly like to characterise in the language that naturally suggests itself; and the attempt to extract from the various details of the legislation a set of harmonious principles, always underlying the specific provisions, is, I am afraid, futile" — *the late Mr. Justice Wills, in 1896.*

CONTENTS

Chapter 6 – HIGHWAY DRAINS

Chapter 7 – SEWAGE DISPOSAL AND SEWAGE DISPOSAL WORKS

Chapter 8 – THE DISCHARGE OF SEWAGE EFFLUENTS

Contents

PREFACE TO THE EIGHTH EDITION

Since the last edition, the most important changes in the law have been the consolidation of the water legislation in 1991, amendments to that legislation contained in the Competition and Service (Utilities) Act 1992 and the implementation of the Urban Waste Water Treatment Directive by regulations made in 1994. Implementation of the Urban Waste Water Treatment Directive in particular will impose significant new standards on sewerage undertakers.

The arrangements for the regulation of water and sewerage undertakers originally found in the Water Act 1989 have now been in operation for a number of years and the strengths and weaknesses of those arrangements are now beginning to emerge, particularly with the major Periodic Review of charges that took effect on 1st April 1995. As a result of of the Environment Act 1995, the National Rivers Authority will be replaced by the new Environment Agency from 1st April 1996 and this has been anticipated in the text. There has also been some case law, particularly in the context of the pollution offences found in the Water Resources Act 1991. All these and other changes have been noted in this edition and the law is stated as at 1st August 1995.

The present edition has been prepared by Professor Stephen Bailey of the University of Nottingham, the editor of *Cross on Local Government Law*, in co-operation with Professor Garner, who is very grateful for the work he has done.

Nottingham　　　　　　　　　　　　　　　　　　　S.H.B
　　　　　　　　　　　　　　　　　　　　　　　　　J.F.G.

PREFACE TO THE FIRST EDITION

It is the purpose of this work to endeavour to bring some degree of order into chaos, and to attempt to achieve what was described by Mr. Justice Wills, over 50 years ago,[1] as "futile", namely to extract from our sanitary legislation a set of harmonious principles. The writer is not rash enough to suggest that such principles have in fact been extracted in the pages that follow, but if this book results in illuminating to any extent what is one of the darkest patches of our statute law, it is considered that the main object of the book will have been achieved. In endeavouring to attain this objective, the author has been greatly assisted by that indispensable friend, "Lumley's Public Health". Unfortunately the assistance of the Legislature, who had the opportunity of abolishing such oddities as "single private drains" in 1936, has not been so extensive. The law relating to future sewers and drains was considerably simplified by the Public Health Act, 1936, but the status of pre-1937 sewers and drains was left to be determined in accordance with the earlier, unsatisfactory, legislation.

The law relating to sewers and drains is commonly regarded as referring to the relevant provisions of the Public Health Acts, and it is so understood in the present work. For this reason therefore, incidental discussion only is included on the allied subject of land drainage, but some comment has been included on the topic of the prevention of river pollution.

The law relating to the Metropolis, being of very specialised nature, is not here dealt with, nor is there any discussion of the law of Scotland or of Northern Ireland.

References are included throughout to the copyright forms of

---

[1]   *See* quotation on the title-page of the present work, taken from Wills J.'s judgment in *Bradford v. Eastbourne Corporation* [1896] 2 Q.B. 205.

Shaw and Sons Ltd. Specimen forms will gladly be supplied on request.

The law is stated in this book as it was on 1st June 1950.

J.F.G.

Bognor Regis

LIST OF ABBREVIATIONS

(except where the contrary appears)

The Secretary of State	*means* the Secretary of State for the Environment and, in Wales, the Secretary of State for Wales, and their predecessors in title (see *post*, p.13).
The 1875 Act	*means* the Public Health Act 1875.
The 1936 Act	*means* the Public Health Act 1936.
The 1961 Act	*means* the Public Health Act 1961.
The 1973 Act	*means* the Water Act 1973.
The 1974 Act	*means* the Control of Pollution Act 1974.
The 1984 Act	*means* the Building Act 1984.
The 1989 Act	*means* the Water Act 1989.
The 1990 Act	*means* the Environmental Protection Act 1990.
The 1991 Act	*means* the Water Industry Act 1991.
The 1992 Act	*means* the Competition and Service Utilities Act 1992.

TABLE OF STATUTES

Table of statutes

TABLE OF STATUTORY INSTRUMENTS

TABLE OF CASES

A

B

E

F

G

M

N

O

P

Y

Chapter 1

INTRODUCTORY

BACKGROUND

The law of sewers and drains has been a neglected area. This is perhaps understandable for, as noted by the House of Lords Select Committee on the European Communities in its report in 1991 on Municipal Waste Water Treatment,

> "Sewerage, more than any other form of waste, lends itself to an 'out of sight, out of mind' attitude. Most of us would rather forget that it exists, let alone discuss what to do with it, and we are able to do so since the means of collecting and treating sewage are buried under roads, or shut away on the edges of towns."[1]

However, as the Committee also affirmed,

> "The efficient control of sewage effluent has always been an index of the state of any civilised society, necessary for aesthetic and health reasons, and as a primary tool in the management of water systems."[2]

A number of factors have combined to give the subject greater prominence. These include the significant growth in domestic concern for environmental matters, graphically illustrated in the present context by objections to the presence of untreated sewage at bathing beaches; increased political and public interest in the provision of water and sewerage services arising from privatisation and from significant increases in the levels of charges; and the impact of European environmental law, most importantly the Bathing Waters Directive of 1976 and the Urban Waste Water Treatment Directive of 1991.[3]

---

[1]   10th Report, 1990-91 H.L. 50-I, p.7.
[2]   *Ibid.*
[3]   Dir. 76/160/EEC and 91/271/EEC.

1

Historically, the prime concern lying behind the provision of sewerage systems has been the protection and promotion of public health. The key developments took place in the second half of the nineteenth century when the establishment of such systems was identified as a high priority by municipal sanitary authorities, under the influence of the Local Government Board, and significant developments in engineering enabled this to be done without (as many feared) posing additional threats to public health.[4] London's sewer system was begun in 1858 and finished in 1865 and there were significant advances in many towns between then and the end of the century.[5] By the 1880s, the major cities had built new sewage treatment plants.[6]

The position in the 1990s is that 96 per cent of the U.K.'s population is connected to the sewerage system (the highest percentage in the EU) and 83 per cent of sewage is treated, including almost all that disposed to inland waters (comparable with the then F.R.G., Denmark and the Netherlands).[7]

The contribution that the sewerage system makes to the preservation of public health is now taken for granted. Concern instead has focused on the impact of the operation of the system on the environment, and on the need for significant attention to the aging infrastructure, which together give rise to a need for very substantial investment.

DEFINITION OF SEWERS AND DRAINS

The definition of the terms "sewer" and "drain" must seem a necessary preliminary to satisfactory discussion of the law which governs them. Upon examination, however, the matter presents some difficulty in view of the absence of comprehensive

---

[4]   See A.S. Wohl, *Endangered Lives: Public Health in Victorian Britain* (1983), Chap. 4, "The Valleys of the Shadow of Death".

[5]   *Ibid.,* pp.107-108.

[6]   *Ibid.,* p.110.

[7]   DoE Memorandum to the House of Lords Select Committee on the European Communities (Report on *Municipal Waste Water Treatment* (1990-91 H.L. 50), Vol. II, p.3).

formal definition. An associated, and vitally important, question is the legal status of pipes and conduits recognised as "sewers" – in particular as between public and private ownership.

(a) Common law

At common law the terms "sewers" and "drains" had no specialised meaning[8] and were used in a non-technical sense to signify a conduit or channel for the carrying off of surface water, sewage or faecal matter. A "sewer" was understood to mean, in general, a large drain or a public drain.

(b) Statute

Such precise definition of these terms as is available is derived not from common law but originally from 19th century sanitary legislation. The earliest major English legislation in this area, the Public Health Act 1848, used the word "drain" to signify a passage for the outflow of sewage from a single building, the word "sewer" meaning any system of drainage which was not a "drain" so defined. Refinements of definition were added by the Public Health Act 1875. These earlier definitions are not now operative but retain some modern relevance in so far as reference to them may be necessary to establish the present status of particular conduits.[9] The current statutory definition is given by section 219(1) of the Water Industry Act 1991, which provides that

> "'drain' means (subject to subsection (2) below) a drain used for the drainage of one building or of any buildings or yards appurtenant to buildings within the same curtilage."

The term "sewer" is, unfortunately, not defined precisely, but

---

[8] In Tudor times the "Commissioners of Sewers" were established by statute to regulate land drainage, especially in the Fens. Here "sewers" were used to signify land drains rather than the modern conduits for sewage. In *Callis on Sewers* (1647), it was said (at p.57) that "a sewer is a fresh water trench compassed in on both sides with a bank, and is a small current or little river".

[9] See Chapter 2.

section 219(1) does state that the term

> "'sewer' includes (without prejudice to subsection (2) below) all sewers and drains (not being drains within the meaning given by this subsection[10]) which are used for the drainage of buildings and yards appurtenant to buildings."

Section 219(2)(a) provides that

> "references to a pipe, including references to a main, a drain or a sewer, shall include references to a tunnel or conduit which serves or is to serve as the pipe in question and to any accessories for the pipe."[11]

Section 219(1) also defines the term "public sewer":

> "'public sewer' means a sewer for the time being vested in a sewerage undertaker[12] in its capacity as such, whether vested in that undertaker by virtue of a scheme under Schedule 2 to this Act or under section 179 above or otherwise;[13] and 'private sewer' shall be construed accordingly."

The distinction in detail between "public" and "private" sewers is of very considerable importance in this branch of the law and is considered in Chapter 2, *post*.

It is therefore a basic principle that both sewers and drains, as understood in the Public Health Acts and later legislation, up to and including the Water Industry Act 1991, should be designed (or used) to drain buildings and constructed objects such as roads, as distinct from land itself. In the application and

---

[10] A connection leading from a public sewer to the curtilage of a single dwelling (sometimes described as a "lateral") is therefore a drain and not a public sewer, even if it was laid by the local authority prior to the coming into force of the Water Act 1973. See *post*, p.53.

[11] These definitions are essentially the same as those found in s.343 of the Public Health Act 1936, which is still in force for the remaining purposes of that Act.

[12] i.e. a company so appointed under the Water Industry Act 1991, s.6.

[13] As to the vesting process, see Chapter 2, *post*.

clarification of these definitions judicial interpretation has been of some importance. The key issue is what is the "essential character" of the channel or conduit in question.[14] This is a question of fact.[15] A number of points emerge from the decisions.

First, the channel of a sewer need not necessarily be an artificial construction.[16] In general, however, a natural stream which was not brought within the definition of "sewer" by the 19th century sanitary legislation would generally not be capable in law now of becoming "a sewer". In *George Legge and Son v Wenlock Corporation*[17] Lord Maugham remarked that,

> "generally speaking, the beds and banks of natural rivers and streams are not sewers within the term as used in the Act [of 1875].... To prevent misconception I will add that no doubt there are circumstances in which the bed and banks of ... a natural stream might, prior to the Act of 1875, have become substantially nothing but a channel for sewage."[18]

It seems clear, in any event, that following section 17 of the 1875 Act and section 3 of the Rivers Pollution Prevention Act 1876 no natural streams could after 1876 have become sewers through the discharge of sewage into them. The discharge of raw sewage into natural watercourses would clearly be a serious breach of pollution control.[19]

Secondly, although it will normally be the case, it does not seem actually to be necessary that a "sewer" should carry sewage or foul matter. In *Ferrand v Hallas Land and Building Company*,[20]

---

14   *Per* Oliver L.J. in *British Railways Board v Tonbridge and Malling District Council* (1981) 79 L.G.R. 565, 575.

15   *Falconar v Corporation of South Shields* (1895) 11 T.L.R. 223, *per* Lord Halsbury.

16   *Falconar v Corporation of South Shields, supra.*

17   [1938] A.C. 204.

18   *Ibid.,* p.219. The *Falconar* case was distinguished on the ground that in that case the legality of the discharge of the sewage into the stream was not in question.

19   See in particular the Water Resources Act 1991, ss.85-104, *post*, pp.148-157.

20   [1893] 2 Q.B. 135.

A.L. Smith L.J. said *obiter*[21]

> "It will be noticed that a sewer need not necessarily convey sewage matter in order to constitute it as a sewer. It would be none the less a sewer within the Act of 1875 if it conveyed only rain or surface water. The draining off of rain or surface water, collected from different premises by different feeders into one main drain, would constitute that main drain a 'sewer' within the meaning of the Act."

Similarly, a pipe has been held to be a "drain" where it only carried off rain water from the roof of a house.[22]

Thirdly, a natural watercourse does not become a "sewer" simply by being piped or culverted. Thus, in *Shepherd v Croft*,[23] a natural underground watercourse was held not to have become a "sewer" by virtue of being piped by the owner of land through which it flowed. Similarly, in *British Railways Board v Tonbridge and Malling District Council*,[24] three natural watercourses had in the 19th century been diverted into a culvert in which the flow passed under a railway embankment. As a result of subsequent residential development upstream the flow of water had markedly increased, albeit through run off from the buildings rather than with foul water. The British Railways Board, as successor to the original railway company, claimed that the culvert had become a sewer and was therefore the responsibility of the (then) water authority for the area. The Court of Appeal held that the disturbance of the natural flow by the embankment and the consequent direction into the culvert did not make the watercourses into "sewers." *Per* Oliver L.J.:[25]

---

21 At p.144.
22 *Holland v Lazarus* (1897) 66 L.J.Q.B. 285, approved by the Court of Appeal in *Silles v Fulham Borough Council* [1903] 1 K.B. 829 (but note the comments of Channell J. in *Heaver v Fulham Borough Council* [1904] 2 K.B. 383, 393-394).
23 [1911] 1 Ch. 521.
24 (1981) 79 L.G.R. 565, C.A.
25 At p.575. His Lordship referred to and adopted the approach of Lord Maugham in the *Wenlock* case, *supra*.

"On the facts as found . . . it is . . . clear that there has been no alteration in the essential character of the three watercourses and the culvert since 1840 and the mere fact that the surface drainage of the built-up area has been collected and diverted into them through a number of outfalls so as to produce a significant increase in the volume of water carried off, cannot possibly constitute them, either individually or collectively, sewers or a sewer within the ordinary meaning of that term."

The Public Health Act 1936 distinguished between "sewers" and watercourses, e.g. in section 30, and one channel could clearly not be both. Consequently the culvert in the instant case was not a "sewer".

Fourthly, a distinct question may arise whether a sewer or drain is "used for drainage of buildings and yards appurtenant to buildings". At first instance in *British Railways Board v Tonbridge and Malling District Council*,[26] Judge Finlay, sitting as a judge of the Chancery Division, held that the culvert was a sewer, but not "used for the drainage of buildings". The test for whether a sewer was so used was one of function.[27] His conclusions were summarised as follows by Oliver L.J. in the Court of Appeal:[28]

"[the test] . . . was not whether the channel concerned in fact carried water or soil deriving from buildings, but what was the function for which the channel was constructed and existed. Here the function of the watercourses and the culvert was to carry away all the surface water from the catchment area as a whole regardless of its origin, and the fact that a part of the flow derived from the outfalls of surface drains associated with buildings and yards did not mean that the culvert was being 'used for the drainage of buildings etc.'"

In view of the decision of the Court of Appeal on the "logically

---

[26] *Supra.*
[27] *Blackdown Properties Ltd. v Ministry of Housing and Local Government* [1967] Ch. 115.
[28] At p.571.

anterior point"[29] of whether the channel constituted a "sewer"[30] this issue did not strictly arise for consideration by the Court of Appeal. Nevertheless, Oliver L.J. noted that the court rejected the submission of counsel for the Board that Judge Finlay had misunderstood or failed to apply the decision of the Court of Appeal in *Hutton v Esher Urban District Council*:[31]

"That case merely established . . . that a purpose-built sewer for the drainage of buildings does not cease to be a statutory sewer simply because, in addition to drainage from buildings, it carried water also from other sources. [Counsel] seeks to derive from that case the precisely converse proposition that a natural stream does become a sewer if, in addition to other waters, it carries water derived from the drainage of buildings. That is a simple *non sequitur* and we mention it only to emphasise that the decision at which we have arrived ought not to be taken as necessarily involving a dissent from the ground upon which the judge decided the case. On the view which we take of [the] first point, it becomes unnecessary to express any opinion as to that ground."[32]

It is clear that a sewer designed for the drainage of buildings does not cease to be a sewer for the purposes of the relevant legislation merely because, without reconstruction, it is not used at all.[33]

Fifthly, it has been said that a "sewer" must cause effluent to flow from one place to another and thus it

"must be in some form a line of flow by which sewage or water of some kind, such as would be conveyed by a sewer,

---

29 *Per* Oliver L.J. at p.571.
30 *Supra.*
31 [1974] Ch. 167.
32 *Per* Oliver L.J. at p.575.
33 *Per* Stamp J. in *Blackdown Properties Ltd. v Ministry of Housing and Local Government* [1967] Ch. 115 at p.123. Similarly, where a sewer is constructed for the purposes of draining a number of premises, it is a "sewer" notwithstanding that it is so far serving one building: *J. Pullan & Sons Ltd. v Leeds City Council* (1990) 7 Constr. L.J. 222, C.A. (accordingly, the authority was bound to declare the sewer vested in itself by virtue of an agreement with the developer).

should be taken from a point to a point and then discharged. It must have a *terminus a quo* and a *terminus ad quem*."[34]

It would therefore seem that a line of pipes terminating in a cesspool would not be a "sewer",[35] nor would a line of pipes with no proper outfall[36] or a conduit linking two cesspools.[37] A cesspool or storage tank is not a part of the sewer, unless it is really a mere catchpit from which an outflow pipe runs to a sewer or other proper outfall.[38] It seems, therefore, that a drain serving any number of buildings, whether or not within the same curtilage, which discharges into a cesspool or cesspit (not being a mere catchpit), is not capable of being a public sewer.[39]

Finally, it should be noted that for the purposes of the provisions of the 1936 Act covering "sanitation and buildings"[40] it was stated that,

"any reference . . . to a drain or to a sewer shall be construed as including a reference to any manholes, ventilating shafts, pumps or other accessories belonging to that drain or sewer . . ."[41]

The Water Industry Act 1991 provides that references to a drain

---

[34] *Per* Buckley L.J. in *Pakenham v Ticehurst R.D.C.* (1903) 67 J.P. 448.
[35] *Meader v West Cowes Local Board* [1892] 3 Ch. 18 and *Butt v Snow* (1903) 67 J.P. 454. It is doubtful, however, whether the principle herein applied relates to a case where a drainage system terminating in private drainage "works" has been approved by the local authority as being initially satisfactory. Thus, a conduit ending in tanks from which the effluent was raised by mechanical means and then discharged, all of which had been constructed by a private individual and approved by the local authority, was held to be a sewer in *Attorney-General v Peacock* [1926] Ch. 241.
[36] *Per* Maugham J. (*obiter*) in *Clark v Epsom R.D.C.* [1929] 1 Ch. 287, 294. However, the mere fact that a particular outfall is not satisfactory or may cause a nuisance does not prevent the line of pipes draining into it from being a "sewer" in law and from having vested in a local authority under the 1875 Act: *ibid.*
[37] *Button v Tottenham U.D.C.* (1898) 62 J.P. 423.
[38] *Pakenham v Ticehurst R.D.C.* (1903) 67 J.P. 448.
[39] As to which see Chapter 2.
[40] Sections 14-90.
[41] Public Health Act 1936, s.90(4); see also s.126, Building Act 1984.

or sewer include references to any "accessories for the pipe".[42]

On the other hand, a pumping main or trunk sewer is none the less a sewer, and in most circumstances will also clearly be a public sewer.

Subject to the above observations, the terms "sewer" and "drain" should be interpreted in accordance with normal practice in the light of their ordinary or "dictionary" meaning.[43] For example, gutters and fall pipes are probably not "drains" in law and are almost certainly not "sewers", even if they serve more than one set of premises. Such a usage would be highly artificial and would seem an unjustified imposition upon the statutory language.

Thus, on the following diagram, the surface water drain taking rain from houses 1, 2 and 3 to the soakaway at point X on A's property is not sewer but a drain, whereas the foul drain leading to the stream at point Y, is a sewer *from* point B.

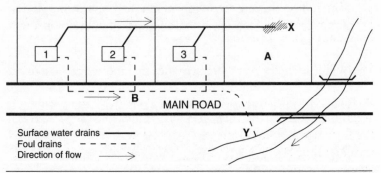

Surface water drains ————
Foul drains   – – – – – –
Direction of flow ———→

---

42 Water Industry Act 1991, s.219(2). "Accessories" in relation to a "water main, sewer or other pipe", includes any manholes, ventilating shafts, inspection chambers, settling tanks, wash-out pipes, pumps, ferrules or stopcocks for the main, sewer or other pipe, or any machinery or other apparatus which is designed or adapted for use in connection with the use or maintenance of the main, sewer or other pipe or of another accessory for it", but not any telecommunication apparatus unless it is in the close vicinity of the pipe or accessory and intended to be used only in connection with its use or maintenance: s.219(1).

43 In the absence of judicial authority, dictionaries may be consulted in the interpretation of statutes, see Asquith J. in *Kerr v Kennedy* [1942] 1 K.B. 409. Also *Maxwell on the Interpretation of Statutes,* 12th edn., p.55; *Craies on Statute Law*, 7th edn., pp.160-161; Bennion, *Statutory Interpretation*, 2nd edn., 1992, pp.849-850.

THE MODERN BACKGROUND TO SEWERAGE SERVICES

Until recent times, controls over the provision and maintenance of sewers and drains in England and Wales were almost exclusively the concern of local authorities, subject only to the minimum of supervision by central government. The law was principally to be found in the Public Health Acts 1848 and 1875, replaced by the Public Health Act 1936. Minor alterations followed, mainly in the Public Health Act 1961. The Water Act 1973 transferred many of the functions of local authorities in this field to ten water authorities and the public sewers of local authorities were thereby vested in those water authorities.[44] More recently, the Water Act 1989 made revolutionary changes in law and administration. This Act was in turn consolidated with other legislation into the Water Industry Act 1991, the Water Resources Act 1991, the Land Drainage Act 1991 and the Water Consolidation (Consequential Provisions) Act 1991.[45] Further amendments were effected by the Competition and Service (Utilities) Act 1992.

Designed to privatise the water industry, the 1989 Act transferred the water and sewerage assets of the water authorities to limited liability companies operating under the regime of the Companies Acts. Individually these successor companies, one for each of the former water authorities, were originally wholly owned by the central government. Then, as from 1st November 1989, the shares in holding companies for the successor companies were offered for sale on the private market. Each successor company

---

[44] The transfer was effected by the Local Authorities (England) (Property etc.) Order 1973 (S.I. 1973 No. 1861), articles 7, 8, and the Local Authorities (Wales) (Property etc.) Order 1973 (S.I. 1973 No. 1863), articles 7, 8. The whole of the local authorities' interests were transferred: see *Sheffield City Council v Yorkshire Water Services* [1991] 1 W.L.R. 58, where Sir Nicolas Browne-Wilkinson V-C rejected the argument that the transferor councils retained an interest in the proceeds of any sale of the assets for profit following privatisation.

[45] See the Law Commission's *Report on the Consolidation of the Legislation relating to Water* (Law Com. No. 198, Cm. 1483, 1991).

was formally appointed by the Secretary of State to operate as a water undertaker and sewerage undertaker for the area of the former water authority, except in cases where before 1989 there was a statutory water company; in those instances the statutory company remained and the successor company was appointed only as a sewerage undertaker.

The Water Act 1989 repealed several key sections of the 1936 Act, in particular section 20 (definition of public sewer) and section 24 (maintenance of certain lengths of public sewer). The remaining provisions of the 1936 Act in relation to sewers were consolidated in the Water Industry Act 1991. Important changes have also been introduced by the Urban Waste Water Treatment (England and Wales) Regulations 1994[46] which implement the Urban Waste Water Treatment Directive.[47] These regulations affect both the collection and treatment of waste water.

The functions of local authorities relating to controls over the drainage of individual premises were left virtually unaltered by the 1989 and 1991 Acts, but the provisions relating to the prevention of river pollution contained in Part II of the Control of Pollution Act 1974 were replaced by new and more stringent controls in the 1989 Act, now found in Part III of the Water Resources Act 1991.[48]

THE AUTHORITIES

The Act of 1989 introduced a plethora of authorities concerned with sewerage services at different levels. This makes a striking change from the straightforward situation before 1973 when the only authorities concerned were the local authorities, subject in very minor respects to the general supervision of the Secretary of State, or formerly the Ministry of Health. These authorities will now be outlined *seriatim*.

---

[46] S.I. 1994 No. 2841.
[47] Dir. 91/271/EEC.
[48] ss.82-104. See *post*, pp.148-157.

(a) The Secretary of State

The Secretary of State[49] has very considerable duties under the Water Industry Act 1991. In the first place it is the duty of the Secretary of State to ensure that a sewerage undertaker is appointed for all areas of England and Wales.[50] Appointments may be made by the Secretary of State or, with the consent of or under a general authorisation given by the Secretary of State, by the Director General of Water Services.[51] The Secretary of State (or Director) may by notice terminate an appointment or vary the area to which it relates. However, in the case of termination or a decrease in area this may only take effect if a replacement undertaker is appointed to ensure continuity. Furthermore, an appointment or variation replacing a company as undertaker may not be made unless the company consents, or the appointment or variation relates only to part of that area none of the premises in which is served by the company,[52] or is made in circumstances set out in the conditions of appointment.[53] The last of these points is dealt with in Condition O of the standard Conditions of Appointment,[54] which states that for the purposes of what is now section 7(1)(c) of the 1991 Act,

> "the only circumstances in which an appointment or variation to which section [7] applies may be made in relation to the area for which the Appointee holds the Appointment as . . . sewerage undertaker . . . are where the Secretary of State has

---

[49] i.e. the Secretary of State for the Environment (for England) or the Secretary of State for Wales (for Wales).

[50] Water Industry Act 1991, s.7(1).

[51] *Ibid.,* s.6. The initial appointments were made by the Secretary of State.

[52] Premises in part of an area are served by an undertaker if they are "drained by means of a relevant sewer" (1991 Act, s.36(3), as amended by the 1992 Act, s.40(5)). A "relevant sewer" is a public sewer, a sewer in relation to which a declaration of vesting has not taken effect or a drain or sewer in respect of which the undertaker has entered an agreement under s.102: s.36(4).

[53] *Ibid.,* s.7(1)-(4)(a), (b), (c). As to the procedure for appointments and variations, see ss.8-10 and Sch. 2, ss.8 and 9, as amended by the Competition and Service (Utilities) Act 1992, s.40(3), (4) and Sch. 2, para. 17.

[54] *Instrument of Appointment of the Water and Sewerage Undertakers* (H.M.S.O., 1989), p.99.

given the Appointee at least 10 years' notice, expiring not earlier than 25 years after the transfer date, to terminate the relevant Appointment in relation to the whole of its area and the said period of notice has expired."

This is the only route by which an appointment may be terminated apart from the making of a special administration order by the High Court.[55] In addition, an "inset appointment" of another company may be made for parts of an undertaker's area where each of the premises in those parts are or are likely to be supplied with not less than 250 megalitres of water in any period of 12 months and the person who is the customer in relation to each of the premises consents in writing.[56]

Once appointed, each sewerage undertaker must comply with a series of duties prescribed by the 1991 Act and regulations, including a duty to provide adequate sewerage arrangements for its area.[57] These duties are enforceable by the Secretary of State or the Director General of Water Services by means of enforcement orders and special administration orders. These are considered below.[58] The Secretary of State may prescribe standards of performance in relation to sewerage services.[59]

The Secretary of State must make a "merger reference" to the Monopolies and Mergers Commission in respect of any actual or prospective merger of two or more "water enterprises", i.e. an enterprise carried on by a water or sewerage undertaker.[60] Mergers are excluded where the assets of the target company do not exceed £30M.[61] In determining whether any matter operates, or may be expected to operate, against the public interest, the

---

[55] See *post*, pp.20-21.
[56] 1991 Act, s.7(4)(bb), (5) and (6), inserted by the Competition and Service (Utilities) Act 1992, s.40.
[57] *Ibid.*, s.94.
[58] pp.17-21.
[59] See *post*, pp.26-28.
[60] 1991 Act, s.32.
[61] *Ibid.*, s.33, and see the Water Enterprises (Merger) Modification Regulations 1994 (S.I. 1994 No.73).

Monopolies Commission is to have regard to the desirability of giving effect to the principle that the Director's ability in carrying out his functions to make comparisons between different water enterprises shall not be prejudiced; and shall have regard to the desirability of achieving any other purpose only so far as it is satisfied that this does not conflict with that principle, or is of substantially greater significance in relation to the public interest than that principle.[62]

The Secretary of State has numerous other detailed powers under the Act, which will be referred to in their appropriate context.

Section 2 of the Water Industry Act 1991 imposes a number of duties on the Secretary of State as to when and how he should exercise and perform his powers and duties relating to the regulation of sewerage undertakers. Accordingly, this should be done in the manner that he considers is best calculated

(a) to secure that the functions of a sewerage undertaker are properly carried out as respects every area of England and Wales;

(b) without prejudice to the generality of (a), to secure that companies appointed as undertakers are able (in particular by securing reasonable returns on their capital) to finance the proper carrying out of their functions as undertakers;

(c) to ensure that all customers and potential customers[63] are protected as respects the fixing and recovery of charges and, in particular, that the interests of customers in rural areas are so protected and that there is no undue discrimination in the fixing of charges;

(d) to ensure that the interests of customers and potential

---

[62] 1991 Act, ss.34 and 35, s.34 as amended by the Competition and Service (Utilities) Act 1992, s.39.

[63] The Secretary of State must take particular account of the interests of pensioners and the disabled: s.2(4).

customers are also protected as respects other terms of service and the quality of services; as respects the non-core activities of a holding company or any activities of a person appearing to the Secretary of State to be connected with that company (in particular by ensuring that transactions are carried out at arm's length and that the company in its capacity as an undertaker keeps separate accounts); and as respects benefits arising from the disposal of land;

(e) to promote economy and efficiency in the carrying out of an undertaker's function; and

(f) to facilitate effective competition with respect to such matters as he considers appropriate between persons holding or seeking appointment as undertakers.

In this list, (a) and (b) are the overriding considerations.[64] The Secretary of State is also subject to general environmental and recreational duties;[65] these are, however, subject to the overriding general duties set out in section 2.

(b) The Director General of Water Services

(i) Appointment and general functions
The Director is an independent officer, originally appointed by the Secretary of State under section 5 of the Water Act 1989, and continued in office by section 1 of the Water Industry Act 1991. He was appointed initially for a five year period but may be re-appointed.[66] His primary duties under the 1991 Act are "to ensure that the water and sewerage companies carry out and finance their functions"; subject to that, he must "protect customers, promote economy and efficiency and facilitate competition".[67]

---

[64] 1991 Act, s.2(1)-(3), as amended by the Competition and Service (Utilities) Act 1992, s.50.

[65] 1991 Act, ss.3-5, discussed in relation to sewerage undertakers, *post*, pp.84-87.

[66] The appointment of the first Director, Ian Byatt, has been extended to six years.

[67] *OFWAT Annual Report 1993* (1993-94 H.C. 416), p.4.

(ii) Modification of conditions of appointment

The Director has power to modify the conditions of appointment of a sewerage undertaker, with the undertaker's consent, although such action cannot relieve the undertaker of its statutory duties and may in certain cases be blocked by the Secretary of State.[68] Where consent cannot be obtained to a proposed modification, he has power to make a "modification reference" to the Monopolies and Mergers Commission requiring it to investigate and report on whether specified matters relating to the carrying on of sewerage functions "operate, or may be expected to operate, against the public interest", and whether this could be remedied or prevented by modification of the Conditions of Appointment.[69] Copies of a report thereafter received must be sent by the Director to the Company concerned and to the Secretary of State and must also be published in such a fashion as may be appropriate to draw it to the attention of "persons likely to be affected by it."[70] Whether this category of persons is limited to the shareholders in the company or extends to the general inhabitants of the sewerage area concerned is unclear. In any event such a report may in due course again lead to a modification of the conditions of appointment of the sewerage undertaker.[71]

(iii) Enforcement orders

The Director or the Secretary of State[72] must make a provisional or final enforcement order under section 18 of the 1991 Act where he is satisfied that an undertaker is contravening[73] any of

---

68   Water Industry Act 1991, s.13.
69   *Ibid.*, s.14.
70   *Ibid.*, s.15.
71   *Ibid.*, s.16. And see also s.17 (modification orders by the Secretary of State following a monopoly reference under s.56(1) of the Fair Trading Act 1973, a merger reference under s.73 of the 1973 Act or a competition reference under s.101 of the Competition Act 1980).
72   Depending on who is the "enforcement authority". The Director is the enforcement authority in relation to the Conditions of Appointment; otherwise it is as specified in the particular statutory provision or provision of subordinate legislation that makes a requirement enforceable under s.18.
73   Or has contravened and is likely to do so again.

the Conditions of Appointment, or any other statutory or other requirement made so enforceable by an enactment or subordinate legislation. A number of provisions of the 1991 Act are expressly made enforceable under section 18.[74] An order must make "such provisions as is requisite for the purpose of securing compliance with that condition or requirement". The order must be a "final" order unless it appears to the Director (or Secretary of State) that it is requisite that a "provisional" order be made instead of taking steps towards a final order. In determining whether it is so requisite, he must have regard in particular to the extent to which any person is likely to sustain loss or damage in consequence of any contravention before a final order may be made. Where a provisional order is made, the Director (or Secretary of State) must confirm it, with or without modifications, if he is satisfied as set out above. If it is not confirmed, it lapses at the end of such period (not exceeding three months) as is determined by or under the order. An enforcement order must require the undertaker, according to the circumstances, to do or not to do specified things, takes effect at such time, being the earliest practicable time as is determined by or under the order, and may be revoked at any time by the enforcement authority who made it.

There are exceptions to the duty to make or confirm an order, if the Director (or Secretary of State) is satisfied

(a) that the contraventions or apprehended contraventions are trivial in nature;[75]

(b) that the undertaker has given and is complying with an undertaking to take all such steps as appear to him for the time being to be appropriate to secure or facilitate

---

[74]   Including the general duties under s.94 of the 1991 Act and the Urban Waste Water Treatment (England and Wales) Regulations 1994 (S.I. 1994 No. 2841). See *post*, pp.62-63, 109-112.

[75]   In Standing Committee D, the Minister, Michael Howard M.P., stated that "It is very unlikely that circumstances giving rise to a danger to health could be properly regarded as trivial" (col. 923, 9th February 1989).

compliance;[76]

(c) that the general duties under Part I of the Act preclude the making or confirmation of the order.[77]

If he is so satisfied he must serve a notice on the undertaker, and publish it.[78]

The procedure for making an order is set out in section 20. The Director (or Secretary of State) must generally give prior notice by publication and by serving a copy on the undertaker, and consider any representations or objections that are duly made.[79] The order itself must similarly be published and served. The undertaker has 42 days from service of the order to challenge its validity in the High Court on the ground that it is *ultra vires* section 18 or the requirements of section 20 have not been complied with. Otherwise, its validity may not be questioned in any legal proceedings whatsoever.[80]

Breach of an enforcement order may give rise to an action for damages,[81] and the enforcement authority may seek an injunction or other appropriate relief to secure compliance.[82]

---

[76] A decision to accept an undertaking may be challenged on an application for judicial review: *R. v Secretary of State for the Environment, ex p. Friends of the Earth Ltd.* [1994] 2 C.M.L.R. 760 (challenge to undertakings accepted from water undertakers following breaches of requirements as to water intended for human consumption rejected on the facts). See *ENDS Report* 231, April 1994, pp.46-47 (R. Macrory). An appeal to the Court of Appeal was dismissed: *The Times*, 8th June 1995. An undertaking is itself enforceable as a requirement under s.18: s.19(2).

[77] 1991 Act, s.19(1). The Minister (*supra* n.75) also indicated that the circumstances in (c) would be unlikely to apply where there was any danger to public health (col. 923-924, 9th February 1989).

[78] *Ibid.,* s.19(3). This does not apply if the Secretary of State so directs under s.208 in the interests of national security.

[79] Again, subject to exceptions for reasons of national security: s.20(9).

[80] 1991 Act, s.21. This would exclude an application for judicial review on any ground before or after the 42-day period: *Smith v East Elloe R.D.C.* [1956] A.C. 736.

[81] See *post*, p.65. Breach of an undertaking does not, however, give rise to a claim for damages.

[82] 1991 Act, s.22.

(iv) Special administration orders

A more draconian procedure is available in the form of "special administration orders"[83] in respect of companies holding appointments as undertakers. Such an order may be made by the High Court on the application of the Secretary of State (or, with the Secretary of State's consent, the Director), if the court is satisfied:

(a) that there has been or is likely to be such a contravention of any principal duty[84] as is serious enough to make it inappropriate for the company to continue to hold its appointment;

(b) that there has been or is likely to be such a contravention of a final or confirmed provisional enforcement order as is similarly serious;

(c) that the company is or is likely to be unable to pay its debts;

(d) that the circumstances would justify presentation of a petition for winding-up under section 440 of the Companies Act 1985;[85] or

(e) that the company is unable or unwilling adequately to participate in arrangements certified by the Secretary of State or the Director to be necessary in relation to a proposal for termination of appointment under Condition O of the Conditions of Appointment.[86]

A special administration order directs that the company's affairs, business and property are to be managed by a person appointed by the High Court to achieve the purposes of the order in a

---

[83] 1991 Act, ss.23-26.

[84] i.e. in relation to sewerage undertakers, a requirement imposed by s.94: see *post*, p.62; no exemption notice must have been served under s.19(3): see *ante*, p.19.

[85] The making of a winding-up order is itself barred by s.25 of the 1991 Act in respect of any company holding an appointment as undertaker. Similarly, voluntary winding-up and insolvency proceedings are barred by s.26.

[86] 1991 Act, s.24.

manner which protects the respective interests of the company's members and creditors. The purposes of such an order are to transfer so much of the undertaking as is necessary to ensure that the functions as undertaker may be properly carried out and to continue carrying out those functions pending the transfer.[87]

(v) The Director General's register

The Director must maintain a public register of such matters as the appointments of undertakers, enforcement orders, undertakings and special administration orders.[88]

(vi) Review and information functions

The Director is under a duty to keep under review the carrying on both in England and Wales and elsewhere of activities connected with the matters in relation to which sewerage undertakers carry out functions; and to collect information with respect to the carrying out by the appointed companies of their functions as sewerage undertakers, and information with respect to the companies themselves, with a view to informing himself of matters with respect to which powers and duties are conferred on him.[89] The Secretary of State may give directions to the Director indicating considerations he should take into account in determining the order of priority in which matters are to be brought under review and in determining whether to exercise his powers under Parts II to V and VII of the 1991 Act.[90]

He must also collect information with respect to the compensation paid by sewerage undertakers under the Customer Service Standards specified in the regulations made by the Secretary of State[91] and the levels of overall performance achieved by sewerage

---

[87] 1991 Act, s.23. Provisions of the Insolvency Act 1986 are applied by Sch. 3. Transfer schemes are governed by Sch. 2.

[88] 1991 Act, s.195. See the Director General of Water Services Register (Inspection and Charges) Order 1989 (S.I. 1989 No.1154), which has effect under this section.

[89] 1991 Act, s.27(1), (2).

[90] *Ibid.*, s.27(3).

[91] See *post*, p.27.

undertakers in connection with the provision of sewerage services.[92] He has power to direct the undertakers to give him relevant information for this purpose.[93] Furthermore he must arrange for the publication, at least annually, of such of the information collected by him or given to him as appears expedient to give to customers or potential customers;[94] and he may direct the undertakers to inform their customers, at least annually, about their overall performance against the specified standards.[95]

(vii) Competition

It is also the Director's duty to provide information, advice and assistance to the Secretary of State or the Director General of Fair Trading relating to the functions of a sewerage undertaker or the carrying out of such functions by an appointed company; this information is to be provided on request or when he considers it expedient to do so.[96] The Director may at the request of the Director General of Fair Trading exercise the latter's functions under Part III of the Fair Trading Act 1973 relating to courses of conduct which are or may be detrimental to the interests of consumers in relation to the provision of sewerage services by sewerage undertakers.[97] He may, concurrently with the Director General of Fair Trading, exercise functions in relation to monopoly situations, and to courses of conduct which have, or are intended to have, or are likely to have, the effect of restricting, distorting or preventing competition in connection with the provision or securing of sewerage services.[98] Each Director must consult the other before exercising the powers under section 31(2) or (3). The latter powers include powers to make references in appropriate cases to the Monopolies and Mergers Commission.

---

[92] 1991 Act, s.95A(1), inserted by the Competition and Service (Utilities) Act 1992, s.31.

[93] *Ibid.,* s.95A(2), (3).

[94] *Ibid.,* s.95A(4), (5).

[95] *Ibid.,* s.96A, inserted by the Competition and Service (Utilities) Act 1992, s.32. This duty is enforceable under s.18, see *ante,* p.17.

[96] *Ibid.,* s.27(4).

[97] *Ibid.,* s.31(1).

[98] *Ibid.,* s.31(2), (3).

(viii) Disputes

Finally, the Director General has powers to consider complaints[99] and to determine disputes. A number of powers to determine disputes were added by the Competition and Service (Utilities) Act 1992.[100] In determining disputes referred to him under the 1991 Act, he must follow such practice and procedure as he considers appropriate, he must give reasons and may order the payment of his costs and expenses.[101] A determination by him is final.[102] However, he is not to determine any such dispute which is the subject of proceedings before a court, or with respect to which judgment has been given by a court.[103]

(ix) Overriding duties

In exercising his powers and performing his duties in relation to the regulation of undertakers, the financial conditions of requisitions and the movement of pipes, he is subject to the general duties set out in section 2 of the 1991 Act; he is also subject to the general environmental and recreational duties in sections 3 to 5 of the Act.[104]

---

[99] See *post*, pp.30-31.

[100] s.35, introducing powers to determine disputes, under, *inter alia*, ss.105 (adoption of sewers), 106 (right to communicate with public sewers), 107 (right of sewerage undertakers to undertake the making of communications with public sewers), 112 (requirement that proposed drain or sewer be constructed so as to form part of a general system), 113 (power to alter drainage system of premises), 116 (power to close or restrict use of public sewers); see *post*, pp.97, 107-108, 117-118, 178-179, 181, 191-192.

[101] Any provision as to costs and expenses is enforceable as if it were a County Court judgment: s.30A(5)(b); in deciding to make any such provision, the Director is to have regard to the conduct and means of the parties and any other relevant circumstances: s.30A(7). The Director's procedures for determining disputes are subject to "informal supervision" by the Council on Tribunals (*Annual Report of the Council on Tribunals 1991-92* (1992-93 H.C. 316), pp.22-23).

[102] This term does not exclude judicial review: *R. v Medical Appeal Tribunal, ex p. Gilmore* [1957] 1 Q.B. 574.

[103] 1991 Act, s.30A, inserted by the Competition and Service (Utilities) Act 1992, s.34.

[104] See *ante*, pp.15-16; *post*, pp.84-87.

(c) The National Rivers Authority

This body corporate, established by the Water Act 1989 and continued by Part I of the Water Resources Act 1991,[105] is primarily responsible for the standards of quality of water in rivers, streams, coastal and estuarine waters and is also concerned with the prevention of water pollution. The Authority is not therefore concerned with sewerage matters other than the discharge of sewage and trade effluent into rivers and streams, and in cases of pollution it may institute proceedings where it considers an offence has been committed.

Between 1974 and 1989, the water authorities were responsible for both the operation of the sewerage system and for enforcing the law on water pollution offences. This dual role was ended by the establishment of the Authority, which describes itself as "the strongest Environmental Protection Agency in Europe" and a very effective "Guardian of the Water Environment."[106] It has adopted an increasingly confrontational approach to its enforcement role.[107] The Authority is to be merged with other bodies[108] to form the Environmental Agency, with effect from 1st April 1996.[109]

(d) Sewerage undertakers

There are now ten companies appointed as sewerage undertakers, originally under the 1989 Act, and operating under the regime of the Companies Acts.[110] The previous water authorities were

---

[105] ss.1-18.
[106] *Annual Report and Accounts 1992-93*, inside front cover.
[107] S. Ball and S. Bell, *Environmental Law* (2nd edn., 1994) pp.112-117; W. Howarth, *The Law of the National Rivers Authority* and "Making Water Polluters Pay: England and Wales" [1994] *Env. Liability* 29.
[108] Waste regulation authorities and Her Majesty's Inspectorate of Pollution.
[109] Environment Act 1995, Part I.
[110] Anglian Water Services Ltd.; Dwr Cymru Cfyngedig; Northumbrian Water Ltd.; North West Water Ltd.; Severn Trent Water Ltd.; Southern Water Services Ltd.; South West Water Services Ltd.; Thames Water Utilities Ltd.; Wessex Water Services Ltd.; Yorkshire Water Services Ltd. On the political background to privatisation, see D. Kinnersley, *Coming Clean: The Politics of Water and the Environment* (1994), Chaps. 4-6.

described as

"a publicly owned utility acting as monopoly supplier of a necessary commodity, enjoying certain statutory powers and subject to certain obligations, but . . . not acting as an instrument or agent of government."[111]

These remarks would apply *a fortiori* to the successor undertakers. An undertaker is, however, a state authority against which EC directives are capable of direct enforcement.[112]

The assets, including public sewers and sewage pumping stations, functions and liabilities of the former water authorities in respect of sewerage were transferred to the ten "successor companies"[113] on 1st September 1989 (the "Transfer Date") under section 4 of the 1989 Act and the Water Authorities (Transfer of Functions) (Appointed Day) Order 1989,[114] under schemes made by the authorities with the approval of the Secretary of State. The Secretary of State also nominated a "holding company" for each "successor company".[115] Shares in the holding companies were initially all owned by H.M. Treasury, but were offered for sale to the public upon terms set out in a Prospectus and Memorandum of Association prepared for each company under the terms of the 1989 Act and in compliance with the Companies Acts on 1st November 1989. In the case of each holding company, a target investment limit for the remaining government shareholding

---

[111] *Per* Bingham M.R. in *A.B. v South West Water Services Ltd.* [1993] Q.B. 507, 532. The authority was accordingly not within one of the categories of cases where exemplary damages can be awarded, viz. "oppressive, arbitrary or unconstitutional action by the servants of the government" (*per* Lord Devlin in *Rookes v Barnard* [1964] A.C.1129, 1226).

[112] *Griffin v South West Water Services Ltd.* [1995] I.R.L.R.15.

[113] Specified by the Water Authorities (Successor Companies) Order 1989 (S.I. 1989 No. 1465).

[114] S.I. 1989 No. 1530. The sewerage undertakers inherited the liability of the predecessor water authorities: see *Dear v Thames Water Co. and Others* (1993) 33 Con. L.R. 43. As to the initial financial arrangements, see the Water Act 1989, ss.84-96.

[115] Water Act 1989, s.83(1); the Water Reorganisation (Holding Compaines of Successor Companies) Order 1989 (S.I. 1989 No. 1531). These companies are plcs.

was specified by the Secretary of State, and was not to exceed 0.5 per cent of the ordinary voting rights.[116] In most areas the same company was appointed to be both water and sewerage undertaker in succession to a former water authority. This was not the case, however, where statutory water companies existing prior to the passing of the 1989 Act continued in existence.

The initial appointments have been for 25 years. The structure of separate "holding companies" and "appointed companies" enables the former to diversify.[117] Only the latter are subject to the regulatory regime enshrined in the 1991 Act. However, the business as undertaker must be kept at arm's length from the other activities of the group.[118] The special "golden" shares in each holding company held by the Secretary of State for the Environment were redeemed on 31st December 1994, opening the way for mergers and takeovers to occur among the companies.[119]

The general duties of the sewerage undertakers are specified by section 94 of the Water Industry Act 1991, under which they must provide and maintain sewers adequate for the drainage of their area and they must properly dispose of the contents of the sewers, and also similarly receive and dispose of trade effluent in accordance with the terms of Chapter III of Part IV of the 1991 Act. When exercising their functions, they must observe the requirements of sections 3 and 4 in preserving and enhancing the natural environment and means for public recreation and access.

Under section 95 of the 1991 Act, performance standards for the provision of sewerage services may be specified by the Secretary of State or by the Director with the approval of the Secretary of State.

---

[116] See the 1989 Act, s.89, and the Water (Target Investment Limit) Order 1990 (S.I. 1990 No. 1083).

[117] See OFWAT Information Note No. 9, *Diversification of Water Companies*.

[118] Guidelines on "transfer pricing" (i.e. the prices paid by the appointed business to the non-appointed business and associates) were issued by the Director in 1994. These prevent cross-subsidisation: see *OFWAT Annual Report 1993* (1993-94 H.C.416), p.10, and s.2 of the 1991 Act (*ante*, pp.15-16).

[119] *OFWAT Annual Report 1994* (1994-95 H.C. 431), p.52.

The matters that may be contained in regulations made by the Secretary of State include

(a) provision for contraventions of prescribed requirements to be treated as breaches of the duty under section 94;

(b) prescription of such standards of performance in connection with the provision of sewerage services as, in his opinion, ought to be achieved in individual cases;[120] and

(c) provision that a sewerage undertaker which fails to meet a prescribed standard shall pay a prescribed amount to any person affected who is of a prescribed description.[121]

The procedure for making regulations is set out in section 96 of the 1991 Act.[122] The Secretary of State has made the Water Supply and Sewerage Services (Customer Service Standards) Regulations 1989,[123] setting standards as to keeping appointments; dealing with account queries and requests about payment arrangements; dealing with complaints about services; flooding from sewers; and giving notice to customers of their rights. In some cases, provision is made for £10 payments (or credits) if standards are not met, without affecting other legal liabilities. In the case of flooding from sewers, the undertaker must remit sewerage charges for the year or pay £1,000 (whichever is the lesser). This obligation does not arise where such a payment has

---

[120] Regulations under this head may include a requirement for an undertaker to inform a person of his rights under the regulations; provide for any dispute to be referred by either party to the Director; provide for the procedure for the reference and the enforceability of the Director's determination; and prescribe circumstances in which a sewerage undertaker is to be exempted from requirements of the regulations: 1991 Act, s.95(4).

[121] *Ibid.*, s.95(1)-(3).

[122] As amended by the Competition and Services (Utilities) Act 1992, s.30 and Sch. 2, para. 25. Regulations are made on the application of the Director, who must first commission research to discover the views of persons likely to be affected and serve copies of the application on affected undertakers and persons or bodies likely to represent persons likely to be affected.

[123] S.I. 1989, No. 1159, as amended by S.I. 1989 No. 1383 and S.I. 1993 No. 500. Following the 1993 amendments, entitlements are extended to all and not just domestic customers.

already been made in the same financial year; or the entry of
effluent is caused by exceptional weather conditions, industrial
action by the undertaker's employees, the actions of the customer,
or any defect, inadequacy or blockage in his drains or sewers; or
a claim is not made within three months. Any disputes as to the
right to a payment may be referred by either party to the Director.

Sewerage undertakers are expressly empowered by section 142
of the Act to make charges for their services, without statutory
restrictions on any amounts. However, the amounts are subject
to close regulation by the Director under the Conditions of
Appointment of each undertaker.[124] Initial charging limits were
set by the Secretary of State for ten years from 1989. Price
increases thereafter are controlled by a percentage formula RPI
+ K, where "RPI" is the rate of inflation in November prior to the
beginning of the charging year in April and "K" is a "figure set
for each company for each year and reflects what a company
needs to charge to finance the provision of services and its
capital expenditure programme."[125] A "Periodic Review" of
charging limits took place in 1994, with new limits effective
from 1st April 1995.[126] Infrastructure charges levied on new
properties connected for sewerage services are not controlled

---

[124] See DoE, Welsh Office, *Instruments of Appointment of the Water and
Sewerage Undertakers* (H.M.S.O., 1989), and Conditions B (Charges), C
(Infrastructure Charges), and D (Charges Schemes).

[125] OFWAT Information Note No. 3, *Why water bills are rising and how they are
controlled* (Revised edn., 1993). See also Note No. 8 on *The K Factor – what
it is and how it can be changed* (Revised edn., 1994).

[126] Such a review was mandatory after 10 years but could be held after 5 at the
option of the Director or the appointees (on this occasion, the Director). See
OFWAT Information Note No. 17, *1994 Review of water charging limits – the
periodic review* (Revised edn, 1993); OFWAT paper, *Setting Price Limits for
Water and Sewerage Services* (November 1993); OFWAT Information Note
No. 30, *Water Industry Referrals on Price Limits to the Monopolies and
Mergers Commission* (1994). The outcome of the Periodic Review was set out
in OFWAT, *Future Charges for Water and Sewerage Services* (1994). Two
water companies objected, but on a reference, the Monopolies and Mergers
Commission came to an almost identical conclusion: OFWAT News Release
PN 19/95, 28th July 1995. On the Periodic Review, see D. Legge, (1994)
Utilities Law Review 85 and (1994) *Utilities Law Review* 115. See also *post*,
p.112.

under this formula but under separate limits; these were also considered in the first Periodic Review.

Each sewerage undertaker must establish a procedure for dealing with complaints by customers or potential customers, after consulting its customer service committee, and with the approval of the Director. The Director may direct an undertaker to review or modify its procedure. The undertaker's duty to establish a procedure or to comply with a direction is enforceable under section 18 of the 1991 Act.[127]

Each undertaker is required by its Conditions of Appointment to produce a Code of Practice for domestic customers, subject to the approval of the Director.[128]

A sewerage undertaker is by section 155 of the 1991 Act given powers to acquire compulsorily land required for the purposes of, or in connection with, the carrying out of its functions, but any order made by an undertaker would be subject to confirmation by the Secretary of State, and the usual procedure of the Acquisition of Land Act 1981 would apply.

(e) Customer service committees

Section 28 and Schedule 4 of the 1991 Act make provision for not more than ten customer service committees to be established in accordance with the section, and the Director is required to allocate each sewerage or water undertaking to one of these committees. In the event, ten committees have been appointed. The Director maintains the committees and assigns duties to them. Each committee is to consist of a chairman appointed by the Director, after consultation with the Secretary of State, and between ten and twenty other members also to be appointed by the Director. The chairman is paid a salary fixed by the Director, and may not be a member of the House of Commons. Each

---

[127] 1991 Act, s.116A, inserted by the Competition and Service (Utilities) Act 1992, s.33.

[128] *OFWAT Annual Report for 1993* (1993-94 H.C. 416), p.20.

committee has a duty under section 29 of the 1991 Act to keep under review all matters appearing to the committee to affect the interests of customers or potential customers of companies allocated to that committee. They must make such representations to the company about any such matters as they consider appropriate. They must investigate any complaint made to them by a customer or potential customer or referred by the Director[129] that relates to the performance of a sewerage undertaker's functions and does not appear to be vexatious or frivolous.

However, three categories of complaint *must* be referred (or referred back) to the Director:

(a) complaints that involve an assertion of a contravention of an undertaker's conditions of appointment;

(b) complaints in relation to the exercise of works powers where the Director is under a duty to investigate;[130]

(c) complaints which the committee is unable to resolve with the undertaker in question after making representations.

If a complaint is made direct to the Director, and is not in categories (a) or (b), he must consider whether the complaint should be referred to a committee. If a complaint does fall into one of those categories, he should consider whether it should be referred to the Secretary of State. Accordingly, the Director *may* deal with complaints outside categories (a) and (b), and *must* consider complaints in categories (a) or (b) (if not referred to the Secretary of State) and category (c).[131] Furthermore, the only

---

[129] Under the 1991 Act, s.30. Statistics of complaints dealt with by CSCs are set out in the OFWAT Annual Reports.

[130] Under the 1991 Act, s.181. See OFWAT Information Note No. 22, *Pipeline Powers on Private Land*.

[131] 1991 Act, s.30(1), (2), (3)(a), (b). In practice, except where the Director is required by law to deal with a complaint, complainants are advised to approach, first, the undertaker and, if still unsatisfied, the appropriate CSC: see OFWAT, *OFWAT Complaints Procedure* (1994). The Director will, however, deal with complaints from suppliers of goods and services to the water and sewerage industry alleging unfair trading practices by water and sewerage companies: *ibid.*, p.11.

remedy for a breach by a committee of any of its duties under section 29 of the 1991 Act is to complain to the Director, and this provides a further category of complaint which he is under a duty to consider.[132] The Director must take such steps in consequence of his consideration of any matter as he considers appropriate.[133] These might include seeking an order under section 18.[134]

(f) Local authorities

Sewerage services in this country have been traditionally a principal function of local authorities, and those at district level in particular. The principal legislation began with the Public Health Act of 1848 and the major consolidating and reforming Act of 1875, establishing the former boroughs, urban and rural sanitary districts. These were followed by the county boroughs, non-county boroughs and urban and rural districts of the Local Government Acts of 1888, 1894 and 1933. Their sewerage services were reformed by the Public Health Act 1936, but were transferred in 1974 to the water authorities,[135] which were, in their turn, succeeded by the appointed companies under the privatisation statute of 1989. However, many powers in relation to the drainage of individual premises have been left with the modern district councils (metropolitan and non-metropolitan), the London boroughs and, from 1st April 1996, the county or county borough councils in Wales. In England, collection of waste is also the responsibility of the district councils, but the controls over the disposal of waste and the licensing of waste disposal sites are the concern of county councils.

---

[132] 1991 Act, ss.29(5), 30(3)(c).

[133] *Ibid.,* s.30(4).

[134] See *ante*, pp.17-19.

[135] The transfer of property, rights and liabilities was effected by the Local Authorities (England) (Property etc.) Order 1973 (S.I. 1973 No. 1861), arts. 8, 9, 18, as amended by S.I. 1974 No. 406, and the Local Authorities (Wales) (Property etc.) Order 1973 (S.I. 1973 No. 1863), arts. 8, 9, 18, as amended by S.I. 1974 No. 404. See the *Local Government Reorganisation in England, Transfer of Property – Memorandum* (H.M.S.O., 1973) and *Supplementary Memorandum* (H.M.S.O., 1974), and DoE Circular 100/73, *Water Act 1973: Water Authorities and Local Authorities.*

The prevention of river pollution was formerly a district council function, but this is now the principal concern of the National Rivers Authority, which is responsible for monitoring the discharge of sewage and trade effluent into rivers and streams. The principal statute concerning river pollution was formerly the Control of Pollution Act 1974, but most of the relevant provisions of the 1974 Act were replaced by the Water Act 1989,[136] now Part III of the Water Resources Act 1991.[137]

The prevention of nuisances, requirements for adequate drainage for individual premises of various kinds, the maintenance and cleansing of sanitary conveniences, the cleansing of stopped up, etc. drains and other detailed provisions of a similar kind remain the responsibility of district councils and London boroughs, virtually unaffected by the 1989 Act. They may also act as agents for sewerage undertakers,[138] although the latter remain statutorily responsible for the discharge of the relevant functions.[139]

(g) The Ombudsmen

Under the Parliamentary Commissioner for Administration Act 1967, complaints of maladministration causing injustice by any officer in central government departments can be referred to the Commissioner (popularly known as the Ombudsman). He may then investigate the complaint and issue a report suggesting remedial action to be taken should he find the complaint well-founded. The complaint may be made by a member of the public, but must be directed through a Member of Parliament.

Similarly, complaints of maladministration causing injustice by a member of the public against a local authority may be made to one of the Local Commissioners for Administration under the

---

[136] See in particular ss.103-124.
[137] ss.82-104.
[138] See *post*, pp.83-84.
[139] *King v Harrow L.B.C.* [1994] E.G.C.S. 76; *R. v Yorkshire Water Services Ltd.*, *The Times*, 19th July 1994 (undertaker fined total of £15,000 for two pollution incidents deemed to have been caused by it, although day-to-day operations were entrusted to an agent local authority).

Local Government Act 1974, whereupon similar action may be taken.

The National Rivers Authority[140] and the Director General of Water Services are subject to the jurisdiction of the Parliamentary Commissioner. The successor sewerage companies and the customer service committees have, however, not been made subject to his jurisdiction. Indeed, the customer service committees perform in general the functions of an ombudsman in relation to water and sewerage services under the Water Industry Act 1991.

THE URBAN WASTE WATER TREATMENT (ENGLAND AND WALES) REGULATIONS 1994

It is convenient at this point to introduce the Urban Waste Water Treatment (England and Wales) Regulations 1994,[141] which implement the Urban Waste Water Treatment Directive.[142] These regulations introduce new standards to be met at specified times in the collection, treatment and disposal of urban waste water. They constitute a new body of law, using terms many of which are not the familiar expressions used hitherto in this area, which supplement the existing structure by imposing new duties on (as appropriate) the Secretary of State, the Director, the National Rivers Authority and the sewerage undertakers.

Key matters regulated include "collecting systems" for "urban

---

[140] Except in relation to its flood defence functions, which fall under the jurisdiction of the Local Government Ombudsman: Parliamentary Commissioner Act 1967, Sch. 2, as amended by the Water Act 1989, Sch. 1, para. 11, and the Water Consolidation (Consequential Provisions) Act 1991, Sch. 1, para. 17; Local Government Act 1974, s.25(1)(d), inserted by the 1989 Act, Sch. 1, para. 12, and amended by the 1991 Act, Sch. 1, para. 25.

[141] S.I. 1994 No. 2841.

[142] Dir. 91/271/EEC. For the text, see *Garner's Environmental Law*, p.IX/681*ff*. On the background to the Directive, see the 10th Report of the House of Lords Select Committee on the Environment, *Municipal Waste Water Treatment* (1990-91 H.L. 50), and A.W. Gurwitz, "Municipal Waste Water and Sewage Sludge Management in the EC" (1991) XIV (2) *Boston College International & Comparative Law Review* 403. On the Regulations, see *ENDS Report* 240, January 1995, p.40.

waste water" and the treatment of discharges of urban waste water into receiving waters. The latter requirements vary when the waters are a "sensitive area" or a "high natural dispersion area", and according to the "population equivalent" of the "agglomeration" from which discharges take place. Special rules apply to discharges of "industrial waste water". The detailed rules will be considered at the appropriate point in this book. A table summarising the implementation requirements is reproduced in the Appendix. The main definitions are set out here.

(a) Definitions

(i) Collecting system

A "collecting system" is a "system of conduits which collects and conducts urban waste water".[143] It will be noted that no distinction is drawn here between sewers and drains.

(ii) Waste water[144]

"Urban waste water" means "domestic waste water or the mixture of domestic waste water with industrial waste water and/or run-off rain water".

"Domestic waste water" means "waste water from residential settlements and services which originates predominantly from the human metabolism and from household activities".

"Industrial waste water" means "any waste water which is discharged from premises used for carrying on any trade or industry,[145] other than domestic waste water and run-off rain water".

(iii) Sensitive areas and high natural dispersion areas[146]

These areas are to be identified by the Secretary of State

---

[143] S.I. 1994 No. 2841, Reg. 2(1).
[144] *Ibid.*
[145] These terms are not defined.
[146] S.I. 1994 No. 2841, Reg. 3.

according to criteria set out in, respectively, Part I and Part II of Schedule 1 to the Regulations, and shown on maps deposited with the National Rivers Authority. The identification is to be reviewed by the Secretary of State no later than 31st December 1997, and thereafter at intervals of no more than four years.

A body of water must be identified as a "sensitive area" if it is in one of three groups:

(a) natural freshwater lakes, other freshwater bodies, estuaries[147] and coastal waters[148] which are found to be eutrophic[149] or which in the near future may become eutrophic if protective action is not taken;

(b) surface freshwaters intended for the abstraction of drinking water which could contain more than the concentration of nitrate laid down in the Drinking Water Directive[150] if action is not taken;

(c) areas where further treatment than secondary[151] or equivalent treatment is necessary to fulfil Council Directives.

A "marine water body or area" can be identified as a high natural dispersion area "if the discharge of waste water does not adversely affect the environment as a result of morphology, hydrology or

---

[147] i.e. "the transitional area at the mouth of a river between fresh-water and coastal waters, the outer (seaward) limits of which are shown on maps kept in accordance with Regulation 12": Reg.2(1).

[148] i.e. "the waters outside the low-water line or the outer limit of an estuary": Reg. 2(1).

[149] "Eutrophication" means "the enrichment of water by nutrients, especially compounds of nitrogen and/or phosphorus, causing an accelerated growth of algae and higher forms of plant life to produce an undesirable disturbance to the balance of organisms present in the water and to the quality of the water concerned." Part I also specifies elements that "might be taken into account when considering which nutrients should be reduced by further treatment".

[150] Dir. 75/440/EEC, concerning the quality required of surface water intended for the abstraction of drinking water in the Member States, as amended by Dir. 79/869/EEC.

[151] i.e. "treatment of urban waste water by a process generally involving biological treatment with a secondary settlement or other process in which the requirements established in Table 1 in Schedule 3 are respected": Reg. 2(1).

specific hydraulic conditions which exist in that area". However, the Secretary of State must take into account the risk that discharged load may be transferred to adjacent areas where it can cause detrimental environmental effects, and must recognise the presence of sensitive areas outside England and Wales. Elements to be taken into consideration are

> "open bays, estuaries and other coastal waters with a good water exchange and not subject to eutrophication or oxygen depletion or which are considered unlikely to become eutrophic or to develop oxygen depletion due to the discharge of urban waste water."

The Secretary of State has designated 36 sensitive areas and 82 high natural dispersion areas.[152] The NRA recommended that a further nine areas should be designated as sensitive areas, but this was rejected by ministers; these areas will, however, be monitored.[153]

(iv) Population equivalent
This is a

> "measurement of organic biodegradable load, and a population equivalent of 1 (1 p.e.) is the organic biodegradable load having a five-day biochemical oxygen demand (BOD 5) of 60g of oxygen per day (the load shall be calculated on the basis of the maximum average weekly load entering the treatment plant during the year, excluding unusual situations such as those due to heavy rain)."[154]

(v) Agglomeration
This means

> "an area where the population and/or economic activities are sufficiently concentrated for urban waste water to be collected

---

[152] Decision of 18th May 1994: see *ENDS Report* 232, May 1994, pp.35-36. The Directive term for "high natural dispersion areas" is "less sensitive areas".
[153] *Ibid.*
[154] Reg. 2(1).

and conducted to an urban waste water treatment plant or to a final discharge point."[155]

Provision is also made in the Regulations for samples and records, and the deposit of maps and certificates with the National Rivers Authority.[156] The Authority must monitor or procure the monitoring by a competent authority or appropriate body

(a) of discharges from urban waste water treatment plants to verify compliance with Schedule 3 of the Regulations;[157]

(b) of amounts and composition of sludges disposed of to surface waters (other than by dumping from ships);

(c) of waters subject to discharges from such plants provided under Regulation 5[158] in cases where it can be expected that the receiving environment will be significantly affected;

(d) to verify that specified discharges and the disposal of sludge to surface waters (other than by dumping from ships) do not adversely affect the environment.[159]

The Secretary of State must every two years publish a situation report on the disposal of urban waste water and sludge in England and Wales, and provide information to the Commission on a programme for the implementation of the Directive.[160]

(b) Costs of implementation

A key factor in developing plans for the implementation of the

---

[155] Reg. 2(1).
[156] Regs. 10, 12.
[157] See *post*, pp.138-139.
[158] See *post*, pp.137-140.
[159] Reg. 11(1). Dumping from ships is to be monitored by the licensing authority under s.24 of the Food and Environmental Protection Act 1985. It is to be phased out by 31st December 1998: Reg. 9.
[160] Reg. 13. A report on the U.K. implementation programme was sent to the European Commission in November 1994: *This Common Inheritance: U.K. Annual Report 1995* (Cm. 2822, 1995), p.53.

Directive has been the cost. At one stage it was estimated that it would require additional capital expenditure of around £10bn at 1993-94 prices; this was subsequently revised down to £6bn plus £0.8bn for discharges to bathing waters, and this was allowed for by the Director General of Water Services in fixing price levels for the ten years from 1995.[161] This expenditure assumed completion of the Bathing Waters Programme consistent with the Directive; the ending of sewage sludge dumping in the sea by 1998 and compliance with the requirements of the directive by the due dates.

---

[161] See OFWAT, *Future Charges for Water and Sewerage Services: The outcome of the Periodic Review* (1994), pp.23, 46-47. See also the *ENDS Report* 228, pp.3-4; 229, p.6. The assumptions made by OFWAT in determining what works are needed to secure compliance with EC rules on bathing quality have, however, been too conservative: see *ENDS Reports* 241, p.9 and 242, p.12, reporting that the NRA has told South West Water that it expected it to press ahead with two schemes, relying on its duty to utilise its powers to ensure the achievement of water quality objectives (see *post*, pp.150-151).

Chapter 2

OWNERSHIP OF SEWERS

INTRODUCTORY

Whether a particular sewer belongs to a private individual or to
a sewerage undertaker is a matter of importance in view of the
positive duty laid upon sewerage undertakers in respect of
sewers owned by them by section 94 of the Water Industry Act
1991, *inter alia*,

> "so to cleanse and maintain those sewers as to ensure that
> [its] . . . area is . . . effectually drained; and . . . to make
> provision for the emptying of those sewers and . . . for
> effectually dealing . . . with [their] . . . contents."

This duty applies generally only to sewers vested in a sewerage
undertaker, i.e. to "public sewers". Owners of private sewers
have certain common law and statutory liabilities in respect of
them, from which they will however be freed if they can
repudiate ownership. A sewerage undertaker is under a general
duty to provide a public sewer for the domestic drainage of
premises in its area where a notice to that effect is served upon
it by an owner, occupier or local authority affected and the
premises either have buildings upon them or will have when
projects in hand are completed.[1] When meeting such a sewer
requisition, the sewerage undertaker may require financial
undertakings and guarantees.[2]

The question of ownership falls to be considered under two
principal headings: first, the circumstances in which a sewer
vests in a sewerage undertaker (such a sewer being known[3] and
hereinafter described as a "public sewer") and, secondly, the

---

[1] Water Industry Act 1991, s.98.
[2] *Ibid.*, s.99.
[3] *Ibid.*, s.189(1).

principles according to which the ownership of private sewers is determined.

PUBLIC SEWERS

(a) The present position

According to section 219(1) of the 1991 Act a "public sewer" is any sewer,

> "for the time being vested in a sewerage undertaker in its capacity as such, whether vested in that undertaker by virtue of a scheme under Schedule 2 to the Water Act 1989 or Schedule 2 to this Act or under section 179 above or otherwise . . . ."

The apparent simplicity of this definition, however, masks issues of considerable complexity. The position as regards a *new* sewer is reasonably straightforward. This vests in the sewerage undertaker if

(i) it is a sewer or disposal main laid by the undertaker itself in exercise of a power conferred by Part VI of the Water Industry Act 1991[4] or otherwise;[5]

(ii) it is a sewer in respect of which a declaration of vesting is made by the undertaker under Chapter II of Part IV of the 1991 Act;[6] or

(iii) it is laid in the area of the undertaker under Part XI of the Highways Act 1980 (making up private streets) and is not a sewer belonging to a road maintained by a highway authority.[7]

Provision is also made by Schedule 2 to the 1991 Act for

---

[4] See ss.158 and 159 of the 1991 Act, replacing powers conferred by s.153 and Sch. 19 of the Water Act 1989, and *post*, pp.73-81.

[5] 1991 Act, s.179(1), (7).

[6] *Ibid.*, s.179(2)(a). See Chapter 4, *post*.

[7] *Ibid.*, s.179(2)(b). See the discussion of the equivalent provision of the Public Health Act 1936, *post*, pp.54-55.

schemes for the transfer of property from a company holding an existing appointment as sewerage undertaker to a new appointee.

However, the position as regards sewers transferred to sewerage undertakers in 1989 is more complex.

All those sewers which on 1st September 1989, the "transfer date"[8] for the purposes of the 1989 Act, were vested in one of the former water authorities vested on that date in the successor company appointed in each case to act as sewerage undertaker. Naturally, the determination of which sewers were so vested will turn upon the interpretation of the legal provisions in force prior to the "transfer date" and these therefore continue to be of relevance.

(b) Sewers transferred from water authority to sewerage undertaker

In determining what sewers were initially transferred to the sewerage undertakers as "public sewers" primary reference must be made to section 20 of the Public Health Act 1936 (as substituted by Schedule 8 of the Water Act 1973) which incorporated by reference a number of earlier provisions. Three basic circumstances were set out in substituted section 20 in which a sewer would become a "public sewer":

(i) sewers and disposal works constructed by, vested in under special arrangements under the Water Act 1973 or otherwise acquired by the former water authority;

(ii) all sewers constructed under Part IX of the Highways Act 1959 (subsequently Part XI of the Highways Act 1980), except sewers belonging to a road maintained by a highway authority;

(iii) all sewers and disposal works with respect to which a

---

8   The Water Authorities (Transfer of Functions) (Appointed Day) Order 1989, S.I. 1989 No. 1530.

> declaration of vesting was made under the Public Health Act 1936.

These categories were

> "in addition to the sewers and sewage disposal works vested in a water authority by virtue of section 254 or 68 of the Local Government Act 1972, as either section applies for the purposes of the Water Act 1973."

These will be considered in conjunction with classification (i).

Each limb will now be considered in turn.

(i) Sewers and disposal works constructed by, vested in or otherwise acquired by the former water authority
> "All sewers and disposal works constructed by the water authority at their expense or vested in the authority in pursuance of arrangements under section 15 of the Water Act 1973, or otherwise acquired by the authority."[9]

Sewers constructed after 1st April 1974 (when the 1973 Act came into force) should present little difficulty. They vested in the water authority if they were constructed either by the authority itself or by the local authority[10] acting pursuant to arrangements made under section 15 of the Water Act 1973.[11] The reference to the "acquisition" of a sewer includes all forms of acquisition, as by operation of the maxim *quicquid plantatur solo, solo cedit*.[12]

Sewers vested in local authorities prior to 1st April 1974 were

---

9   Public Health Act 1936, s.20(1)(a), substituted by the Water Act 1973, Sch. 8, para. 33.
10 Usually a district or London borough council or the Common Council of the City of London: Water Act 1973, s.15(10) (as originally enacted); Sch. 4A, para. 9, as substituted by the Water Act 1983, s.6(2).
11 See s.15(2)(c) of the Water Act 1973 as originally enacted. A new s.15 was substituted by the Water Act 1983, s.6(1): this made no mention of the vesting of sewers constructed by the local authority.
12 *Royco Homes v Eatonwill Construction Ltd., Three Rivers District Council (Third Party)* [1979] Ch. 276.

transferred to the water authorities on that date.[13] The determination of what sewers were then vested in local authorities rested upon section 20 of the Public Health Act 1936 *in its original form*.

EXCURSUS: THE PUBLIC HEALTH ACT 1936 IN ITS ORIGINAL FORM

This had *five* classifications of sewer for the purpose. Two of these were to all intents and purposes identical with classifications (ii) and (iii), discussed below,[14] but the other three are as mentioned here, and therefore all sewers coming within any of these provisions are still public sewers. The three paragraphs of section 20(1) in its original form considered here were as follows:

(i) **Sewers within the meaning of the Public Health Act 1875 and sewerage disposal works** which, by virtue of the provisions of that Act, were, immediately prior to the 1st October 1937,[15] vested in the local authority.

In order to appreciate the effect of this provision, it is necessary to consider the relevant provisions of the Act of 1875, and the effect of the considerable case law arising therefrom, and the meaning of "sewer", as explained in Chapter 1, must also be borne in mind.

(A) MEANING OF "SEWER" IN 1875 ACT

The word "sewer" was defined by section 4 of the 1875 Act to include "sewers and drains of every description, except drains to which the word 'drain' interpreted as aforesaid applies, and except drains vested in or under the control of any authority having the management of roads and not being a local authority

---

13 Water Act 1973, ss. 14(2) and 34(1), Sch. 6, Part I, paras. 4, 5, applying the Local Government Act 1972, ss.254 and 68. See the Local Authorities (England) (Property etc.) Order 1973 (S.I. 1973 No. 1861), Art. 8, as amended by S.I. 1974 No. 406; and the Local Authorities (Wales) (Property etc.) Order 1973 (S.I. 1973 No. 1863), Art. 8, as amended by S.I. 1974 No. 404.
14 pp.54, 55.
15 The date of the commencement of the 1936 Act: see s.347(1).

under this Act"; "drain" in turn was defined in the same section to mean[16] "any drain of and used for the drainage of one building only, or premises within the same curtilage, and made merely for the purpose of communicating therefrom with a cesspool or other like receptacle for drainage, or with a sewer into which the drainage of two or more buildings or premises occupied by different persons is conveyed." Speaking generally, therefore, by virtue of these definitions, a sewer was, for the purposes of the 1875 Act, any drain (or "line of pipes," to use a neutral expression), which served more than one building, or premises not within the same curtilage.[17] Even by reducing the provisions to this comparatively simple proposition one does not, however, explain the position fully, for the courts have had to consider the meanings in this connection of the term "building," and of the expression "within the same curtilage".

"Building" and "house" are not here necessarily synonymous, and it has been held to be a question of fact whether two semi-detached houses are a single building,[18] and the court, in a later case,[19] refused to lay down any general rule on the point. "Curtilage" is a legal term of ancient vintage, but none the less does not seem to be capable of very precise definition; in *Harris v Scurfield*,[20] it was said[21] "there is no definition of a curtilage

---

[16] *Not* "include", as in the definition of "sewer". Strictly, a definition introduced by the word "includes" is not a definition at all; it leaves the word explained with its "ordinary" or dictionary meaning and adds to that meaning other terms not ordinarily included in the dictionary meaning. "Means", however, has an exclusionary effect – the definition is to be substituted for the word or words in the statute.

[17] Whether or not the sewer was laid in private land, if it were so laid, there would be no right to connect thereto, without the consent of the landowner.

[18] Two such houses were held to be a single building for this purpose in *Hedley v Webb* [1901] 2 Ch. 126, but the converse had been held for the purposes of the Lands Clauses Consolidation Act 1845, on slightly different facts, in *Harvie v South Devon Railway Co.* (1874) 32 L.T. 1.

[19] *Humphrey v Young* [1903] 1 K.B. 44. In *Birch v Wigan Corporation* [1953] 1 Q.B. 136, a single house was held not to be capable of being part of a building for the purposes of the closing order provisions of the Housing Act 1936 but this would not necessarily apply in the present context.

[20] (1904) 68 J.P. 516.

[21] *Per* Alverstone L.C.J. at p.517.

which would include the case of a number of houses separately occupied by different people, simply because there is a common access and to some extent common accommodation." In one case,[22] two blocks of buildings belonging to the same owner and containing 46 sets of apartments, were separated by a passageway some 20 feet wide, one end of which was open to a public highway. On the particular facts of the method of construction of these buildings, the court held that the two blocks were premises within the same curtilage. On the other hand, an arcade with a number of houses and shops on either side, and roofed over, with gates at either end, was held not to be buildings or premises within the same curtilage for the present purposes.[23] In the Scottish case of *Sinclair-Lockhart's Trustees v Central Land Board*[24] the Court of Session concluded that "the ground which is used for the comfortable enjoyment of a house or other building may be regarded in law as being within the curtilage of that house or building . . ." It may, thus, in general be taken that the "curtilage" of a building is that land used for its normal enjoyment.

The whole question of the meaning of drain for the purposes of the 1875 Act was reconsidered by the House of Lords in *Weaver v Family Housing Association (York) Ltd.*[25] Their Lordships in considering whether a row of eight houses could be regarded as one building, said that all the following matters were relevant, although they were not all to be given equal weight:

- structural unity;
- unit of ownership;
- occupation by separate tenants, without intercommunication;
- existence of a single comprehensive system of drainage;
- separate cold stores;
- separate outside lavatories.

---

22 *Pilbrow v St. Leonard's Shoreditch Vestry* [1895] 1 Q.B. 433.
23 *St. Martin's-in-the-Field Vestry v Bird* [1895] 1 Q.B. 428.
24 (1950) 1 P.&C.R. 195, affirmed (1951) 1 P.&C.R. 320.
25 (1975) 74 L.G.R. 255.

Whilst refusing to interfere with the finding of the court below that these were separate buildings, their Lordships said that it was essentially a question of fact.

In a subsequent case,[26] Walton J. applied the cases discussed above including *Weaver*, and found that two separately occupied cottages, built onto one another and owned by the same landlord, were a single building, and that the water closets in the garden serving the cottages were within the curtilage of the building. "Curtilage" said his Lordship, was an "enclosure", or "land within an enclosure".

The essential point under this heading, therefore, is that the particular conduit (in order to be a public sewer) should drain two or more buildings.[27] The connection of a second building to an existing drain serving one building only, although done illegally and without the consent of the local authority, was nevertheless capable of operating to convert the drain into a public sewer as from the point of junction.[28] On the other hand, if one of the two premises drained by a public sewer was subsequently disconnected therefrom, such an action would not normally operate so as to make the sewer once more a drain.[29]

---

[26] *Cook v Minion* (1978) 37 P.&C.R. 58.

[27] *Travis v Uttley* [1894] 1 Q.B. 233; *Holland v Lazarus* (1897) 66 L.J.Q.B. 285.

[28] *St. Matthew, Bethnal Green, Vestry v London School Board* [1898] A.C. 190, and compare *Holland v Lazarus* (1897) 66 L.J.Q.B. 285. Both these decisions were on the provisions of the Metropolis Management Acts, but there seems to be no reason why the principle therein applied should not apply also to cases under the Public Health Acts.

[29] *St. Leonard, Shoreditch, Vestry v Phelan* [1896] 1 Q.B. 533; but see also *Kershaw v Smith* [1913] 2 K.B. 455, in which Avory J. refused to agree with the principle "once a sewer always a sewer", and held that a sewer which by reconstruction had become a drain serving but one building, could be no longer vested in the local authority as a public sewer. Where there was no such reconstruction, however, it was held that a sewer did not cease to be a sewer for the purposes of the 1936 Act just because it was not used as such: *Blackdown Properties Ltd. v Minister of Housing and Local Government* [1967] Ch. 115. "Vesting" does not mean complete ownership, but merely the giving of an interest sufficient to enable the local authority to perform its duties; if those duties cease by a change in the factual situation then the vesting comes to an end; see also *Bradford v Eastbourne Corporation* [1896] 2 Q.B. 205, and article by J.F. Garner at 20 Conv. N.S. 208.

Moreover, because a particular line of pipes served a number of premises, it did not necessarily follow that that conduit must be a public sewer from end to end.[30] That portion of the conduit which received the drainage of one building only would be a drain,[31] while the remainder could be a public sewer. If the conduit had been constructed by the local authority, or by a private individual with the approval of the local authority,[32] with the intention of it receiving the drainage of more than one building, it would normally be a public sewer, although no buildings might have been actually connected thereto.[33]

(B) "VESTING" UNDER 1875 ACT

Having decided that the particular line of pipes in question was a "sewer" within section 4 of the Act of 1875, it is then necessary to consider the effect of section 13 of that Act (now repealed), which read as follows:

> "All existing and future sewers within the district of a local authority, together with all buildings, works, materials and things belonging thereto,[34] except –
>
> (1) Sewers made by any person for his own profit, or by any company for the profit of the shareholders; and
>
> (2) Sewers made and used[35] for the purpose of draining, preserving, or improving land under any local or private Act of Parliament, or for the purpose of irrigating land; and
>
> (3) Sewers under the authority of any commissioners of sewers appointed by the Crown;
>
> shall vest in and be under the control of such local authority:

---

[30] As was suggested in *Travis v Uttley, supra.*
[31] *Beckenham U.D.C. v Wood* (1896) 60 J.P. 490.
[32] *Turner v Handsworth U.D.C.* [1909] 1 Ch. 381.
[33] *Turner v Handsworth U.D.C.* and *Beckenham U.D.C. v Wood., supra.*
[34] The position of sewage works, etc. is discussed *post*, Chapter 7.
[35] The test here is probably the *primary* use for which the sewer in question was made. Difficulties may arise in practice where a land drain is also used for the conveyance of sewage.

Provided that sewers within the district of a local authority
which have been or which may hereafter be constructed by
or transferred to some other local authority or by or to a
sewage board or other authority empowered under any Act
of Parliament to construct sewers shall (subject to any
agreement to the contrary) vest in and be under the control
of the authority who constructed the same, or to whom the
same have been transferred."

The second and third[36] exceptions from the general proposition
in this section are virtually self-explanatory,[37] and do not normally
give rise to difficulties, but the exception of sewers made "by any
person for his own profit" has been the subject of considerable
judicial interpretation. Whether or not a particular sewer was
made for profit is essentially a question of fact.[38] Thus, a sewer
constructed by a builder laying out a building estate was still
capable of not having been made for profit, although the builder
proposed to sell off the houses, when constructed, and make a
profit out of the transaction.[39] On the other hand, "profit" in the

---

[36]   The second exception clearly deals with land drainage; the third deals with
     sewers that are not normally the concern of the local authority as such (except
     with the consent of the appropriate government department under e.g. s.327
     of the Act of 1875). The proviso to the section does not cause difficulty, this
     relating to public sewers constructed by a public body for public use.

[37]   It is largely a question of fact and degree as to whether a land drain has become
     a sewer. If the ditch takes a considerable amount of surface water from houses,
     this may make it a sewer: *Ferrand v Hellas Land & Building Co.* [1893] 2 Q.B.
     135; but see *R. v Godmanchester L.B.* (1886) L.R. 1 Q.B. 328.

[38]   *Southstrand Estate Development Co. v East Preston R.D.C.* [1934] Ch. 254;
     unfortunately, it is only too often in this branch of the law that one finds that
     a particular matter is to be treated by the courts as a "question of fact". The
     result is that every such problem must be considered in relation to all the
     relevant circumstances, and reference to previously decided cases, except
     perhaps to indicate which circumstances are likely to be considered relevant,
     is not of any great assistance.

[39]   *Ferrand v Hallas Land & Building Co.* [1893] 2 Q.B. 135; *Pinnock v
     Waterworth* (1887) 3 T.L.R. 563; the fact that the builder intends to reimburse
     himself for his expenses in constructing the sewer does not affect the position;
     Vowles v Colmer (1895) 64 L.J. Ch. 414, which was followed in *Solihull
     R.D.C. v Ford* (1932) 30 L.G.R. 483. "'Made for profit' is not the same thing
     as 'made for use'," said Huddleston B. in *Bonella v Twickenham Local Board*
     (1887) 18 Q.B.D. 577.

section does not necessarily mean a direct money payment, and a land drain constructed for the purpose of enabling the land to be used more economically would normally be held to be one made for profit.[40]

To summarise the effect, therefore, of this first class of sewers vested in the local authority under section 20 of the 1936 Act in its original form, it seems that every "line of pipes" which was a "sewer" and was constructed prior to 1st October 1937, for the drainage of more than one building, or for premises not within the same curtilage, and which was not made for profit, vested in the former local authority under the 1875 Act, and would normally have been vested in the water authority under section 20 of the 1936 Act in its new form.[41] It is also clear that a sewer constructed mainly for the purpose of taking surface water from buildings is none the less capable of being a public sewer, although it may also take land drainage.[42]

(ii) All combined drains constructed before the 1st October 1937,[43] which would, immediately prior to that date, have vested in the local authority as sewers by virtue of the 1875 Act.

This classification also needs a consideration of the pre-1936 Act law for its appreciation. It will be noted in the first place that it concerns only "combined drains". This expression was not defined in the 1875 Act, nor was a definition included in the 1936 Act; it must therefore be construed as a technical term, referring to the common practice of builders and others engaged in the construction of drains. Generally speaking, buildings may be said to be drained in combination where a common line of pipes

---

[40] *Croysdale v Sunbury-on-Thames U.D.C.* [1898] 2 Ch. 515. A sewer constructed for the purpose of draining agricultural land will also normally be held to have been one made for profit and hence not a sewer within the section: *Phillimore v Watford R.D.C.* [1913] 2 Ch. 434, and see *Vare v Joy* (1920) 124 L.T. 148.

[41] Subject to the possible exception of "single private drains", considered under class (ii), below.

[42] *Hutton v Esher U.D.C.* [1974] 1 Ch. 167.

[43] The date of commencement of the 1936 Act: see s.347(1).

takes the effluent from the internal drains of the several buildings through private land to a cesspool, cesspit or "other receptacle for drainage", or to a sewer. By reason of the definitions of "sewer" and "drain" in section 4 of the Act of 1875, every combined drain having a proper outfall was itself a sewer and under section 13 of the same Act, vested in the local authority. The paragraph does not, therefore, seem strictly to be necessary, as every combined drain/public sewer would remain vested in the local authority under class (i), discussed above.

"Vesting" in the local authority under section 13 of the 1875 Act did not, however, give the authority an absolute right of ownership in the sewer in question,[44] as the section did not make the sewers the property of the authority so as to place them to all intents and purposes in the same position as if they were the private owners of the sewers. Thus the authority had no power to stop up a sewer vested in them, or physically to disconnect drains therefrom.[45] This limitation on the effect of the statutory vesting was important after the passing of the Public Health Acts Amendment Act 1890,[46] section 19 of which read as follows:

"(1) Where two or more houses belonging to different owners are connected with a public sewer by a single private drain, an application may be made under section 41 of the

---

[44] *Attorney-General v Dorking Union* (1882) 20 Ch. D. 595: "We must remember that the vesting of the sewers in the local authority gives them a very limited right of ownership": *per* Jessel M.R. at p.604.

[45] *Ogilvie v Blything Union Rural Sanitary Authority* (1891) 65 L.T. 338; (1892) 67 L.T. 18. "It has been clearly held that the vesting is not a giving of the property of the sewer and in the soil surrounding it to the local authority, but gives such ownership and such rights only as are necessary for the purpose of carrying out the duties of a local authority with regard to the subject matter": *per* Lord Russell C. J. in *Bradford v Mayor of Eastbourne* [1896] 2 Q.B. 205. In *Newcastle Corporation v Woolstanton Ltd.* [1947] 1 All E.R. 218, it was held that a gas undertaking has no natural right of support (apart from statute) for the land surrounding its gas mains, but only an implied right of support for the mains themselves (and see Chapter 5 *post*); it seems that this principle applies equally to public sewers.

[46] And provided the section had been adopted by the local authority concerned, this being an adoptive Act; the section was repealed by the 1936 Act.

Act of 1875[47] (relating to complaints as to nuisances from drains), and the local authority may recover any expenses incurred by them in executing any works under the powers conferred on them by that section from the owners of the houses in such shares and proportions as shall be settled by their surveyor or (in case of dispute) by a court of summary jurisdiction.

(2) Such expenses may be recovered summarily or may be declared by the urban authority to be private improvement expenses under the Public Health Acts, and may be recovered accordingly.

(3) For the purposes of this section the expression 'drain' includes a drain used for the drainage of more than one building."

The term "single private drain" in this section was not given a statutory definition, but it received much judicial consideration. The section is considered further later,[48] suffice it here to summarise the cases by describing the expression as a drainage pipe provided for a single house or for a group of houses in common, which is exclusive and private to that house or those houses.[49] Many of these drains which serve more than one house will also be combined drains and, if constructed before 1st October 1937, would therefore have vested in the local authority under the present paragraph; unless the two or more houses served by a particular drain were one building, or premises within the same curtilage.[50] It is submitted that the present paragraph in so far as it relates to section 19 of the 1890 Act was included in the 1936 Act *ex abundanti cautela*, and so as to

---

[47] Under this section the local authority, on complaint made to it of a nuisance in a drain, privy, cesspool, etc., could take certain action to secure the abatement of the nuisance, and if necessary take default action, its expenses in so doing being recoverable from the owner of the premises concerned.

[48] See Chapter 5, *post*.

[49] *Kingston-upon-Hull Corporation v North Eastern Railway Co.* [1916] 1 Ch. 31; the houses must be in separate ownership for s.19 of the 1890 Act to apply.

[50] See definitions of "sewer" and "drain" in s.4 of the 1875 Act: *supra*, p.43.

answer the argument that the 1890 Act at least in part divested the property in a sewer previously vested under the 1875 Act; it was argued (wrongly as it seems) for instance,[51] that a single private drain could not also be a public sewer.[52]

A similar position would appear to arise in connection with the common form provision in many local Acts,[53] in force before the passing of the 1936 Act, by which the effect of the section of the 1890 Act above discussed was made applicable to a "single private drain" serving two or more houses owned by the same person, or by different persons.[54] Such a provision also would not, it is submitted, have affected the vesting of the sewer under the Act of 1875.[55]

The present paragraph in the 1936 Act also referred to "statutory schemes",[56] the commonest examples of which in practice were the planning schemes prepared under the Town and Country Planning Act 1932, and its predecessors. Such schemes frequently made provision for the combined drainage of houses;[57] this

---

[51] e.g. in *Hill v Aldershot Corporation* [1933] 1 K.B. 259.

[52] In *Pemsel and Wilson v Tucker* [1907] 2 Ch. 191, a "single private drain" within the meaning of s.19 of the Act of 1890 was held none the less to have vested in the local authority as a sewer; the 1890 Act did not operate to prevent this vesting, and the owner of the property concerned therefore could not convey to a purchaser the property in the sewer.

[53] "Enactment" includes any enactment in a provisional order confirmed by Parliament: s.343(1) of the 1936 Act.

[54] See e.g. s.49 of the Kingston-upon-Hull Corporation Act 1903, considered by the court in *Kingston-upon-Hull v North-Eastern Railway Co.*, *supra*.

[55] *Ibid.*

[56] Defined by s.343(1) of the 1936 Act as meaning schemes "made under any enactment".

[57] A combined drainage agreement is valid and enforceable by the local authority (*Butt v Snow* (1903) 67 J.P. 454) with whom it is made, but only against the original owner, as the stipulations in the agreement will be positive in character and would not, therefore, run with the land as would restrictive covenants (see e.g. *Haywood v Brunswick Building Society* (1882) 8 Q.B.D. 403). By incorporating such agreements in the local authority's planning scheme under the Town and Country Planning Act 1932, this difficulty of enforceability was overcome. The agreements made under such a scheme frequently provided that the financial responsibility of maintaining the drains in question would remain with the private owners concerned.

paragraph will cover any combined drain constructed under such a scheme before 1st October 1937.

Other local Acts may contain different provisions which would be affected by this paragraph;[58] these obviously cannot be dealt with in detail in the present context.

Before temporarily leaving the subject of combined drains, it should, perhaps, be mentioned that the term is not here used in the sense sometimes used by engineers and other technicians, namely, to indicate that the particular drain is used for the conveyance of both foul and surface water.

(iii) Sewers constructed by the local authority at their expense or acquired by them.

It will be observed that this class of public sewer refers only to sewers properly so-called,[59] but includes sewers constructed either prior or subsequent to the commencement of the 1936 Act. Moreover, it would include a sewer constructed by the predecessors in title of the local authority, either as landowner or as sanitary authority, by virtue of the reference to "acquisition". In *Royco Homes Ltd. v Eatonwill Construction Ltd.*[60] it was held that a sewer which had been constructed by private individuals which lay under a roadway which subsequently became vested in the local authority, as highway authority, prior to 1974 thereupon became a public sewer, as having been "acquired" by

---

[58] Under the Metropolis Management Acts, the term "drain" was defined to include "any drain for draining any group or block of houses by a combined operation under the order of any vestry" (see s.250 of the Metropolis Management Act 1855). The Public Health Acts applied to central London only with modifications; cases decided on the statutes relating to London should therefore be read and applied with caution and reserve. A number of local Acts provided that the local authority should be enabled to order the provision of combined drainage; such cases, outside the Metropolis, might have operated prior to the 1936 Act, to prevent such combined drains from vesting in the local authority (see e.g. s.81 of the Wimbledon Corporation Act 1914, discussed in *Grant v Derwent* [1929] 1 Ch. 390).

[59] See *ante*, pp.3-10.

[60] [1978] 2 All E.R. 821.

them. Because the soil was acquired, the line of pipes within it was also acquired upon the principle *quicquid plantatur solo, solo cedit.*

The sewer need not have been constructed by the local authority in its capacity of local sanitary authority; it may, for example, have been constructed for the purpose of draining the authority's housing estate, under the Housing Act 1957; in such a case, the proviso would normally apply, and the sewer did not become a public one until the authority had declared it to be such. No particular formality had to be observed in the making of such a declaration; an ordinary resolution of the authority was probably sufficient. This provision applied also to sewers constructed by a local authority outside their own district, under sections 15 and 16 of the 1936 Act.[61]

The proviso did not appear in the re-enacted version of section 20, but in view of the terms of section 20(1)(a) this is immaterial as the paragraph refers to sewers constructed by the water authority not by the local authority. There was therefore no question of a sewer constructed by the local authority after 1st April 1974 becoming a public sewer, unless and until it was "adopted" by the water authority or arrangements were made under section 15 of the 1973 Act.

A sewer constructed by the local authority, but at the expense of some other person[62] did not vest in the authority under this provision, and (if constructed after the commencement of the Act) remained a private sewer.

(ii) Sewers constructed under Part XI of the Highways Act 1980
It remains to consider the second paragraph of section 20 of the 1936 Act as substituted by Schedule 8 of the 1973 Act, itself repealed by the 1989 Act.

---

[61] Now repealed.
[62] e.g. under s.36 of the 1936 Act (see s.36(3)); or by agreement with the owner or occupier of the premises concerned, under s.275, *ibid.*

"All sewers constructed under [Part XI of the Highways Act 1980][63] except sewers belonging to a road maintained by the highway authority."

This paragraph refers to the procedure for the making up of private streets at the expense, partial or complete, of the frontagers, under Part XI of the Highways Act 1980.[64] These provisions enable the "street works authority"[65] to require a private street to be sewered, levelled, paved, metalled, flagged, channelled, made good[66] or lighted to the satisfaction of the authority; any one or more of these operations can be required to be executed at the same time. Once a sewer was constructed under these provisions, it became a public sewer and vested in the water authority. Where the street works authority had expressed itself as satisfied with a particular system of sewering, it could not require the owners of the private street in question to construct a further sewer, should this subsequently become necessary.[67]

Highway drains vest in the highway authority,[68] and consequently the exception in the present paragraph provided that where the private street works action was confined to the construction of a highway drain or sewer, any sewer so constructed would vest in the highway authority and would not be a "public sewer".

(iii) Declarations of vesting

"All sewers and sewage disposal works with respect to which a declaration of vesting under the foregoing provisions of this Act has taken effect."

---

[63] This replaced a reference to Part IX of the Highways Act 1959 in the version of s.20 originally substituted by the 1973 Act.

[64] There is now only one such procedure, that under "the code of 1892"; the former procedure by way of "the code of 1875" was abolished by the Local Government Act 1972. See *post*, p.132.

[65] See *post*, p.132, n.45.

[66] This particular operation did not appear in the code of 1875; otherwise the two codes were similar.

[67] *Bonella v Twickenham Local Board* (1888) 20 Q.B.D. 63; *Poole Corporation v Blake* [1956] 1 Q.B. 206.

[68] See *post*, Chapter 6.

Section 17 of the Public Health Act 1936 enabled the water authority to adopt any sewer in or serving its area by a declaration of vesting, provided that the sewer's construction had not been completed before 1st October 1937.

(c) Conclusion

In summary a "public sewer" under the 1991 Act is broadly any sewer vested in a sewerage undertaker in its capacity as such[69] whether by transfer from the former authorities including the effect of "historical" provisions considered above, or by construction *de novo*. Any other sewer is a private sewer, and will be vested not in a sewerage undertaker, but in some other public or private body or individual.

THE EFFECT OF PUBLIC OWNERSHIP

If a particular conduit is in law a public sewer, it will be vested in the sewerage undertaker, but its ownership thereof will be limited, as above explained[70] to the purposes of fulfilling its functions as undertaker. Further, it will not be able to interfere with private rights enjoyed in respect of the particular conduit before it became a public sewer,[71] nor may it physically disconnect any drains from the public sewer (except under section 113 of the Water Industry Act 1991).[72] However, the following consequences will apply in the event of a conduit being in law a public sewer:

(a) the sewerage undertaker will be under a duty to maintain, cleanse and empty it;[73]

(b) provided he has a means of access thereto an adjoining landowner will have a right to cause the drains of his premises to connect thereto;[74]

---

69   Section 219(1).
70   *Ante*, p.50.
71   See e.g. *R. v Staines Local Board* (1888) 60 L.T. 261.
72   *Ogilvie v Blything Union R.S.A.* (1891) 65 L.T. 338.
73   1991 Act, s.94, *post*, p.109.
74   *Ibid.*, s.106, *post*, p.175*ff.*

(c) the sewerage undertaker will not be able to take proceedings (e.g. in nuisance) in respect of any effluent therefrom;

(d) the *local* authority may be able to prevent building over the sewer[75] and the sewerage undertaker will be able to take proceedings if anyone interferes with its property.[76]

Thus, for example, in the diagram on page 58, the drain, although it serves more than one premises, is *not* a public sewer (whether constructed before or after 1st October 1937); indeed it is not a sewer at all, as it does not lead to a proper outfall (*ante*, page 9). Therefore, if flooding occurs at the shaded area, the sewerage undertaker would not itself be liable, but the local authority could probably commence nuisance proceedings against the persons responsible, who will presumably be the owners of A, B and C. If there is a highway drain connected at point E, this will not affect the position, as the frontagers would be liable. However, if Lovers' Lane were adopted by the highway authority, and the flooding was shown to be due to the surface water from the highway, that authority would (presumably) be held liable.

Further, if a new house is built on plot D, the owner will have no right to cause his house drains to connect with this existing drain; he would have to negotiate terms with the owners of A, B and C.

PRIVATE SEWERS

A sewer which is not a public sewer must be a private sewer, and there is no point, in law, of distinguishing between a private sewer and a drain.[77] "Sewer" will normally be used to describe a conduit draining more than one property, and "drain" will be

---

[75] Building Act 1984, s.18, *post*, p.119.

[76] *Post*, p.120.

[77] A drain, *stricto sensu*, cannot be vested in the sewerage undertaker in its capacity as such, although it may, of course, belong to the undertaker in its capacity as landowner, or by virtue of its draining the undertaker's own property. See also definition of "private sewer" in s.343(1) of the 1936 Act and s.219(1) of the 1991 Act.

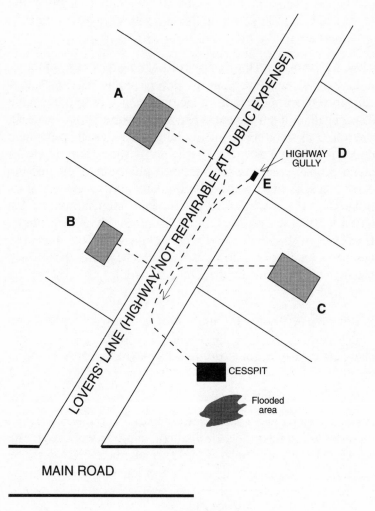

A

HIGHWAY
GULLY

D

E

B

LOVERS' LANE (HIGHWAY NOT REPAIRABLE AT PUBLIC EXPENSE)

C

CESSPIT

Flooded
area

MAIN ROAD

Foul drain – – – – – – – –

used to signify a channel draining a single property,[78] but the distinction has no legal significance. The all important question is whether a particular sewer is a *public* sewer.

In practice, however, the subsidiary question may arise, in whom is a particular private sewer or drain vested? If the sewer drains the premises and runs through the land of but a single owner, it is normally clear that such owner is the owner of the sewer; if the sewer is used to drain the property of another person, the legal position (in the absence of any express agreement or provision in the relevant title deeds) will be presumed to be that the owner of the tenement has granted an easement of drainage through his property – provided the requirements for presuming such an easement are present. Thus (apart from an express grant), the right must have continued for the statutory period for prescription of 20 years,[79] the dominant owner must have enjoyed the easement claimed as a benefit for his property of which he is owner in fee simple, the use of the sewer must be claimed "as of right",[80] and the right claimed must be to drain through a well defined channel.[81]

---

[78] Buildings drained "in combination" are, however, said to be served by a combined "drain".

[79] Prescription Act 1832. User for 20 years may be defeated by evidence proving that no easement had in fact been granted (for all prescription depends on a presumed grant), but user for 40 years is indefeasible, except by proof that the user had originally been by agreement or consent (see s.2 of the Act of 1832). A right to cause sewage to flow across another's land or into a public sewer cannot be acquired secretly without the knowledge of the owner of the servient tenement: *Liverpool Corporation v Coghill* [1918] 1 Ch. 307.

[80] The user must therefore have commenced "*nec vi nec clam nec precario*", i.e. permission must not have been obtained by force, or the user must not have commenced secretly and in such circumstances that the owner of the servient tenement could not have been aware of the drain in question, or with the permission of the owner of the servient tenement, as in such last-mentioned case, the right would be limited to the terms of such permission. On these points, see such cases as *Union Lighterage Co. v London Graving Dock Co.* [1902] 2 Ch. 557, and *Lyell v Hothfield* [1914] 3 K.B. 911.

[81] This proposition follows, it is submitted, from the law relating to the acquisition of rights to watercourses; thus, in *Acton v Blundell* (1843) 12 M.&W. 324, it was held that a landowner could have no rights in water percolating in an undefined channel through his land in such manner as to enable him to prevent an adjoining owner from diverting such water.

It is frequently important to decide whether a particular person has an easement to lay a private sewer or drain through another person's land,[82] for if the conduit is there with the permission of the landowner in such circumstances that an easement has been created, that landowner will not be able to require the removal of the conduit without making payment of compensation to the person entitled to use the drain.[83] However, when taking proceedings for the abatement of a nuisance[84] in a private sewer or drain, or caused thereby, the local authority is not concerned to ascertain whether the persons whose premises are drained by the conduit in question have a legal right to cause their drainage to flow through such conduit;[85] they will be the persons by "whose act, default, or sufferance"[86] the nuisance has arisen or is continuing, and abatement proceedings may, therefore, properly

---

82   The right to lay a drain and to cause drainage to flow through such drain will normally carry with it the ancillary right to enter on the land and effect necessary works of repair, maintenance or renewal to the drain; see *Pomfret v Ricroft* (1669) 1 Saund. 321. It would not, of course, under such a right be competent to increase the size of the drain. In *Simmons v Midford* [1969] 2 Ch. 415, it was held, on the facts of that case, that a grant of an easement of drainage amounted to an exclusive right to use the line of pipes in question.

83   An easement is a legal interest provided it is created by grant (express, implied or presumed from long use) and limited for an interest equivalent to an estate in fee simple absolute in possession or a term of years absolute: Law of Property Act 1925, s.1(2)(a). If the easement of drainage in question is a legal interest, it will be enforceable against subsequent purchasers of the servient tenement. If it has been limited in such a manner that it is capable of subsisting only as an equitable interest in the land, it will none the less still be enforceable against subsequent owners, provided it is registered as an equitable easement under s.2(5) of the Land Charges Act 1972 (Class D (iii)). Easements granted for drains to serve an estate to be developed subsequent to the time of the grant should be limited so as to take effect within the perpetuity period: *Dunn v Blackdown Properties Ltd.* [1961] 1 Ch. 433. However, in the case of deeds coming into effect after 1964, an easement which is in fact exercised within the perpetuity period will not be invalidated simply because it could have first been exercised after the end of that period; one is now entitled to "wait and see" if there will be a breach of the perpetuity rule: Perpetuities and Accumulations Act 1964, s.3.

84   Under the Environmental Protection Act 1990, Pt. III, or s.59 of the Building Act 1984.

85   *Brown v Bussell* (1868) L.R. 3 Q.B. 251.

86   See s.79(7) of the 1990 Act (definition of "person responsible" for a statutory nuisance).

be taken against them.[87] On the other hand, the landowner who stops up a private sewer laid through his land without his consent may be liable in nuisance abatement proceedings brought by the local authority, as he would then be the person who had caused the nuisance.[88] The owner of a private sewer or drain may be liable in private nuisance to another landowner who has sustained injury as a consequence of his failure to cleanse the sewer, etc.[89]

---

[87] If the drain is really a public sewer vested in the sewerage undertaker, apparently no nuisance proceedings can be taken against a person draining into it, and in respect of whom it might otherwise be said that he was causing a nuisance: *Fordom v Parsons* [1894] 2 Q.B. 780. The judgment of Kennedy J. in *Wincanton R.D.C. v Parsons* [1905] 2 K.B. 34, however, suggests that the fact that the conduit in question was a public sewer would not necessarily constitute a defence in nuisance proceedings. It is submitted that this decision, in so far as this point is concerned, would not be followed (see *Lumley's Public Health*, 12th edn., Vol. III, p.2278).

[88] *Riddell v Spear* (1879) 43 J.P. 317; but it should be noted that in this case the sewer in question had become a public sewer before the action complained of was taken.

[89] *Sedleigh-Denfield v O'Callaghan* [1940] A.C. 880.

Chapter 3

CONSTRUCTION OF PUBLIC SEWERS

DUTY TO PROVIDE SYSTEM OF PUBLIC SEWERS

(a) The basic duty

Under section 94(1)(a) of the Water Industry Act 1991, it is the duty of every sewerage undertaker

> "to provide, improve and extend such a system of public sewers (whether inside its area or elsewhere) . . . as to ensure that that area is and continues to be effectually drained; . . . ."

this provision being in effect a repetition of the former section 14 of the Water Act 1973, which itself derived from section 14 of the Public Health Act 1936 and indirectly from section 15 of the 1875 Act.

The duty under section 94 is supplemented by Regulation 4 of the Urban Waste Water Treatment Regulations 1994.[1] Thus, the duty under section 94(1)(a) is to include a duty to ensure that collecting systems[2] which satisfy the requirements of Schedule 2 to the regulations are provided:

(a) where the urban waste water[2] discharges into receiving waters which are a sensitive area,[2] by December 31st, 1998, for every agglomeration[2] with a population equivalent[2] of more than 10,000; and

(b) without prejudice to (a), by December 31st, 2000, for every agglomeration with a population equivalent of more than 15,000; and by December 31st, 2005, for every agglomeration with a population equivalent of between 2,000 and 15,000.

These requirements do not apply where either the National

---

[1] S.I. 1994 No. 2841.
[2] These expressions are defined in Reg. 2(1); see *ante*, pp.33-37.

Rivers Authority certifies that the establishment of a collecting system is not justified because it would produce no environmental benefit; or the Secretary of State certifies that this is not justified because it would entail excessive costs. In either case, individual systems or other appropriate systems must be provided that the Authority certifies achieve the same level of environmental protection.[3]

The requirements for collecting systems specified by Schedule 2 are that systems shall take into account waste water treatment requirements, and that the design, construction and maintenance of such systems shall be undertaken in accordance with the best technical knowledge not entailing excessive costs, notably regarding:

(a) volume and characteristics of urban waste water;

(b) prevention of leaks; and

(c) limitation of pollution of receiving waters due to storm water overflows.

(b) Consequences of default

Under the Public Health Act 1875 it was provided that where a local authority failed to provide its district with adequate sewers or to maintain those provided, a complaint could be made to the Local Government Board which could then make a default order requiring the authority to perform its statutory duties.

Under the 1875 (and sc. 1936) legislation, the existence of the default power was held to exclude the grant of *mandamus*.[4] Furthermore, it was held in a number of cases that no action for damages or a mandatory injunction lay for breach of duty or negligence in respect of harm arising from the inadequacy of a

---

[3]   Reg. 4(1)-(3).
[4]   *Pasmore v Oswaldtwistle U.D.C.* [1898] A.C. 387 (*mandamus* not available to compel a local authority under the 1875 Act to provide an adequate sewerage system).

sewerage system constructed by the responsible authority itself and which was adequate originally.[5] It was unclear whether the principle recognised in these cases was an aspect of a wider principle that a local authority was not liable for "non-feasance" as distinct from "misfeasance".[6] In any event the sanitary authority could be held liable if it caused, adopted or continued a nuisance.[7]

So far as modern sewerage undertakers, which are limited companies vested with statutory functions rather than public authorities, are concerned it is provided that the duty under section 94 of the 1991 Act is enforceable under section 18 of that

---

[5]   *Glossop v Heston and Isleworth Local Board* (1879) 12 Ch. D. 102 (mandatory injunction refused); *Att.-Gen. v Dorking Union Guardians* (1882) 20 Ch. D. 595; *Robinson v. Workington Corporation* [1897] 1 Q.B. 619 (claim for damages rejected where the case was admitted to be one of non-feasance in that the defendants had not replaced an existing, inadequate, sewer; the duty was owed to the district as a whole not any individual and the default power was the only remedy); *Pride of Derby and Derbyshire Angling Association v British Celanese Ltd. and others* [1953] 1 Ch. 149 (general principle recognised, see Evershed M.R. at pp.169-179, but distinguished as here the defendant corporation was itself discharging polluting effluent from its own sewage disposal works into the River Derwent); *Smeaton v Ilford Corporation* [1954] 1 Ch. 450 (corporation not liable in nuisance arising simply from the overloading of its sewers).

[6]   The existence of any such general doctrine outside highway cases was denied by Evershed M.R. and Denning L.J. in the *Pride of Derby* case, *supra* at pp.175-176, 187-189, respectively.

[7]   See *post*, p.124. In the *Pride of Derby* case, Denning L.J. stated *obiter* (pp.189-191) that where the sanitary authority as local authority was itself responsible for or permitted additional building that rendered a sewerage system inadequate, "they are themselves guilty of the nuisance" (p.190); the old "non-feasance" cases had "little or no application in the present day" as in the 19th century local authorities had no powers to control additional buildings (pp.190-191). However, his Lordship also accepted that no evidence had been given of the building or planning activities of Derby Corporation and so it was not right to base the decision on the point. It is submitted that these dicta are unsound; in particular, a local authority cannot be said to have "caused" a nuisance through the grant of a planning permission. In any event the dicta cannot apply now that the functions of sewerage undertaker and planning authority have been separated: see *Dear v Thames Water* (1993) 33 Con. L.R. 43, where Judge Bowsher Q.C. (Official Referee) held that the *Glossop* case, *supra* n.5, was still good law, and not to be regarded as qualified by the principle of *Leakey v National Trust*, *post*, p.173 (alternatively, if the cases could be reconciled, it was within the application of the reasonableness test).

Act by the Secretary of State or (with the consent of or in accordance with a general authorisation given by the Secretary of State) by the Director General of Water Services. Section 18 enables the Secretary of State or the Director to make a final or provisional "enforcement order".[8] Section 18(8) provides that

"Where any act or omission constitutes a contravention of a condition of an appointment under Chapter I of this Part or of a statutory or other requirement enforceable under this section, the only remedies for that contravention, apart from those available by virtue of this section, shall be those for which express provision is made by or under any enactment and those that are available in respect of that act or omission otherwise than by virtue of its constituting such a contravention."

This makes the section 18 remedies for breach (*inter alia*) of duties under section 94 exclusive, apart from any other remedies expressly provided under statute, and any causes of action arising from the same act or omission but not relying in terms on the fact of non-compliance with section 94.[9] Contravention of an enforcement order is actionable by a person affected who sustains loss or damage, subject to a defence that the company has taken all reasonable steps and exercised all due diligence.[10] The relevant enforcement authority (i.e. the Secretary of State or the Director, as the case may be) may seek an injunction.[11] If the Secretary of State is satisfied that there has been a contravention, he *must* make an enforcement order unless one of the exceptions applies. If he is not so satisfied, it is unclear whether a person

---

8   See *ante*, pp.17-19.
9   See *Dear v Thames Water* (1993) 33 Con. L.R. 43, where Judge Bowsher Q.C., Official Referee, held that the forerunner of s.18 (the Water Act 1989, s.20) precluded an action against a sewerage undertaker in respect of any alleged negligence or nuisance occurring after 31st August 1989, in respect of any matters coming within the enforcement procedure. It is submitted that an application for judicial review based on a breach of s.94 would also be barred by s.18(8).
10   1991 Act, s.22(1)-(3).
11   *Ibid.*, s.22(4), (5).

who claims to have been prejudiced by a breach of duty may challenge that decision on application for judicial review.[12]

Sections 23 and 24 of the 1991 Act provide for the issue of special administration orders by the High Court in certain cases of default.[13] Such an order is issued where the court is satisfied upon petition by the Secretary of State or, with the consent of the Secretary of State, by the Director General of Water Services that, *inter alia*, there has been or is likely to be a contravention by a sewerage undertaker of a requirement imposed by section 94 sufficiently serious to justify its deprivation of its appointment.[14] The degree of "seriousness" of default which will be required before such an order will be issued will clearly emerge only from the practical jurisprudence of the court in applying the provision, should this in fact prove necessary.

The position of a water authority in respect of the period 1st April 1974 to 31st August 1989 was different. There was no provision for a default power in the Water Act 1973, and the general duty to provide for the effectual draining of the area under section 14 (unlike other powers[15]) was not made subject to the Minister's default power in section 322(1) of the Public Health Act 1936.

---

[12] *Cf. R. v Secretary of State for the Environment, ex. p. Jaywick Sands Freeholders Association Ltd.* [1975] J.P.L. 663, where the Divisional Court stated *obiter* that there were grounds for quashing the Secretary of State's decision to refuse to exercise his default power under s.322(1) of the Public Health Act 1936 (see *post*, p.246) where there had been a delay of over 20 years in providing sewers (and water supply) for 773 holiday chalets. The matter would have been remitted to the Secretary of State had responsibility not by then been transferred from the local authority (Clacton U.D.C.) to the water authority. Lord Widgery C.J. said that "the Secretary of State did not have the power to direct the water authority to do the work as it was not the defaulting authority in the first place" (p 663). Note, however, that this case concerned a default *power* and so does not necessarily apply to the s.18 powers. In *R. v Secretary of State for the Environment, ex p. Friends of the Earth Ltd., The Times*, 8th June 1995, the Court of Appeal entertained but rejected on the merits an application for judicial review of the Secretary of State's decision to accept undertakings under s.19 of the 1991 Act: see p.19, n.76, *ante*.

[13] See *ante*, pp.20-21.

[14] Section 25(2).

[15] See the Water Act 1973, s.14(2).

Accordingly, the section 14 duty was in principle enforceable by *mandamus*, although liability in negligence or for breach of statutory duty arising out of non-compliance was limited.[16]

For the individual consumer, or potential consumer, some further aid might be found in the duties imposed upon customer service committees under section 28 of the 1991 Act.[17]

Like that under the former section 14 of the 1973 Act, the duty of sewer provision under section 94 of the 1991 Act does not include the provision of land drains or drains required for agricultural purposes. The duty is only to provide *public sewers*, which is to say those which will vest in the sewerage undertaker under section 179 when constructed.[18]

REQUISITION NOTICES

Under section 98 of the Water Industry Act 1991, a sewerage undertaker is under a duty to provide a public sewer for the drainage for domestic purposes of premises in a locality in its area where it is required so to do by a notice served upon it by one or more persons entitled to make such a demand. A notice may be served by:

---

[16] *Dear v Thames Water and others* (1993) 33 Con. L.R. 43. In *Weaver v West Yorkshire Water Authority* [1981] C.L.Y. 2874 the public sewer running beneath the plaintiff's house became blocked at an interceptor trap by foreign bodies (including newspapers) put into the system by third parties. The plaintiff's cellar was consequently flooded with sewage and she declined an offer to remove and seal up the trap. The sewer was adequate for the houses it served. The plaintiff lost an initial claim that the pipe concerned was not a public sewer (see *Weaver v Family Housing Association (York) Ltd.* (1975) 74 L.G.R. 255) but then sought redress against the water authority by an ordinary action for damages and for an injunction under s.14 requiring diversion of the sewer. Glidewell J. held that the facts did not disclose a breach of the section and that an individual had no right to bring an action for damages in such a case even had there been a breach (*cf.* the *Glossop* case, *ante*, p.64, n.5). An application for judicial review (unreported, C.A. 17th July 1985) also failed because the Court of Appeal, upholding the Divisional Court, held that on the facts there was no evidence that the drainage was not effectual and, therefore, no grounds for judicial review were disclosed.

[17] See *ante*, p.29.

[18] Section 219(1).

(a) an owner of any premises in the locality concerned;

(b) an occupier of such premises;

(c) a local authority within whose area the locality is in whole or part located;

(d) the Commission for the New Towns, the Development Board for Rural Wales or the development corporation of a new town where the locality lies in whole or part within an area of their responsibility; and

(e) an urban development corporation where the locality is situated in whole or part within an area designated as an urban development area under Part XVI of the Local Government, Planning and Land Act 1980.[19]

A requisition notice may only be served in respect of domestic drainage of premises upon which there either are buildings or will be when current proposals for construction are carried out.[20] Drainage for "domestic purposes" in this context is carefully defined.[21] Where there are buildings upon premises in the locality concerned, domestic drainage is taken to mean

(i) the removal from the buildings and associated land of the contents of lavatories;

(ii) the removal from such buildings and land of water which has been used for cooking or washing, other than in connection with a laundry business or the business of preparing food and drink for consumption otherwise than on the premises; and

(iii) the removal from such buildings and land of surface water.[22]

---

[19] Section 98(2).
[20] Section 98(1)(b).
[21] Section 98(5).
[22] Section 98(5) and 117(1) (definition of "domestic sewerage purposes").

Where a person is proposing to erect buildings upon the premises concerned, "domestic purposes" has the same meaning as in relation to existing buildings but must be specified in the requisition in relation to stated times after the erection of the buildings.[23] Where a requisition notice is served upon a sewerage undertaker in due order under section 98, the sewerage undertaker has, in effect, a period of six months from the day upon which any financial conditions which may be set are satisfied or that upon which the points at which private sewers and drains leading from the premises will connect with the public sewer are agreed, whichever shall be the later, in which to meet the requisition before it will be considered to be in default.[24] The points of connection with the public sewer should be agreed between the parties, i.e. those making the requisition and the sewerage undertaker,[25] or in default be determined by a single arbitrator appointed by agreement or, if this is not achieved, by the President of the Institution of Civil Engineers.[26]

The duty of the sewerage undertaker to provide a public sewer under the provisions of section 98 is stated by section 98(3) to be owed to the person making the requisition or to each of the persons joining in doing so. Any breach of this duty which causes loss or damage to be sustained by a person to whom the duty is owed is actionable at the suit of that person;[27] it is, however, a defence to such an action for the sewerage undertaker to show that it took all reasonable steps and exercised all due diligence in seeking to avoid the breach.[28]

Where a sewer is requisitioned, the sewerage undertaker may impose financial conditions upon those making the requisition,

---

[23] Section 98(5)(b).
[24] Section 101(1).
[25] Section 101(3).
[26] Section 101(4).
[27] Section 98(4).
[28] Section 98(4). The reference to a "water" undertaker in the original version of s.98(4) was replaced by a reference to a "sewerage" undertaker by the Competition and Service (Utilities) Act 1992, Sch. 2, para. 26, correcting an obvious drafting error.

except in the case of a local authority.[29] The detail of such conditions is set out in section 99 of the 1991 Act. The sewerage undertaker may require from the person or persons requisitioning a sewer undertakings binding them to pay to it in each of the twelve years following the provision of the sewer an amount not exceeding the "relevant deficit"[30] as defined for the year in question, if there should be one, in respect of the cost of making the sewerage provision requisitioned.[31]

Where a deposit is demanded under section 99 by way of security by a sewerage undertaker, interest may be payable by the undertaker upon the sums so retained.[32] Disputes upon financial undertakings under section 99 are to be referred to a single arbitrator appointed by agreement between the parties or, in default thereof, by the President of the Institution of Civil Engineers.[33]

---

[29]   Section 98(1)(c).

[30]   The relevant deficit upon a sewer for any year is "the amount (if any) by which the drainage charges payable for the use during that year of that sewer are exceeded by the annual borrowing costs of a loan of the amount required for the provision of that sewer": s.100. For this purpose the "annual borrowing costs" is the aggregate amount for the year representing the interest payments and capital repayments "if an amount equal to so much of the costs reasonably incurred in providing that sewer as were not incurred in the provision of additional capacity had been borrowed, by the sewerage undertaker providing the sewer", upon (a) the basis of payments and repayments by twelve equal annual instalments and (b) an interest rate calculated upon such a basis as may have been determined by the undertaker with the approval of the Director or, in default, by the Director himself: s.100(2)(3).

[31]   The cost of provision includes costs arising from provision of such other public sewers and pumping stations as may be rendered necessary by the provision of the new sewer and a proportion (if any) which is reasonable of the costs incurred in the provision of any resulting necessary additional capacity in any other public sewer which was provided in the previous 12 years pursuant to s.98 or s.71 of the Water Act 1989 or s.16 of the 1973 Act or any equivalent local statutory provision: s.100(5), (6).

[32]   Interest is payable on each sum of 50p so deposited for every three months during which it is held by the undertaker. The rate is determined by the undertaker with the approval of the Director or, in default, by the Director himself: s.99(4), (5).

[33]   Section 99(6).

PROVISION OF PUBLIC SEWERS OTHER THAN BY REQUISITION

The Environment Act 1995,[34] inserting section 101A in the Water Industry Act 1991, introduces a new obligation for sewerage undertakers to provide a public sewer in specified circumstances. Without prejudice to the duty under section 98 of the 1991 Act,[35] it is the duty of a sewerage undertaker to provide a public sewer to be used for the drainage for domestic sewerage purposes of premises in a particular locality in its area if three conditions are satisfied.[36] These are:

(a) that the premises in question (or any of them) are premises on which there are buildings each of which[37] was erected before, or substantially completed by, 20th June 1995;

(b) that the drains or sewers used for the drainage for domestic sewerage purposes of the premises in question do not, either directly or through an intermediate drain or sewer, connect with a public sewer; and

(c) that the drainage of any of the premises in question is giving, or likely to give, rise to such adverse effects to the environment or amenity that it is appropriate, having regard to guidance issued by the Secretary of State[38] and all other relevant considerations, to provide a public sewer for the drainage for domestic sewerage purposes of the premises in question.[39]

Without prejudice to the generality of (c), regard is to be had, so far as relevant, in determining whether it is appropriate for a sewer to be provided, to:

---

[34] Sch. 22, para. 103. In force from a day to be appointed.
[35] *Ante*, p.67.
[36] s.101A(1).
[37] Except any shed, glasshouse or other outbuilding appurtenant to a dwelling and not designed or occupied as living accommodation.
[38] Issued under s.101A(4) after consultation with the Director, the Environment Agency and such other bodies or persons as he considers appropriate: s.101A(5).
[39] s.101A(2).

(a) the geology of the locality in question or any other locality;

(b) the number of premises with buildings which might reasonably be expected to be drained by means of that sewer;

(c) the costs of providing that sewer;

(d) the nature and extent of adverse effects to the environment or amenity if the premises or locality are not drained by a public sewer;

(e) the extent to which it is practicable for those effects to be overcome other than by the provision of public sewers (through section 101A or otherwise), and the costs of so overcoming those effects.[40]

The duty under section 101A(1) is enforceable under section 18 of the 1991 Act.[41] Any dispute between a sewerage undertaker and an owner or occupier of premises in its area as to whether the duty under section 101A(1) arises, the domestic sewerage purposes for which a sewer should be provided, or the time by which any such duty should be performed, is to be determined by the Environment Agency, whose decision is final.[42] An undertaker is only to be taken to be in breach of its duty where, and to the extent that, it has accepted, or the Environment Agency has determined, that it is under such a duty and that the time by which the duty is to that extent to be performed has passed.[43]

This new provision was introduced as a last-minute amendment to the Environment Bill in the House of Commons "to make easier the provision of first-time connection to mains sewerage of existing premises."[44] It is to be seen in the context of the repeal

---

[40] s.101A(3).
[41] See *ante*, pp.17-19.
[42] s.101A(7)-(9).
[43] s.101A(10).
[44] Sir Paul Beresford, Parliamentary Under Secretary of State for Environment, Vol. 262 H.C.Deb., 28th June 1995, col. 1047.

of section 151 of the 1991 Act which authorises the Secretary of State to make grants to support the provision of sewerage services in rural areas.[45] The power of the sewerage undertaker to charge for any services provided in the course of carrying out its duty under section 100A(1) is to be exercised through a charges scheme applicable to the undertaker's customers generally.[46]

RIGHTS TO LAY SEWERS

Under sections 158 and 159 of the Water Industry Act 1991, sewerage undertakers are empowered to lay and maintain pipes in pursuance of their statutory functions,[47] both within and without their designated areas.[48] The provisions make a distinction between "street works" and works on, over or under "other land" and these categories must be considered separately.

(a) Power to carry out street works

Sections 158 and 161(1) of the 1991 Act empower a sewerage undertaker

(a) to lay a sewer or disposal main in, under or over any street and to keep it there;

(b) to inspect, maintain, adjust, repair or alter any sewer or disposal main in, under or over any street;

(c) to carry out in a street all such works as are necessary to

---

[45] See *post*, pp.140-141.

[46] 1991 Act, ss.142(3A) and 143(3A), inserted by the Environment Act 1995, Sch. 22, paras. 114, 115. See *post*, p.112*ff*.

[47] These powers are applicable to the functioning of both water undertakers and sewerage undertakers.

[48] Section 192(3). By subs. (2A), inserted by the Competiton and Service (Utilities) Act 1992, s.47, in the case of the exercise of a power under ss.158 or 159 to construct a public sewer other than a storm water overflow sewer outside an undertaker's area, the undertaker must give notice to, and obtain the consent of, the undertaker for the other area (or the Director if consent is refused).

ensure that water in a waterworks used, or potentially to be used, by a water undertaker for purposes of water supply is not polluted or contaminated;[49] and

(d) to carry out any works requisite for or incidental to any of these purposes including, in particular,

(i) breaking up or opening a street,

(ii) tunnelling or boring under a street,

(iii) breaking up or opening a sewer, drain or tunnel, and

(iv) moving or removing earth and other materials.

By section 158(11) of the 1991 Act,[50] where a company replaces a relevant undertaker as sewerage undertaker under an inset appointment, any pipe serving the relevant premises is deemed to be a "sewer" for the purposes of sections 158 and 159.[51] The New Roads and Street Works Act 1991[52] now defines the term "street" as meaning

"the whole or part of any of the following, irrespective of whether it is a thoroughfare –

(a) any highway, road, lane, footway, alley or passage,

(b) any square or court, and

(c) any land laid out as a way whether it is for the time being formed as a way or not."

A highway must be a way over which members of the public have a right to pass and re-pass on their lawful occasions, but it need not necessarily be maintainable at the public expense and this may be taken to be the case also for the purposes of the 1991 Act.

[49] 1991 Act, s.161(1).
[50] Inserted by the Competiton and Service (Utilities) Act 1992, s.40(6).
[51] See *ante*, p.14.
[52] s.48(1). This definition is applied for the purposes of the Water Industry Act 1991 by *ibid*., s.219(1).

When carrying out street works a sewerage undertaker must comply with the street works code set out in Part III of the New Roads and Street Works Act 1991[53] relating to the break-up of streets. In most circumstances notice must be given to the highway authority before the works are commenced[54] and openings made in the road must be adequately guarded and lit at night; proper traffic signs must also be placed and operated as may be required;[55] and unnecessary delay and obstruction must be avoided.[56] In carrying out such works a sewerage undertaker is under an express duty

(a) to do as little damage as possible and

(b) to pay compensation for any loss or damage resulting therefrom.[57]

Where dispute arises upon matters of compensation, the amount is to be settled by a single arbitrator appointed by agreement between the parties or, in default, by the Director.[58] This duty relates primarily to property damage done during the performance of works. It is however clear that a sewerage undertaker will be under a general duty of care to any member of the public who sustains injury as a consequence of its performance of works upon the public highway.[59] In exercising its power to construct a sewer in, under or over a street, a sewerage undertaker will also be under a general duty to do so in a proper and reasonably careful manner. If the sewerage undertaker's negligence in constructing the sewer causes subsidence or otherwise damages the highway, it will be liable in damages to any lawful user of the highway who suffers injury in consequence.[60]

---

53   See *Cross on Local Government Law* (8th edn., 1991), paras. 14.52-14.57.
54   New Roads and Street Works Act 1991, s.54.
55   *Ibid*, s.65.
56   *Ibid*, s.66.
57   Water Industry Act 1991, Sch. 12, para. 1(2).
58   *Ibid*., para. 1(3), as amended by the Competition and Service (Utilities) Act 1992, Sch. 2, para. 29.
59   See e.g. *Kimber v Gas Light & Coke Co.* [1918] 1 K.B. 439.
60   See, in relation to former authorities, *Smith v West Dudley Local Board* (1878) 3 C.P.D. 423 and *Shoreditch Corporation v Bull* (1904) 68 J.P. 415.

Moreover if a sewerage undertaker fails properly to maintain a sewer it will be liable to any lawful user of the highway who suffers damage as a result.[61] On the other hand if the sewer itself is properly laid and maintained no liability will arise from the mere fact of the presence of the sewer in the highway because it is there pursuant to statutory authority.[62] If a properly laid and protected sewer should be damaged as a result of some misuse of the highway above it (e.g. by driving an exceptionally heavy vehicle along it in circumstances amounting to negligence), it seems probable that the sewerage undertaker in whom the sewer is vested could recover damages from the person responsible.[63]

Certain special provisions are made in respect of works upon streets under the control of railway undertakers[64] or a navigation authority.[65] The general power of a sewerage undertaker to undertake street works is inapplicable to a street which is not a highway maintainable at public expense within the meaning of the Highways Act 1980 and is controlled, managed or maintainable by railway undertakers or a navigation authority or forms part of a level crossing belonging to such a company or authority or other person, except with the consent of such company, authority or person. This restriction does not, however,

---

61   See, in relation to former authorities, *Skilton v Epsom and Ewell U.D.C.* [1937] 1 K.B. 112.

62   Such an action must be founded upon negligence: *Lambert v Lowestoft Corporation* [1901] 1 K.B. 590 and *Thompson v Brighton Corporation* [1894] 1 Q.B. 332. Similar considerations will apply if a sewer is laid in the bed of a watercourse, but no responsibility could attach to the sewerage undertaker if the sewer is initially properly laid but subsequently obstructs the flow of water in the river due to some change in the river not the responsibility of the undertaker: *Radstock Co-operative and Industrial Society Co. Ltd. v Norton-Radstock U.D.C.* [1968] Ch. 605.

63   See *Driscoll v Poplar Board of Works* (1897) 62 J.P. 40. It might also be possible to recover damages from the highway authority where a sewer is damaged by the use of exceptionally heavy equipment for highway repairs: see *Gas Light and Coke Co. v Vestry of St. Mary Abbots* (1885) 15 Q.B.D. 1.

64   For this purpose "railway undertakers" means the British Railways Board, London Regional Transport or any other person authorised by or under any enactment to construct or operate a railway (1991 Act, s.219(1)).

65   1991 Act, Sch. 13, para. 3(1).

apply to emergency works within the meaning of the New Roads and Street Works Act 1991.[66] In other circumstances consents given under this provision may be made subject to reasonable conditions but may not be unreasonably withheld. Disputes as to the granting or withholding of such consents are to be resolved by a single arbitrator appointed by agreement or, in default of such agreement, by the President of the Institution of Civil Engineers. Contravention of the restrictions without reasonable excuse is a criminal offence for which an offender will incur liability to a fine not exceeding level 3 on the standard scale.

A further specific restriction is imposed by Schedule 13 of the Water Industry Act 1991. It is provided that powers to perform works conferred by the 1991 Act do not authorise the carrying out of actions without consent of certain specified undertakings which, whether directly or indirectly, would injuriously affect works or property vested in such an undertaker in that capacity as such or with the use of any such works or property.[67] Any disputes upon such consent are to be referred to a single arbitrator appointed by agreement or, in default thereof, by the President of the Institution of Civil Engineers.[68] The undertakings specified for this purpose are those of

(a) the National Rivers Authority, the Civil Aviation Authority, the Coal Authority and the Post Office;

---

[66] 1991 Act, Sch. 13, para. 3(2). As to "emergency works" under the New Roads and Street Works Act 1991, see *ibid.*, s.52.

[67] 1991 Act, Sch. 13, para. 1(1). It is further provided that no power to perform works under the 1991 Act authorises works prejudicial to the performance of statutory functions by any of the specified undertakers (Sch. 13, para. 2). Further, nothing in the 1991 Act confers power to interfere without consent with any sluices, floodgates, sewers, groynes, sea defences or other works used for the drainage, preservation or improvement of any land under any local statutory provision or with any works used by any person for the irrigation of land (s.186(1)). Where, other than in the exercise of compulsory powers, a sewerage undertaker proposes to construct or alter an inland water not forming part of a main river for the purposes of Part IV of the Water Resources Act 1991 or to alter works thereon or in, the undertaker must first consult with the internal drainage board for the district (s.186(5)).

[68] Sch. 13, para. 1(3), (4).

(b) a water or sewerage undertaker;

(c) any undertaking consisting in the running of a telecommunications code system within the meaning of Schedule 4 to the Telecommunications Act 1984;

(d) an airport to which Part V of the Airports Act 1986 applies;

(e) a public gas supplier within the meaning of Part I of the Gas Act 1986;

(f) an undertaking licensed to generate, transmit or supply electricity under Part I of the Electricity Act 1989;

(g) a navigation, harbour or conservancy authority or an internal drainage board;

(h) the British Railways Board, London Regional Transport or any other enterprise authorised to construct or to operate a railway;

(i) any public utility carried on by a local authority under any Act or any order having the force of an Act; and

(j) the undertaking of any licensed operator, within the meaning of the Coal Industry Act 1994.[69]

(b) Powers to carry out works upon other land

Under sections 159 and 161(2) of the Water Industry Act 1991, a sewerage undertaker[70] has power in respect of land not in, under or over a street

(a) to lay a sewer or disposal main, above or below the surface;

(b) to inspect, maintain, adjust or alter a sewer or disposal main;

---

[69] Sch. 13, para. 1(5), as amended by the Coal Industry Act 1994, Sch. 9, para. 42.

[70] As to the powers of companies by virtue of inset appointments, see *ante*, p.14 and *post*, pp.67, 74.

(c) to carry out works requisite for the aversion of pollution or contamination of water in a water works;[71]

(d) to carry out works requisite for or incidental to any such works.

This power was originally inserted in parenthesis in section 16 of the 1875 Act and was at that time made subject to a requirement that the power should be exercised only where the (then) local authority's surveyor had stated that passing through the private land in question was necessary.[72] This requirement no longer specifically applies. Before power under the paragraph may be exercised, "reasonable notice" of the proposed exercise must be given to the owner and occupier of the land concerned.[73] The precise form of notice is not stated by the Act but "reasonable notice" is defined to mean

(i) in case of operations to lay a sewer or disposal main, a three month period;

(ii) in case of alteration of an existing pipe, a period of forty-two days.[74]

These time limits do not, however, apply in cases of emergency or where a sewerage undertaker is to lay a pipe in compliance with its duty under section 94 of the 1991 Act to provide a public sewer for domestic drainage.[75]

Under former equivalent powers it was held that a public sewer so constructed need not necessarily lead at either end (or at both ends) to a public sewer, although it normally will do so; it might be constructed to serve as a link between two private sewers.[76] Presumably in such a case the authority must acquire rights from

---

[71] This provision is of primary relevance to water undertakers but may have some significance for sewerage undertakers.

[72] See e.g. *Lewis v Weston-super-Mare Local Board* (1888) 40 Ch. D. 55.

[73] 1991 Act, s.159(4). Shaw's Form PH85 is appropriate.

[74] *Ibid.*, s.159(5).

[75] *Ibid.*, s.159(6).

[76] *Moore v Frimley and Camberley U.D.C.* (1965) 63 L.G.R. 194.

the owner of at least one of the private sewers to allow effluent from the public sewer to flow through that private sewer.

Also under earlier equivalent powers it was held that where construction of a sewer necessarily involved the demolition of a building such action lay within the authority conferred.[77] It also appears that for this purpose a right of water to a mill is also "land".[78]

No land need be acquired in order to lay a sewer under these provisions and if a recalcitrant owner were to object to the performance of such works a notice under section 159 would generally suffice without need of recourse to compulsory purchase procedures.[79] None the less, the performance of such works has an effect equivalent to compulsory purchase and provision is therefore made by the 1991 Act for the payment of compensation. If the value of land over which powers conferred by sections 159, 161(2) and 163 of the 1991 Act have been exercised or land held with such land[80] is depreciated by the exercise of its powers over "other lands" (i.e. non-street works) by a sewerage undertaker then the persons entitled to an interest so depreciated will be entitled to equivalent compensation from the undertaker.[81] Further, if a person entitled to an interest in such land sustains loss or damage attributable to the exercise of such powers by a sewerage undertaker, which whilst not a depreciation of the

---

77 *Hutton v Esher U.D.C.* [1974] Ch. 167.

78 *Cleckheaton U.D.C. v Firth* (1898) 62 J.P. 536. The Act does not specifically define "land", but Sch. 1 to the Interpretation Act 1978 states that the term includes buildings and other structures, land covered with water, and any estate, interest, easement, servitude or right in or over land.

79 See *Thornton v Nutter* (1867) 31 J.P. 419 in respect of equivalent earlier provisions.

80 This definition is given by Sch. 12, para. 2(5).

81 Schedule 12, para. 2. See e.g. *Collins and Collins v Thames Water Utilities Ltd.* [1994] 49 E.G.116, where the Lands Tribunal held on the facts that the value of a house had not been depreciated by the construction of a sewer under part of the back garden. Judge Marder Q.C., President, inclined to the view but did not decide that the Tribunal could take into account any enhancement of value as a result of the works: here, the house was now on mains drainage, replacing a septic tank.

value of the interest is a matter in respect of which disturbance compensation would have been payable in case of a compulsory acquisition under section 155,[82] compensation will also be payable. Compensation will also be payable where damage or injurious affection is caused by its performance of works to land which is not the land immediately concerned. The amount of compensation in respect of depreciation in value is assessed in accordance with the rules set out in section 5 of the Land Compensation Act 1961, subject to any necessary modifications.[83] Any dispute as to the amount of compensation is to be settled by the Lands Tribunal in the light of sections 2 and 4 of the Land Compensation Act 1961, again subject to any necessary modifications.[84] If the interest in respect of which compensation is to be paid is burdened with a mortgage,

(i) the assessment is made as if the interest were not so burdened,

(ii) a claim may also be made by the mortgagee but without prejudice to the claim of the holder of the interest,

(iii) no compensation is payable in respect of the interest of the mortgagee *per se*, as distinct from the interest which is subject to the mortgage, and

(iv) any such compensation will be paid to the mortgagee, or the first if there is more than one, and then applied as if it were the proceeds of sale.[85]

In respect of all land compensation claims in respect of works by sewerage undertakers, the Secretary of State has power by regulation to authorise advance payments.[86]

---

[82] See below.
[83] Schedule 12, para. 3(2).
[84] *Ibid.*, para. 3(1).
[85] *Ibid.*, para. 3(3).
[86] *Ibid.*, para. 2(4). See the Water and Sewerage (Works) (Advance Payments) Regulations 1989 (S.I. 1989 No. 1379).

(c) Powers of entry in relation to the performance of works

A person so authorised in writing by a sewerage undertaker may enter premises[87] for the purposes of determining whether it is appropriate or practical for the undertaker to exercise any power conferred by sections 158, 159, 161(1), (2) of the 1991 Act; or for determining how such a power should be exercised; or for the actual exercise of such a power.[88] The works so authorised include experimental borings to ascertain the nature of the subsoil and the removal for analysis of samples of water, effluent, land or articles necessary for determining the appropriateness of the exercise of powers. Such powers of entry may, however, only be exercised at a reasonable time and upon seven days' notice to the occupier or in an emergency.[89] However, under Part II of Schedule 6 to the 1991 Act,[90] a Justice of the Peace who is satisfied upon sworn information in writing that there are reasonable grounds for the exercise of a power conferred by, *inter alia*, section 168 and that

(a) the exercise of the power has been refused;

(b) such a refusal is reasonably apprehended;

(c) the premises concerned are unoccupied;

(d) the owner is temporarily absent;

(e) the matter is urgent; or

(f) an application for admission would defeat the purpose of entry,

may by warrant authorise the sewerage undertaker to designate a person to exercise the powers in relation to the premises

---

[87] Including land where entry is needed to gain access to other land where works are to be performed, etc.: *Dwr Cymru Cyfyngedig v Williams, The Times*, 9th October 1991, D.C.

[88] 1991 Act, s.168.

[89] *Ibid.*, Sch. 6, Part II, para. 6.

[90] Para. 7.

concerned, by force if need be. Such a warrant will remain in force until such time as the purposes for which it was issued have been fulfilled.

(d) Powers to acquire land

A sewerage undertaker may be authorised by the Secretary of State to purchase land in England and Wales which is required for the performance of its functions; such an authorisation may include the creation of new rights and interests and the extinguishment of pre-existing rights.[91] The land compulsorily acquired by a sewerage undertaker may include land required for giving in exchange for, or for any right in, land which forms part of a common, open space or a fuel or field garden allotment.[92] Compulsory purchases by a sewerage undertaker are generally governed by the procedures under the Acquisition of Land Act 1981 with certain specific exceptions.[93]

(e) Restrictions upon disposal of land

A sewerage undertaker may not dispose of an interest in or right over any land which was transferred to it in accordance with a scheme under Schedule 2 of the 1989 Act or, in the case of a statutory water company, was held by it in the financial year ending with 31st March 1990;[94] or has since then been held by the company in connection with the performance of its functions as a sewerage undertaker; or was transferred from a company so holding it in accordance with a scheme under Schedule 2 of the 1991 Act, except with the consent of, or in accordance with a

---

[91] 1991 Act, s.155(1), (2).

[92] *Ibid.,* s.155(3).

[93] In particular in relation to the acquisition of mineral rights, in which case, by virtue of s.188 of the Act, Sch. 14 of the 1991 Act is substituted for Sch. 2 of the Acquisition of Land Act 1981. Note also that certain modifications are made by Sch. 9 to the 1991 Act in cases where a right over land is acquired by the creation of a new right.

[94] i.e. including the transfer date (1st September 1989): The Water Authorities (Transfer of Functions) (Appointed Day) Order 1989, S.I. 1989 No. 1530.

general authorisation given by, the Secretary of State. Such an authorisation will be set out in a notice served by the Secretary of State and may be made subject to conditions.[95] Such conditions may include requirements that

(a) prior to disposal an opportunity of acquiring the land or right must be offered to a specified person;

(b) the company has complied with the conditions of its appointment relating to disposal of lands or interest in land;

(c) in a case of land in a National Park, the (Norfolk or Suffolk) Broads or in an area of outstanding natural beauty or special scientific interest the undertaker should consult with the Countryside Commission and/or the Nature Conservancy Council and/or enter into such agreements under section 39 of the Wildlife and Countryside Act 1981[96] or under section 156(6) of the 1991 Act[97] as the Secretary of State may determine.[98]

(f) Environmental duties of sewerage undertakers

Sewerage undertakers as such will be less significant landowners than water undertakers, although they may often of course be in fact the same body, but may still hold considerable areas of land and therefore be vested with considerable environmental responsibilities. The 1991 Act provides by section 3 that in formulating or considering proposals in relation to the performance of its functions, a sewerage undertaker is under a duty, so far as is consistent with its statutory duties, to bear a number of environmental interests in mind. The interests

---

[95]   1991 Act, ss.156(1)-(3), 219(1) (definition of "protected land").

[96]   These are management agreements.

[97]   Section 156(6) provides for the entry into a covenant between a company and the Secretary of State relating to freedom of access to the land by members of the public or other persons or the use or management of the land. Such a covenant binds all persons deriving title from or under that company and will be enforceable by the Secretary of State accordingly.

[98]   1991 Act s.156(4), (5).

concerned are crudely divisible into the areas of access and conservation as such.

As to access, a sewerage undertaker must have regard to the importance of preserving public access to woodland, mountains, moors, heathland, downs, cliffs, foreshore and other places of natural beauty.[99] Similar emphasis is placed upon access to buildings, sites and objects of archaeological, architectural or historic interest.[100] A parallel duty in respect of recreational access to water and land associated with water is imposed subject to obtaining the consent of any relevant navigation, harbour or conservancy authorities and having due regard for freedom of navigation as such.[101] In deciding what measures in fact to adopt in particular connection with public access to water and land associated with water, an undertaker is under a duty to take into account the needs of the chronically sick or disabled.[102] There is, however, no express or implied duty to make recreational facilities available free of charge.[103] The duties to consider so imposed are clearly subject to the primary performance of the statutory function of a sewerage undertaker and may consequently be less stringent than might at first appear.

Rather stricter obligations are imposed upon sewerage undertakers with reference to certain sites of special interest under section 4 of the 1991 Act. The areas so protected fall into two broad groups. The first are those which the Nature Conservancy Council notifies to the undertaker as of special interest by reason of its flora, fauna or geological or physiographical features and which is likely to be affected by its activities.[104] The second group are those in a National Park or the Norfolk and Suffolk Broads[105] which a National Park authority

---

[99] 1991 Act, s.3(3)(a).
[100] *Ibid.,* s.3(3)(b).
[101] *Ibid.,* s.3(5). In the nature of things this is clearly a matter of more relevance to water undertakers than to sewerage undertakers.
[102] *Ibid.,* s.3(6).
[103] *Ibid.,* s.3(8).
[104] *Ibid.,* s.4(1).
[105] As defined in the Norfolk and Suffolk Broads Act 1988 (1991 Act, s.4(6)).

or the Broads Authority considers to be of particular importance in terms of the general environmental duties set out in section 3 of the 1991 Act and which may be affected by the activities of, *inter alia*, a sewerage undertaker. In either situation the National Park authority or Broads Authority must notify the fact, and the details of its concern, to the undertaker and to any other body whose works or operations might affect the land. Upon receipt of such a notification the sewerage undertaker, or other body concerned, must consult with the notifying body before carrying out any works, operations or activities which appear in the undertaker's opinion to be likely to destroy or damage any flora, fauna or geological or physiographical features which make the land of special interest or significantly to prejudice access or environmental factors within the meaning of section 3 of the Act which render land in a National Park or the Broads of "importance".[106] A general exception is provided in cases of "emergency", provided that what is done and the nature of the emergency are notified to the Nature Conservancy Council, the National Park authority or the Broads Authority, as might be appropriate in a given case, as soon as possible.[107] The possible necessity for emergency works without time for consultation is evident and this provision takes account of it although the exception is very widely phrased. A rather more alarming prospect is opened by the provision that the general duty of consultation is stated to exist in respect of works, etc. "which appear to that" undertaker to be potentially damaging. The subjectivity of this standard may give rise to uncertainty in practice. Some relief is offered however by section 5 of the 1991 Act. Under that section the Secretary of State has powers by order to issue or approve codes of practice giving guidance, *inter alia*, to sewerage undertakers upon such matters and encouraging what appears to him to be desirable practices. In making such an order, the Secretary of State must consult the National Rivers Authority, the Countryside Commission, the Nature Conservancy

---

[106] Section 9(5).
[107] Section 9(4).

Council, the Historic Buildings and Monuments Commission for England, the Sports Council, the Sports Council of Wales, all such water and sewerage undertakers and other persons which he may find appropriate.[108] Such a code does not in itself form part of the requirements of sections 3 and 4, nor does contravention of it give rise to civil or criminal liability but the Secretary of State and the Minister will be under a duty to take into account whether there has been or is likely to be a contravention in determining when and how to exercise his powers under the 1991 Act.[109] These powers include, of course, ultimately the power to deprive a company of its appointment as a sewerage undertaker. The *Code of Practice on Conservation, Access and Recreation* has effect under these provisions.[110]

The environmental and recreational duties are expressly made subject to the overriding general duties set out in section 2 of the 1991 Act.[111]

(g) Duty to remove pipes

Where a sewerage undertaker keeps a sewer or disposal main[112] or other apparatus, on, under or over land and a person with an interest in that land or adjacent land requires it to alter or remove the pipe or apparatus upon the ground that this is necessary to facilitate a proposed improvement of the land, the undertaker must in most cases comply unless the demand is unreasonable.[113] No definition of "unreasonableness" for this purpose is given and the issue, if it comes in a practical form, will presumably be determined on a case by case basis. A notice of requirement for the alteration or removal of a pipe cannot impose a duty upon an

---

[108] 1991 Act, s.5(4).

[109] *Ibid.,* s.5(2).

[110] See the Water and Sewerage (Conservation, Access and Recreation) (Code of Practice) Order 1989 (S.I. 1989 No. 1152).

[111] See *ante*, p.15.

[112] i.e. a "relevant pipe": 1991 Act, s.158(7), applied by s.185(9).

[113] 1991 Act, s.185(1), (2). "Improvement" includes all development or changes of use but not improvements with respect to water supply or sewerage (s.185(9)).

undertaker to alter or remove any pipe or apparatus in, under or over a street.[114]

Where a sewerage undertaker carries out works pursuant to such a notice it will be entitled to recover its reasonable expenses in doing so from the person who made the requirement[115] and may make it a condition of compliance that reasonable security be provided in respect of the payment of such expenses.[116] Where such a security is deposited the undertaker must pay interest upon each sum of 50p so deposited for each three months period in which it remains deposited with it. The rate of interest will be determined by the undertaker, with the approval of the Director General of Water Services or, in default, by the Director himself.[117] The duty of the sewerage undertaker to comply with such a demand is enforced by the Director through an enforcement order under section 18 of the 1991 Act.[118]

(h) Planning controls in respect of sewerage works

Where the operations or activities of a sewerage undertaker amount to "development" within the meaning of section 55 of the Town and Country Planning Act 1990, the fact that they are authorised by the 1991 Act does not exempt them from the requirement for planning permission.[119] Under the Town and Country Planning (General Permitted Development) Order 1995,[120] a number of classes of development by or on behalf of a sewerage undertaker are "permitted development" and so do not require an express grant of planning permission.[121] These are

"A (a) development not above ground level required in

---

114 Section 185(3).
115 Section 185(5).
116 Section 185(4).
117 Section 185(6).
118 Section 185(8). As to s.18 enforcement orders, see *ante*, pp.17-19.
119 Section 190.
120 S.I. 1995 No. 418, replacing S.I. 1988 No. 1813, as amended.
121 Unless a direction has been given under Article 4 of the order restricting what would otherwise be permitted development.

connection with the provision, improvement, maintenance or repair of a sewer, outfall pipe, sludge main[122] or associated apparatus;[123]

(b) the provision of a building, plant, machinery or apparatus in, on, over or under land for the purpose of survey or investigation;[124]

(c) the maintenance, improvement or repair of works for measuring the flow in any watercourse or channel;

(d) any works authorised by or required in connection with an order made under section 73 of the Water Resources Act 1991 (power to make ordinary and emergency drought orders);

(e) any other development in, on, over or under their operational land, other than the provision of a building but including the extension or alteration of a building."[125]

---

[122] i.e. "a pipe or system of pipes (together with any pumps or other machinery or apparatus associated with it) for the conveyance of the residue of water or sewage treated in a water or sewage treatment works as the case may be, including final effluent or the products of the dewatering or incineration of such residue, or partly for any of those purposes and partly for the conveyance of trade effluent or its residue: Sch. 1, Part 16.A.3.

[123] "Associated apparatus" means "pumps, machinery or apparatus associated with the relevant sewer, main or pipe": Sch. 1, Part 16.A.3.

[124] Subject to the condition that after 6 months (or, if sooner, on the completion of the survey or investigation), all such operations cease, and all such buildings, etc. are removed and the land restored as soon as reasonably practicable to its former condition (or any other condition agreed with the local planning authority): Sch. 1, Part 16.A.2.

[125] 1995 Order, Sch. 1, Part 16A. Development is not permitted by Class A(e) if: (a) it would consist of or include the extension or alteration of a building so that (i) its design or external appearance would be materially affected; (ii) the height or the cubic content of the original building would be exceeded by more than 25%; or (iii) the floor space of the original building would be exceeded by more than 1,000 square metres; or (b) it would consist of the installation or erection of any plant or machinery exceeding 15 metres in height or the height of anything it replaces, whichever is the greater.

(i) Sewer maps

Sewerage undertakers are under a duty to keep records of the locations and particulars of all sewers and disposal mains vested in them; all sewers in respect of which a vesting declaration has been, or deemed to have been, made by the undertaker under Chapter II of Part IV of the Water Industry Act 1991 but has not taken effect and all drains or sewers to which an agreement to make such a declaration made, or deemed to have been made, under section 104 of the 1991 Act relates.[126] For each pipe particulars must be noted of whether it is a drain, sewer or disposal main, of the nature of the effluent flowing through it and of whether it is vested in the undertaker or, if not, whether it is the subject of a vesting declaration under Chapter II of Part IV of the 1991 Act or any agreement under section 104 of the 1991 Act.[127] Separate records must be kept by the sewerage undertaker in relation to each local authority the area of which is in whole or part coincident with its own. Copies of such records are required to be supplied, and updated, to the local authorities concerned without charge and such records must also be made available for inspection by members of the public, free of charge, at all reasonable times at an office of the undertaker.[128] Similarly a local authority must make available to the public for inspection without charge at reasonable hours at its office information so supplied in the form of a map.[129]

In the keeping of such records there may obviously arise difficulties in the seeking out of the requisite information and the 1991 Act seeks to some extent to take account of this. A sewerage undertaker is not required to record drains, sewers or disposal mains laid prior to 1st September 1989 (the "Transfer

---

[126] 1991 Act, s.199(1).

[127] *Ibid.,* s.199(2).

[128] *Ibid.,* ss.199(3), (4), 200.

[129] *Ibid.,* ss.199(4), 200. Local authority for the purposes of the Inner Temple and the Middle Temple includes respectively their Sub-Treasurer and Under Treasurer (s.200(5)).

Date")[130] if it had no knowledge of or reasonable grounds to suspect their presence or it is not reasonably practicable for it to discover their course.[131] Moreover, a sewerage undertaker is not under a duty at any time within the ten years running from 1st September 1989 (the "Transfer Date") to record any drain, sewer or disposal main laid before that date unless particulars of it were shown immediately prior to that date upon a map kept by a local authority under the former equivalent section 32 of the 1936 Act or it is the subject of a vesting declaration or an agreement therefore within that period.[132] The duties thus imposed upon sewerage undertakers may be enforced by the Secretary of State through an enforcement order under section 18 of the 1991 Act.[133]

(j) Complaints in respect of works on private land

Where a sewerage undertaker exercises its powers under or by virtue of sections 159 or 161(2) of the 1991 Act to perform works upon private land, complaints in respect of the works may be addressed to the Director General of Water Services who will then in general be under a duty to investigate them.[134] Such complaints would clearly include violations of codes of working practice.[135] Exceptions to the duty of investigation are provided where the complaint appears to the Director to be vexatious or frivolous, where he is not satisfied that the matter has been drawn to the attention of the sewerage undertaker concerned with a reasonable opportunity for investigation and action or the complaint was first made more than twelve months, or such longer period as the Director in a special case may allow, since

---

[130] The Water Authorities (Transfer of Functions) (Appointed Day) Order 1989 (S.I. 1989 No. 1530).

[131] Section 199(7).

[132] Section 199(8).

[133] Section 199(9). As to s.18 enforcement orders, see *ante*, pp.17-19.

[134] Section 181(1).

[135] i.e. in particular codes made under s.182, see above. Such a contravention would not *of itself* give rise to any civil or criminal liability but would be a matter to be taken into account by the Director (s.182(3)).

the matter came to the complainant's attention.[136] Such complaints may be made to the Director or to the appropriate Customer Service Committee.[137] A sewerage undertaker is under a duty to provide the information and assistance which the Director might reasonably require in the course of such an investigation.[138]

If, upon investigation of a complaint the Director is satisfied that a sewerage undertaker has failed adequately to consult the complainant before and during the exercise of its statutory powers or has inflicted loss, damage or inconvenience upon the complainant by acting unreasonably in the exercise of its powers, he may direct the undertaker to pay compensation up to the sum of £5,000 to the complainant.[139] Before making such an award the representations made to the Director by the complainant and/ or the undertaker must be considered.[140]

Such compensation may not, however, be awarded in respect of loss, damage or inconvenience which is compensatable under any other enactment, unless the sum so recoverable would not seem an adequate reflection of the unreasonableness of the undertaker's conduct.[141]

NEW CONNECTIONS WITH PUBLIC SEWERS

Section 110A of the Water Industry Act 1991[142] provides that the Director may require an established undertaker to permit a "main connection"[143] into its sewage system by another undertaker or a person who has applied for an appointment or variation of

---

136 Water Industry Act 1991, s.181(2).
137 *Ibid.,* s.181. As to Customer Service Committees, see ss.28 and 29 and Sch. 4 to the 1991 Act. Their role is considered in Chapter 1, *ante.*
138 Section 181(3). This duty may be the subject of an enforcement order under s.18 (s.181(6)).
139 Section 181(4).
140 Section 181(3)(b).
141 Section 181(5).
142 Inserted by the Competition and Service (Utilities) Act 1992, s.45.
143 i.e. a connection between a sewer or disposal main and a sewer or disposal main, or a connection which allows a sewer or disposal main to discharge directly into a sewerage disposal works: s.110A(3).

an appointment under section 8 of the 1991 Act replacing a company as undertaker.[144] The Director must first consult the National Rivers Authority, and must have regard to the desirability of

(a) facilitating effective competition within the sewerage services industry;

(b) the existing undertaker's recovering its expenses and securing a reasonable return on capital;

(c) the existing undertaker's being able to meet its existing and likely future obligations to provide sewerage services without having to incur unreasonable expenditure in carrying out works;

(d) not putting at risk the ability of the existing undertaker to meet such obligations.

---

[144] See *ante*, pp.13-14.

Chapter 4

CONSTRUCTION OF SEWERS BY PRIVATE INDIVIDUALS[1]

INTRODUCTORY

The construction of a drain or sewer for the purpose of draining one's land or premises is a natural incident of the ownership of that land which will not normally give rise to a cause of action in third parties. Liability in private nuisance might, however, arise if

(i) the work interferes with neighbouring land, e.g. by physical damage, encroachment, disturbance of easements or other natural rights;

(ii) there is unreasonable interference with the comfort or convenience of the occupier;

(iii) there is negligence or malicious interference with the natural drainage of neighbouring land, such interference not being an inevitable consequence of the reasonable use and development of the land with due care for the avoidance of harm.[2]

Failure to take reasonable steps to maintain a private sewer may also give rise to liability in private nuisance on ordinary principles.

A landowner will not, however, be liable for damages where non-negligent and proper construction work sets natural agencies in motion which drain subterranean water and cause subsidence.[3]

---

[1] The expression "private individual" is used in this chapter as including any body corporate other than a sewerage undertaker.

[2] *Home Brewery Co. Ltd. v William Davis & Co. (Leicester) Ltd.* [1987] Q.B. 339.

[3] *Popplewell v Hodkinson* (1869) L.R. 4 Exch. 248; it was an essential feature of the case that the natural agencies in question could not reasonably have been foreseen. See also *Stephens v Anglian Water Authority* [1987] 1 W.L.R. 1381.

In contrast, liability may arise where the support of land is removed as a consequence of construction of drains or sewers concomitant upon mineral extraction.[4] Once the landowner has caused sewage or other matter to collect on his land (in the drain pipes, or in a cesspool or tank), he may be held strictly liable for any escape.[5] Liability under this principle – an application of the famous "Rule in *Rylands v Fletcher*" – will attach irrespective of the proof of any negligence but it is now a prerequisite of liability that the damage is foreseeable[6] and the law recognises a number of special defences.[7]

The right to cause sewage matter to flow under or across another's land is thus one which must be acquired by prescription[8] or by express or implied grant or reservation. The details of such matters form part of the law of easements. In the present context we are concerned rather with relations between the sewerage undertaker and a private individual proposing to construct a sewer;[9] the construction of drains by private individuals is considered later.[10]

---

[4]   *Stephens v Anglian Water Authority* [1987] 1 W.L.R. 1381 at p.1384.

[5]   *Rylands v Fletcher* (1868) L.R. 3 H.L. 330; see e.g. *Jones v Bedwellty U.D.C.* (1916) 80 J.P. Jo. 192. "I think it clear that the principle of *Rylands v Fletcher* would apply to the owner of a sewer, whether he himself made the sewer or not . . . . His duty at common law would be to see that the sewage in his sewer did not escape to the injury of others": *per* Parker J. in *Jones v Llanrwst U.D.C.* [1911] 1 Ch. 393; *Humphries v Cousins* (1877) 2 C.P.D. 239: "It was the defendant's duty to keep the sewage which he was himself bound to receive from passing from his own premises to the plaintiff's premises, otherwise than along the old accustomed channel": *per* Denman J. at p.244.

[6]   *Cambridge Water Co. v Eastern Counties Leather plc* [1994] 2 A.C. 264, H.L. *Humphries v Cousins, supra,* seems inconsistent with this principle and must be taken to have been overruled on this point: *cf.* Lord Goff at pp.302, 306.

[7]   Including act of god and act of a stranger: see generally W.V.H. Rogers, *Winfield and Jolowicz on Tort* (4th edn., 1994), pp.454-462.

[8]   See *ante,* Chapter 2, pp.59-60.

[9]   A private individual has none of the special powers discussed in Chapter 3, *ante,* p.73*ff.* Thus, the breaking up of the surface of a street for the purpose of laying a private sewer (as distinct from making a communication with a public sewer) may be done only by agreement with the highway or other appropriate authority.

[10] See Chapter 9, *post,* p.182*ff.* The difference between private sewers and private drains is that between sewers and drains generally; see *ante,* Chapter 1, pp.2-10 and Chapter 2.

THE CONSTRUCTION OF PRIVATE SEWERS

There is no express provision in the 1936 or 1989 Acts requiring a private individual proposing to construct a sewer to submit plans thereof to, or to obtain the approval of, the local authority or the sewerage undertaker, but such proposals are in effect regulated as a consequence of the following provisions:

(a) New buildings

Satisfactory provision must be made for the drainage[11] of any new building or an extension of a building, and the plans required to be submitted under the Building Regulations 1991 in respect thereof must be rejected by the local authority if such provision is not shown to be made, unless the authority is satisfied that it may properly dispense with any such provision.[12] Obviously, it is in the interests of any landowner carrying out an extensive private sewerage scheme to obtain the prior approval of the authority to any such proposals, otherwise he may find when he proposes to connect new buildings thereto that the new sewers so provided are not considered to provide a satisfactory means of drainage of such buildings.[13]

(b) Existing buildings

If any private sewer or drain[14] of an existing building is "insufficient"[15] or, in the case of a sewer or drain communicating directly or indirectly with a public sewer, is so defective as to

---

[11]   As defined in the Building Act 1984, s.21(2), i.e. including "the conveyance, by means of a sink and other necessary appliance, of refuse water and the conveyance of rainwater from roofs."

[12]   Building Act 1984, s.21(1).

[13]   Unfortunately, as there is no express provision requiring such approval to be obtained, any observations of the authority on such proposals could be but informal, and would not be legally binding on the authority. As to connections with existing public sewers, see ss.106 and 107 of the Water Industry Act 1991, Chapter 9, *post*, p.175*ff*.

[14]   Or cesspool, soil pipe, rain-water pipe, spout, sink or other necessary appliance: Building Act 1984, s.59(1)(b), *post*, Chapter 9, p.196.

[15]   This term is not defined or explained in the Act, but see *post*, p.216.

admit subsoil water, or if it is in such a condition as to be prejudicial to health or a nuisance,[16] the local authority may, in any such case, by notice[17] require the defect to be remedied or the nuisance abated.[18] In the event of failure to comply with a notice under this section, the authority may itself act in default and recover its expenses in so doing from the owner of the property for the time being. On completion of the work the expenses become a charge upon the premises.[19] In practice this section provides the local authority with a most effective means of control over the condition, etc. of private drains and sewers.

(c) Special cases

The sewerage undertaker may, in certain circumstances, require any person[20] proposing to construct a drain or sewer to construct it according to the different specifications of the authority. The authority may specify alterations "as regards material or size of pipes, depth, fall, direction or outfall or otherwise".[21] This power may be exercised by the undertaker only when it considers[22] that

---

[16] As to the effect of this phrase see *post*, p.199.

[17] The notice must indicate the nature of the works to be executed and state the time within which they are to be executed: 1984 Act, s.99(1). It must be in writing (s.99). As to authentication and service of documents, see ss.93, 94. The requirement as to writing is mandatory: *Epping Forest District Council v Essex Rendering* [1983] 1 W.L.R. 158, H.L., a decision on the equivalent s.283 of the Public Health Act 1936. There is no prescribed form but see Shaw's Form PN23D.

[18] Building Act 1984, s.59. See further *post*, pp.195-197.

[19] *Ibid.*, s.107, and *post*, Chapter 11, pp.239-240.

[20] "Person" here must include a county council, and therefore it seems that a sewerage undertaker may take action under this section against the county council acting under the private street works code contained in the Highways Act 1980, Part XI.

[21] 1991 Act, s.112(1). The words "or otherwise" normally suggest that the *ejusdem generis* rule is to be applied, but it is submitted that the rule is not applicable in the present context, as the terms used are of different *genera* (see e.g. *R. v Payne* (1866) 35 L.J.M.C. 170, and *Maxwell on the Interpretation of Statutes*, 12th edn., pp.297-306; *Craies on Statute Law*, 7th edn., pp.178-186).

[22] Provided there are reasonable grounds on which the undertaker could come to such a decision, it seems that the courts could not intervene to question the actual decision.

the "proposed drain or sewer is, or is likely to be, needed to form part of a general sewerage system which that undertaker provides or proposes to provide".[23]

Failure to comply with the sewerage undertaker's requirements will be a breach of a duty owed to the undertaker and any loss or damage which it suffers in consequence will be actionable at its suit.[24] A person aggrieved by the requirements may appeal within 28 days to the Director General of Water Services.[25]

Where a person[26] reconstructs a drain that communicates with a sewer or other drain, or executes any other works to such a drain or premises served by such a drain so as permanently to discontinue its use, he must take certain steps. He must disconnect and seal unnecessary or disused drains at such points as the local authority may reasonably require.[27] In addition he must give at least 48 hours' notice to the local authority before complying with this requirement.[28] It it the aim of this provision to prevent abandoned drains becoming a health hazard. The local authority is not given any powers to take action itself in default of compliance with this provision, but failure to give the notice referred to renders the offender liable to a fine on conviction. It is also an offence, again punishable by fine, for any person knowingly to fail to comply with the duty created by section 62(1). In the case of a demolition of a building, the local authority has further powers of control.[29]

(d) Planning control

Direct detailed control over the construction of private sewerage

---

[23]   1991 Act, s.112(1).

[24]   *Ibid.*, s.112(5).

[25]   *Ibid.*, s.112(2), (3), as amended by the Competition and Service (Utilities) Act 1992, s.35(10).

[26]   The section applies to any person, including apparently a contractor, and it is not confined to cases where a new sewer is being constructed.

[27]   Building Act 1984, s.62(1).

[28]   *Ibid.*, s.62(4).

[29]   *Ibid.*, s.80.

or drainage schemes is maintained under the Town and Country Planning Act 1990. These controls are enforceable by the local planning authority which for this purpose will be the district council.[30]

Under this Act the construction of works such as private sewerage schemes, being engineering operations in, on or over land, amounts to development.[31] Express planning permission from the local planning authority is therefore required before it may be undertaken.

(e) Other provisions

The general law places few, if any, major obstacles to the construction of a private sewer or connecting drain. However care must be taken that all necessary easements or other rights can be obtained from other landowners. It is also important to avoid creating a common law nuisance as a result of the construction. If it is intended to connect a new drain or private sewer to an existing *private* drain or sewer, the consent of the owners of the land through which that existing conduit runs must be obtained. The owner of the land from which the existing effluent originates will have obtained an easement and the burden thereby placed on the servient owner cannot be increased without his consent.[32]

The construction of works for the supply of sewage to land for agriculture purposes by owners of limited interests in land (e.g. a tenant for life under the Settled Land Act 1925) is deemed to be an improvement of land within the Improvement of Land Act 1864,[33] and the construction of sewers and drainage is an authorised improvement, the cost of which may be expended out

---

[30] See Town and Country Planning Act 1990, ss.1, 62 and Sch. 1.

[31] See definition of "development" in s.55 of the 1990 Act. The 1990 Act provides no definition of the phrase "engineering operations" except to extend it to include the formation or laying out of means of access to highways: see s.336(1).

[32] See such cases as *Bracewell v Appleby* [1975] Ch. 408.

[33] Public Health Act 1936, s.33.

of capital moneys and is not liable to be replaced by instalments under the Settled Land Act 1925.[34]

THE ADOPTION OF SEWERS

Provided the appropriate procedure is followed, the sewerage undertaker may at any time "adopt" any sewer,[35] or any part thereof,[36] or any sewage disposal works, situate within its area, the construction whereof was not completed before the 1st October 1937.[37]

(a) Effect of a declaration

The effect of any such declaration is to cause the sewer to vest in the undertaker as from the date of such declaration.[38] It should be noted, however, that any person who, immediately before the making of a vesting declaration, was entitled to use the sewer, shall be entitled to use it (or any sewer substituted therefor), to the same extent as if the declaration had not been made.[39] A sewerage undertaker would probably not be liable for any damage caused by an improperly or negligently constructed sewer which had vested in it by virtue of statute[40] "whether with or against their will";[41] nor would it matter that the damage occurred after the vesting of the sewer in the undertaker. However, it would seem that this immunity from liability would not protect an undertaker who had adopted a defective private sewer under

---

34   Settled Land Act 1925, s.83 and Third Schedule, Part I.
35   The provision applies only to sewers, not to drains; but see also s.104 of the 1991 Act, *post*, p.106.
36   1991 Act, s.102(3).
37   *Ibid.*, s.102. The date mentioned was the date of commencement of the 1936 Act: see s.347(1) thereof. As to the general vesting of sewers and works in undertakers, see pp.40-56 *ante*.
38   *Cf.* Chapter 2, *ante*, p.40.
39   1991 Act, s.102(6).
40   e.g. under s.13 of the 1875 Act; *ante*, p.47.
41   *Per* Atkin J. in *Morris v Mynyddislwyn U.D.C.* (1917) 81 J.P. 262. In the Court of Appeal it was simply held on this point that the pipe in question did not constitute a nuisance: [1917] 2 K.B. 309.

the present provision, as in such circumstances it could be held to have taken positive action with regard to the sewer.

(b) Procedure

When a sewerage undertaker proposes to adopt a sewer by a declaration of vesting under the section,[42] the following procedure must be observed:

(i) Notice[43] of the proposal must be given to the owners of the sewer or works in question, including the owners of easements in relation to the sewer.

(ii) In the rare case where the sewer, etc. in question is situate outside the area of the "adopting" sewerage undertaker it must give notice[44] of its proposal to the undertaker in whose area the sewer is situate, and may not proceed to make the vesting declaration until *either* the other undertaker has consented thereto, *or* the Secretary of State, on application to him,[45] has "dispensed with the necessity for such consent, either unconditionally or subject to such conditions as he may think fit to impose".[46]

(iii) No vesting declaration may be made (except on the

---

[42] The owner himself may make application to the undertaker for a declaration to be made (1991 Act, s.102(2)); in any such case, the undertaker should make its decision on such application within two months. It is suggested that a declaration of vesting should be made in respect of the sewers on any new private estate when the building has been completed, provided of course the sewers have been properly constructed. Where the sewers can be said to form part of a street, adoption of the street may include adoption of the sewer, but in any case of doubt the procedure of the present section should be followed.

[43] The notice must be in writing: 1991 Act, s.219(1) (definition of "notice"), and must be served in the prescribed manner (*ibid.*, s.216). In *Epping Forest District Council v Essex Rendering* [1983] 1 W.L.R. 158, the House of Lords decided that the requirement as to writing is mandatory. The notice itself need not be in any particular form, but Shaw's Form PN4 is appropriate.

[44] See preceding note; the same notice will serve for this purpose also.

[45] No provision is made in the section for an inquiry, but the Secretary of State has power to convene one under the 1991 Act, s.215.

[46] 1991 Act, s.103.

application of such body) in respect of any sewer, or of any part thereof, which is vested in another sewerage undertaker, a local authority,[47] a county council,[48]any railway undertakers[49] or dock undertakers.[50]

When the notice under (i) above has been served, the adopting sewerage undertaker may not proceed further until *either* two months[51] have elapsed[52] without an appeal against its proposals being lodged[53] *or* until any such appeal has been determined.[54] Any owner of a sewer[55] aggrieved by the proposal of the undertaker to make a vesting declaration, may appeal to the Director General of Water Services within two months[51] after the notice of the proposal was served upon him; and a similar right of appeal is open to any owner who is aggrieved by the refusal of a sewerage undertaker to make a vesting declaration under the section on his application.[56]

The relationship between "adoption" and the other means whereby a sewer may become a public sewer, should not be overlooked. Thus, in the following diagram, the whole of the drainage system serving the 13 houses in Lovers' Close (having

---

[47] i.e. a district or London borough council or the Common Council of the City of London: 1991 Act, s.219(1).

[48] This will be of particular importance with reference to highway sewers: see Chapter 6, *post*, p.125.

[49] i.e. the British Railways Board, London Regional Transport, any other person authorised by or under any enactment to construct, work or carry on any railway: 1991 Act, s.219(1).

[50] Provided the sewer, etc. in question is situate in or on land which belongs to them and is held or used by them for the purposes of their undertaking.

[51] i.e. two calendar months: Interpretation Act 1978, Sch. 1.

[52] Presumably, from the date of service of the notice.

[53] See below, n.56.

[54] 1991 Act, s.102(4).

[55] Presumably, this means the owner of the sewer, etc. in question; "owner" is defined for the purposes of the 1991 Act in s.219(1) thereof.

[56] 1991 Act, s.105(1), as amended by the Competition and Service (Utilities) Act 1992, s.35(7), substituting a reference to the Director for one to the Secretary of State. This right of appeal may be exercised at any time after he has received notice of the authority's refusal of his application, or, if he receives no such notice, at any time after the expiration of two months from the making of his application (1991 Act, s.105(3)).

been constructed after 1936 by a private developer) could be adopted by the sewerage undertaker by resolution under section 102; the lengths F-C and E-B would then become public sewers. On the other hand if the roadway of Lovers' Close is made up under the private street works code (Highways Act 1980, Part XI), the sewers in the highway (i.e. length F-C) alone will vest in the sewerage undertaker under section 179(2)(b) of the 1991 Act, leaving length E-B as a private sewer.

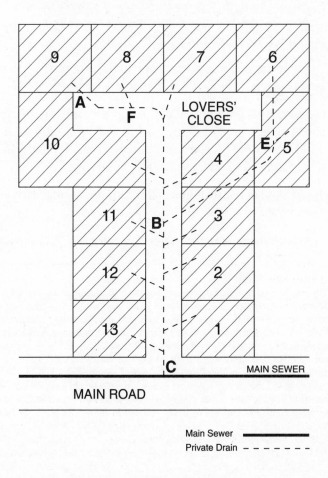

(c) Refusal or failure to make a declaration

When the sewerage undertaker considers the question whether to make a vesting declaration in respect of a particular sewer, etc., or when the Director considers an appeal under the section, regard must be had to all the circumstances of the case. More specifically the following matters must be taken into account:[57]

(a) whether the sewer, or works in question is or are adapted to, or required for, any general system of sewerage or sewage disposal which the undertaker has provided, or proposes to provide, for its area or any part thereof;

(b) whether the sewer is constructed under a highway or under land reserved by a planning scheme[58] for a street;[59]

(c) the number of buildings which the sewer is intended to serve, and whether, regard being had to the proximity of other buildings or the prospect of future development, it is likely to be required to serve additional buildings;[60]

(d) the method of construction and state of repair of the sewer or works; *and*

(e) in a case where an owner objects, whether the making of the

---

[57] 1991 Act, ss.102(5), 105(7).

[58] This expression as it appeared in s.17 of the Public Health Act 1936 was not deleted from the present section by the Town and Country Planning Act 1947 or by any corresponding provisions in the Town and Country Planning Acts 1971 or 1990: but it is submitted that it must be understood to refer to a confirmed development plan under the 1990 Act. It should be noted that the definition of "planning scheme" in s.343(1) of the 1936 Act was repealed by the Ninth Schedule of the Town and Country Planning Act 1947.

[59] In view of the undertaker's powers of entry and the local authority's power to prevent building over sewers, adoption should not be refused on this ground merely because sewers are in back gardens: *Re Westfield Drive, Bolton-le-Sands* (DoE Appeal Decision, October 15, 1987, WS/5527/AB/17), cited in J. Bates, *Water and Drainage Law*, para. 9.37.

[60] This does not set a minimum figure in respect of the present or future number of buildings; each case is treated on its merits: *Re Portman Close, Dartford* (DoE Appeal Decision, February 5, 1987, WS/5274/AB/1), cited in Bates, *op. cit.*, para. 9.37.

proposed vesting declaration would be seriously detrimental[61] to him.

These five considerations are not paramount. Although they must be considered particularly they may be outweighed by other material considerations. However it is not clear whether "all the circumstances of the case" covers financial issues such as the burden of repair and maintenance charges. In *R. v Secretary of State for Wales and A.B. Hutten*,[62] the Secretary of State, contrary to his inspector's recommendation, directed a water authority (as predecessor to the present sewerage undertaker) to adopt defective private sewers because it was "less inequitable" for the water authority to bear the financial burden of repair and maintenance than for it to be borne by the owners of the private estate served by the sewers. On an application for judicial review, Macpherson J. seems to have held that there was insufficient evidence available to the Secretary of State for him to justify his decision on that ground; the court did not directly decide whether the financial burden was a relevant consideration in such circumstances. It is submitted that the declaration should normally depend upon the condition of the sewers and drains concerned and only in exceptional circumstances should personal factors, including that of financial equity, be a relevant circumstance within section 102.

On an appeal,[63] either against the proposals of the undertaker to

---

[61] There is no elucidation in the section of this somewhat obscure expression. However, it has been stated on an appeal that it must be shown that there is an increased likelihood either that the sewer would overflow on to his land or that a structural failure of some sort will occur or that some onerous liability may fall on him as a result of the declaration; however, given the other powers available to an undertaker to deal with such matters, adoption is likely to be considered as beneficial to the owner: *Re Stennet Ave., Spalding* (DoE Appeal Decision, October 8, 1987, WS/5530/AB/22), cited in Bates, *op. cit.,* para. 9.36.

[62] [1987] J.P.L. 711.

[63] Appeals may be lodged by simple letter addressed to the Director; there are no rules of procedure governing their conduct, except that if the rules of "natural justice" were not observed on a particular appeal, the proceedings could presumably be quashed by the courts.

make a declaration, or its refusal to make a declaration, the Director may allow or disallow the undertaker's proposals, or may make any declaration the undertaker might have made. In addition, he may specify conditions (including conditions as to the payment of compensation[64] by the sewerage undertaker[65]), and may direct that any declaration he had made should not take effect unless any such conditions are accepted.[66]

AGREEMENTS FOR THE ADOPTION OF SEWERS

Under section 104 of the Water Industry Act 1991, a sewerage undertaker may agree with any person who is constructing[67] or proposing to construct a sewer or sewage disposal works that, providing the sewer, etc. is constructed in the manner specified in the agreement, the undertaker will make a vesting declaration on completion of the work, or on some specified date or the happening of some future event. Any such agreement is enforceable against the sewerage undertaker by the owner or occupier for the time being of any premises served by the sewer, etc.[68]

---

[64] The undertakers themselves have no power to agree to make compensation to the owner, nor can they be compelled to do so, except on appeal to the Director. Even if the owner can prove that he has sustained damage as a consequence of the undertaker having exercised its powers under the section, any right to compensation (except through an appeal to the Director) is excluded specifically by the 1991 Act, Sch. 12, para. 4(5).

[65] But not payment *to* the undertaker: *Re Robin's Close, Broadstone* (DoE Appeal Decision, January 19, 1981, WS/5533/AB/1), cited in J. Bates, *Water and Drainage Law*, para. 9.37.

[66] 1991 Act, s.105(5), as amended by the Competition and Service (Utilities) Act 1992, s.35(7); the conditions must be accepted, presumably, by the appellant. This power will be used sparingly as it is considered that the fact that the sewer will become available for public use is not a ground for compensation; if the owner has lost any potential profit from the adoption, compensation will only be considered if the sewer was constructed for some purpose beneficial to the owner over and above its normal sanitary purpose, so that it might contain an element of value which public use of the sewer would destroy: *Re Battenhall Road, Worcester* (DoE Appeal Decision, December 23, 1971, WS/1857/AB/1), cited in Bates, *op. cit.,* para. 9.36.

[67] Which includes extension work.

[68] 1991 Act, s.104(1), (5).

Where a person constructing or proposing to construct a drain, sewer or sewage disposal works has applied to the sewerage undertaker in due form for an adoption agreement under section 104 and this has been refused, that person may appeal to the Director General of Water Services.[69] Upon such an appeal the Director may refuse the application or enter into such an agreement as the undertaker might have entered into either upon terms which he considers reasonable or upon terms offered by the undertaker with suitable modifications.[70] Such an agreement will be entered into "on behalf of" the undertaker. The Director has decided that, generally, sewer works should be adopted provided that

(a) the development and associated sewer works have been planned in a way which provides for efficient drainage of the properties concerned;

(b) the design and standard of construction comply with the standards prevailing at the time the proposal for adoption is made, as set out in *Sewers for Adoption* (4th edn.);

(c) the sewer works are in a satisfactory condition (i.e. with no outstanding maintenance problems);

(d) the sewer works are compatible with the undertaker's existing sewer system, so that adoption would not present operational problems for the undertaker; and

(e) there is easy access to the sewers for maintenance purposes, which generally means that the sewer must be laid in the highway or land open to the public.

The underlying principle is that adoption by the undertaker should not impose costs on it which could have been avoided; however, the Director also accepts that even necessary and unavoidable costs may be so high that it would be unreasonable

---

[69] 1991 Act, s.105(2), as amended by the 1992 Act, s.35(7).
[70] 1991 Act, s.105(6), as amended by *ibid*.

for the sewerage undertaker to agree to adopt them.[71]

No agreement may be entered into under this section in respect of a sewer, etc. situate within the area of another sewerage undertaker, until that undertaker has consented thereto or the Director has, on an application made to him, dispensed with the need for such consent.[72]

---

[71]   *OFWAT Annual Report 1994* (1994-95 H.C. 431), p.29.
[72]   1991 Act, s.105(7), as amended by *ibid.*, and compare the power of the Secretary of State under s.103(1), (2), *ante*, p.101.

Chapter 5

MAINTENANCE AND USE OF PUBLIC SEWERS

GENERAL DUTIES OF SEWERAGE UNDERTAKERS

Under section 94(1) of the Water Industry Act 1991 it is the duty of every sewerage undertaker "so to cleanse and maintain . . . [public] sewers [whether inside its area or elsewhere] as to ensure that . . . [its] area is and continues to be effectually drained;" also "to make provision for the emptying of . . . [public] sewers and such further provision . . . as is necessary from time to time for effectually dealing, by means of sewage disposal works or otherwise, with the contents of those sewers."

This duty includes an obligation to have regard to existing and likely future obligations and to make allowance for the discharge of trade effluent[1] into the undertaker's public sewers and the disposal thereof. The modern provision is derived from section 23 of the 1936 Act and it is suggested that here, as in the former case, "maintain" must include all ordinary works of repair,[2] and that "cleanse" must include the clearance of obstructions. The duty to "empty" public sewers would seem to include a duty to provide and maintain a proper outfall,[3] and to cause the sewage or other contents of the sewer to flow in the direction of the outfall. These duties must necessarily be taken to apply to all the public sewers vested in a sewerage undertaker, whether or not laid through private land. Powers of entry are provided for the performance of such works in emergency or at a reasonable time and upon seven days' notice to the occupier by section 168 and Schedule 6, Part II to the 1991 Act. The exercise of such power

---

[1]   "Trade Effluent" has here the same meaning as in Chapter III of Part IV of the 1991 Act (ss.118-141): see s.141(1).

[2]   As to the provision of new sewers see Chapter 3, *ante*.

[3]   As to the duty to provide a proper outfall under former provisions, see *R. v Tynemouth R.D.C.* [1896] 2 Q.B. 451.

of entry will, of course, be limited strictly to that which is necessary for the performance of the undertaker's lawful purposes and if the right is exceeded the undertaker and its agents will be liable in damages as trespassers *ab initio*.[4]

Under the modern, as under former, provisions the duty to "maintain" must not be exaggerated. In *Radstock Co-operative and Industrial Society v Norton-Radstock U.D.C.*[5] Ungoed-Thomas J. said[6] "I fail to see that the statutory obligation to 'maintain' the sewer includes any such extended obligation to maintain lands or conditions outside the sewer, as the plaintiffs suggest, or that it involves obligations to third parties like the plaintiffs who are complete strangers to the sewer." In that case a public sewer had been properly constructed in a river bed but, with no fault on the part of the responsible authority, the river bed was in course of time washed away and the pipe became exposed and caused eddies in the flow of water which damaged the plaintiff's property. The plaintiff claimed, *inter alia*, in nuisance but failed both at first instance and in the Court of Appeal.[7]

A more marginal question might arise were a plaintiff to be injured as a result (for example) of the defective state of a manhole cover situated in private premises.[8] A sewerage undertaker is, of course, under an ordinary duty of care in respect of such a structure,[9] even if it was not aware of the existence of the sewer itself, but it is not clear whether in such a case the court

---

[4] The *Six Carpenters Case* (1610) 1 Sm. L.C. 134, *cf.* Lord Denning "Freedom under the Law" at p.112 and W.V.H. Rogers, *Winfield and Jolowicz on Tort* (14th edn., 1994), pp.393-394.

[5] [1967] Ch. 1094; this point was not discussed in the Court of Appeal: see [1968] Ch. 605.

[6] At p.1118.

[7] [1968] Ch. 605.

[8] Such a cover will normally form part of the sewer: 1989 Act, s.189(1) by reference to Public Health Act 1936, s.90(4).

[9] The standard of care differs according to whether the injured person is a visitor or a person other than a visitor: Occupiers' Liability Act 1957, s.1(3)(a) and 2(2) and Occupiers' Liabilty Act 1984.

would be prepared to hold a sewerage undertaker liable on the ground that it had not carried out a system of regular inspections of sewers upon private property. Presumably the case would turn on the commonly accepted practice amongst sewerage undertakers in this regard.

The duty imposed by section 94 must be performed in a fashion which does not contravene other provisions of the 1991 legislation, in particular the offence of polluting controlled waters under the Water Resources Act 1991.[10]

The duty to cleanse, maintain and empty public sewers imposed by section 94 of the 1991 Act is expressly made enforceable by the Secretary of State or, with his special consent or general authorisation, the Director General of Water Services.[11]

The obligation to comply with a valid provisional or final order under section 18 is owed to "any person who may be affected by a contravention" and such a contravention will be actionable at the suit of any such person who suffers consequent loss or damage.[12] It will be a defence to such a civil action for the sewerage undertaker to show that it "took all reasonable steps and exercised all due diligence to avoid contravening the order."[13] Without prejudice to the possibility of such a civil action, the Secretary of State or the Director General of Water Services, as the case might be, may take civil proceedings for the enforcement of a section 18 order by injunction or other appropriate relief.[14]

A further remedy for contravention of section 94 of the 1989 Act by a sewerage undertaker is provided by the draconian possibility of a special administration order under sections 23 and 24 of the 1991 Act.[15]

---

[10] See *post*, pp.148-157.
[11] Section 94(3). See *ante*, pp.17-19 on powers to make enforcement orders.
[12] Section 22(1), (2).
[13] Section 22(3).
[14] Section 22(4).
[15] See *ante*, pp.20-21.

In addition to these statutory remedies it must be considered that a sewerage undertaker will be liable in civil proceedings for damages or an injunction if negligent or improper maintenance can be shown or if a complaint arises from some positive action by the undertaker whereby legal rights have been infringed.[16]

THE POWER TO CHARGE FOR SEWERAGE SERVICES

Power to charge for provision of sewerage services is conferred upon sewerage undertakers by section 142 of the 1991 Act. The power so conferred is wide ranging and, except in so far as the Act otherwise provides, allows a sewerage undertaker to

> "fix charges . . . by reference to such matters and adopt . . . such methods and principles for the calculation and imposition of the charges, as appear to the undertaker to be appropriate."[17]

Charging limits are, however, set by the Director General of Water Services.[18]

Charges may be fixed either by agreement with the customers concerned or in accordance with a "charges scheme" under section 143 of the 1991 Act.[19] A "charges scheme" may

(a) fix the charges to be paid for any services performed by a sewerage undertaker in the course of its statutory functions;

(b) fix the charges to be paid where, in circumstances specified by the Scheme, a trade effluent notice is served on the undertaker under section 119 of the 1991 Act, a consent required under Chapter III of Part IV of the Act is given by

---

16 See e.g. *Dear v Thames Water Co. and others* (1993) 33 Con. L.R. 43 (where negligence was not proved and the defendants were found not to be responsible for any nuisance arising from the flooding of a watercourse). Proceedings based simply on a contravention of s.94 are, however, barred by s.18(8): see *ante*, p.65.
17 Section 142(4).
18 See *ante*, pp.28-29.
19 Section 142(2).

the undertaker, or a discharge is made pursuant to such a consent;[20]

(c) provide for the times and methods of payment of the charges it fixes.

A scheme may make variant provisions for different cases, including different circumstances and localities and may contain supplemental, consequential and transitional provisions and may revoke or amend and earlier scheme.[21] Even where such a charges scheme is in force, a sewerage undertaker may still conclude charging agreements with customers in particular cases and enter into agreements as to discharge of trade effluent under Chapter III of Part IV of the 1991 Act.[22]

For the purpose of levying charges for sewerage services, services are generally taken to be supplied to the occupiers for the time being of premises which are drained by a sewer or drain connecting, directly or intermediately, with a public sewer provided by the undertaker concerned for the carriage off of both foul or surface water or both, or of premises benefitting from facilities draining into a sewer or drain so connected.[23]

A person may remain liable for sewerage charges after vacating premises if he fails to inform the undertaker of the termination of occupation with at least two working days' notice. Liability will then arise for the charges ending no later than the earliest of

(i) where information of termination of occupation is given less than two days before, or at any time after, such termination, the twenty-eighth day after information is given,

---

[20] In such a case the person liable to pay the charges will be the person who serves the notice, the person to whom consent is given, or any person who makes a discharge pursuant to such a consent. Such a charge may comprise a single charge for the whole period of the consent, separate charges in respect of different parts of the period. or both such types of charge (s.143(2), (3)).

[21] Section 143(4).

[22] Section 143(5).

[23] Section 144(1)(b).

(ii) the day on which the meter would normally have been read,

(iii) the day on which a new occupier informs the undertaker of his occupation.[24]

Although the point is not expressly made by the 1991 Act, it may reasonably be presumed that no charges could be levied for remedying faults or defects which were a direct consequence of the sewerage undertaker's own negligence or misfeasance.

Under earlier provisions, it was doubtful whether "cleansing" was included within the same category as "maintenance", the latter broadly involving constructional works but the former not doing so. Consequently, the 6th edition of this book concluded at p.71 that,

"the legislature understood the two terms ["maintain" and "cleanse"] as being mutually exclusive and . . . [t]he cost, therefore, of the clearance of obstructions, would seem not to be recoverable . . ."

Under the present (1991) provision the position is somewhat clarified. Section 94(1) provides for duties to "provide [etc.] . . . a system of public sewers . . . and . . . to cleanse and maintain [them] . . .; and to make provision for the emptying of those sewers . . ." Section 142(1)(a) then empowers sewerage undertakers "to fix charges for any services provided in the course of carrying out its functions." Such "functions" are those defined by section 94 and there would thus seem to be no reason why the "cleansing" of sewers should not now be considered a chargeable "service" under the 1991 Act.

A sewerage undertaker is not entitled to recover a charge simply in respect of becoming the supplier of sewerage services to domestic premises or to require payment for a declaration of vesting under Chapter II of Part IV of the 1991 Act.[25] Nor may

---

24   Section 144(2), (3), (4).
25   Section 146(1)(b), (2), (3).

a charge be levied upon a highway authority in respect of the drainage of a highway or the disposal of the contents of any such drain or sewer.[26] A sewerage undertaker may, however, levy a connection charge in respect of new connections to a public sewer where there has been no prior such connection.[27] Where a new public sewer connection is requisitioned, the sewerage undertaker may also require financial guarantees.[28]

The level of charging for sewerage services may not after 31st March 2000 be fixed by reference to a rating valuation list. Charges so fixed will not be recoverable in respect of services supplied after that date.[29]

A sewerage undertaker may choose to fix its charges by reference to volume.[30] Where this is done, or notice of such intent has been given, the undertaker has power to install a meter to measure the discharge of effluent in a drain or private sewer connecting with a public sewer and also to enter upon premises for the maintenance, repair, disconnection or removal of such meters.[31] The power of entry for purposes of installation, maintenance, etc. will be conferred by the undertaker upon designated persons, who may enter premises only at a reasonable time and after seven days' notice has been given to the occupier.[32] However, if it is shown to a Justice of the Peace upon sworn information in writing that there are grounds for the installation, maintenance, repair, disconnection or removal of a meter and that the exercise of the power has been refused or such refusal is reasonably anticipated, the premises are unoccupied, the occupier is temporarily absent, the case is urgent or an application for admission would defeat the object of the entry, the Justice may by warrant authorise

---

26 Section 146(4).
27 Section 146(2)(b).
28 See *ante*.
29 1991 Act, s.145. A "rating valuation list" is one maintained for rating purposes under ss.41 or 52 of the Local Government Finance Act 1988, s.67 of the General Rate Act 1967 or other enactments.
30 Section 149 (authorising the Secretary of State to make regulations).
31 Section 162.
32 Section 172 and Sch. 6, Pt. II.

entry, by force if need be.[33]

The expenses of installation of a meter will generally be borne by the sewerage undertaker but an occupier must, in particular, bear the element of the expense arising from compliance with a request to position the meter in a place other than that reasonably proposed by the undertaker.[34] Once a meter has been installed it will be a criminal offence to tamper with it.[35]

Where sewerage services are provided by a person other than a sewerage undertaker, the Director General of Water Services may by order prescribe maximum charges which may be levied by such a person who makes direct or indirect use of the services of a sewerage undertaker in the supply of such services.[36] Where such an order is made it is the duty of the Director to publish it in a manner which he considers appropriate for the purpose of bringing it to the attention of persons likely to be affected.[37]

A sewerage undertaker may not levy charges in contravention of any local statutory provision expressly precluding the making of charges for the supply of specified services.[38]

The Secretary of State may by regulations provide for billing disputes (i.e. disputes between a customer and a sewerage undertaker concerning the amount of the charge the undertaker is entitled to recover for the provision of sewerage services other than by carrying out trade effluent functions) to be referred to the Director for determination.[39]

Recovery of charges and/or expenses in performance of works will normally be as for a simple contract debt in any court of

---

[33] Sch. 6, Pt. II.
[34] Section 148(1), (4).
[35] Sections 175-177.
[36] Section 150.
[37] Section 150(3).
[38] Section 142(5).
[39] Section 150A, inserted by the Competition and Service (Utilities) Act 1992, s.36.

competent jurisdiction, generally the County Court. The legality of the charges levied and/or the expenses claimed will be matters which the court may take into account in proceedings for recovery. The statutory authority of a sewerage undertaker may also, of course, independently be tested in the courts by persons affected by their proposed or actual exercise.

PERFORMANCE OF SEWERAGE FUNCTIONS BY LOCAL AUTHORITIES

A sewerage undertaker may enter into an arrangement whereby a local authority, the Commission for the New Towns, a New Towns development corporation, the Development Board for Rural Wales or an urban development corporation in an urban development area will carry out sewerage functions in the whole or part of the undertaker's area.[40] Such an arrangement may provide for the exercise by the authority, etc. of any of the undertaker's functions and powers which may be specified; no such arrangement will however affect the availability of remedies against the undertaker in respect of sewerage functions or failures in their performance.[41] Except in so far as a specific arrangement may otherwise provide, a local authority acting under such an arrangement may itself delegate its sewerage functions under section 101 of the Local Government Act 1972.[42]

THE ALTERATION AND CLOSURE OF PUBLIC SEWERS

Under section 116 of the 1991 Act,[43] a sewerage undertaker has power to discontinue and prohibit the use of any public sewer vested in it. Under the 1991 Act, the duty is imposed upon

---

[40] 1991 Act, s.97(1), (5).
[41] *Ibid.*, s.97(2), (3). The liability of the local authority as agent can be no geater than the liability of the undertaker, apart from any acts of individual misfeasance: *Dear v Thames Water and others* (1993) 33 Con. L.R. 43.
[42] *Ibid.*, s.97(4).
[43] As amended by the Competition and Service (Utilities) Act 1992, s.35(12).

sewerage undertakers by section 94 to "provide, improve and extend . . . a system of public sewers (whether inside their area or elsewhere) . . . to ensure that that area is and continues to be effectually drained";[44] and their power to perform works on land includes that "to inspect, maintain, adjust, repair or alter any relevant pipe".[45] This power would seem *prima facie* to include also powers of necessary closure, e.g. when a public sewer has been replaced. These powers may only, however, be exercised in pursuance of the duty under section 94 to secure effectual drainage in the area of the undertaker concerned and, clearly, the alteration or closure of a public sewer in such a fashion as to deprive a part of the area of effectual drainage would be a breach of the statutory duty of the undertaker under section 94.

A discontinuance or prohibition under section 116 may be for all purposes, for the purpose of foul water drainage or for surface water drainage. Before a person lawfully using a sewer for any purpose is deprived of the use of the sewer for that purpose, the undertaker must provide a sewer equally effective for his use and, at the undertaker's own expense, carry out work necessary to make that person's drains or sewers communicate with the replacement sewer provided. Any dispute as to the effectiveness of a sewer provided may be referred by either party to the Director for determination under section 30A of the 1991 Act.[46]

THE PRESERVATION OF PUBLIC SEWERS

The integrity of public sewers may be threatened by a number of external influences, in particular by the impact of external works and by the abuse of the pipes themselves. The latter issue is considered below.[47]

---

[44]   Section 94(1)(a).
[45]   Sections 158(1)(b) and 159(1)(b).
[46]   Section 116(4), inserted by the Competition and Service (Utilities) Act 1992, s.35(12). See *ante*, p.23.
[47]   See p.120.

(a) Buildings over sewers

In general no new building may be erected over any sewer or drain shown on the sewer map without the consent of the undertaker. The limitation arises from section 18 of the Building Act 1984[48] and the Building Regulations 1991.[49] The responsible local authority is under a duty to reject any plans for the erection or extension of a building submitted to them under the Regulations which is proposed to be erected over any such sewer or drain, or to be erected on such a site or in such a manner as would result in its interfering with the use of any such sewer or drain, unless it is satisfied that in the particular circumstances it may "properly" consent to the proposal. In the exercise of this discretion, the local authority must notify the sewerage undertaker, which may then impose "requirements" with which it is the authority's duty to comply provided they are reasonable.[50] Work carried out in contravention of the Regulations may be removed by the local authority at the building owner's expense[51] and such construction will normally constitute an offence under the Regulations.

The term "building" is not defined generally for the purposes of the 1984 Act, but it is normally understood as signifying any construction or erection capable of enclosing some area of ground.[52] In the present context, however, the underlying purpose is clearly the prevention of damage to sewers, and to provide the sewerage undertaker with ready access thereto and it has been suggested that "a building to be within the section must be one

---

[48] Amended by the Water Act 1989, Sch. 8, para. 6, the Buildings (Inner London) Regulations 1987 (S.I. 1987 No. 798) and the Water Consolidation (Consequential Provisions) Act 1991, Sch. 1. The section does not apply to the Temples: s.18(6).

[49] S.I. 1991 No. 2768, as amended by S.I. 1992 No. 1180. Made by the Secretary of State under the Building Act 1984. The restriction therefore applies only to buildings for which plans must be submitted under the Regulations.

[50] 1984 Act, s.18(3), inserted by the Water Act 1989, Sch. 8, para. 6.

[51] Provided that the work is in actual contravention of the Act or the Regulations and also provided that the appropriate procedure is observed: see s.36 of the 1984 Act.

[52] See e.g. *Slaughter v Sunderland Corporation* (1891) 60 L.J.M.C. 91.

which, by reason of its weight or otherwise, may cause an injury to the sewer over which it has been built, or one which, by reason of its size or otherwise, prevents access being gained to the sewer".[53]

(b) Injuries to sewers

In addition to the safeguards contained in section 18 of the Building Act 1984, a sewerage undertaker has sufficient ownership in a public sewer[54] to entitle it to bring an action for nuisance for damages or an injunction in a case of injury to its sewers.[55] In practice, however, it may more commonly be convenient for the local authority in the area concerned to take proceedings in public nuisance against the person responsible,[56] as most injuries to public sewers will result in such a nuisance.[57]

Such an action would be brought by the local authority and would not directly involve the sewerage undertaker, unless, in an unusual case, as defendant. If the sewerage undertaker felt

---

[53]   *Urban Housing Co. Ltd. v City of Oxford* [1939] 3 All E.R. 839, *per* Bennett J. at p.850, where he suggested that two walls, each 7 feet high and 9 inches thick were not "buildings" within the meaning of the earlier 1875 Act. Sir Wilfrid Greene M.R., however, in the Court of Appeal in the same case ([1940] Ch. 70 at p.86, upholding the judgment of Bennett J.) said that he would have been disposed to take the view that these walls were buildings within the section, as "there must be, on the face of it, some slight interference, or might be some slight interference owing to their presence, with the facility of repairing or re-laying the sewers". Both these observations were, however, *obiter*.

[54]   See Chapter 2, pp.56-57 *ante*.

[55]   See e.g. *Cleckheaton U.D.C. v Firth* (1898) 62 J.P. 536, although in that case it was held that the defendant was legally entitled to do the act complained of. In *Gas Light and Coke Co. v St. Mary Abbotts Kensington Vestry* (1885) 15 Q.B.D. 1, an injunction was granted to prevent the highway authority from using a heavy steam roller for repairs in such a manner as would injure gas mains laid in the highway at a depth and protected sufficiently against all ordinary traffic, and in *Driscoll v Poplar Board of Works* (1897) 62 J.P. 40, the same principle was applied in an action for damages.

[56]   If the person responsible cannot be found, however, the owner of the sewer or drain concerned, i.e. the sewerage undertaker, may be liable in public nuisance: *Rhymney Iron Co. v Gelligaer U.D.C.* [1917] 1 K.B. 589.

[57]   See e.g. *Riddell v Spear* (1879) 40 L.T. 130.

impelled to take action on its own behalf, it seems that it would be limited to the rights arising from its ownership of the sewer in question.

(c) Support of sewers: removal of minerals

The Public Health Act 1875 (Support of Sewers) Amendment Act 1883 formerly regulated the rights of a water authority to subjacent support of any "sanitary work"[58] which was vested in it or under its control. The owners of the subsoil could not prejudice support of such works by the removal of minerals other than coal, etc. by the National Coal Board without giving notice to the water authority, which might then within 30 days require the minerals to be left unworked or specify and define the nature of the support which was required to be left.

It is now, however, provided that the 1883 Act does not apply after the 1st September 1989 ("The Transfer Date")[59] in relation to any "sanitary work" of a person other than a local authority or any sanitary works carried out under section 97 of the 1991 Act (performance of sewerage functions by local authorities).[60] It would therefore seem that this statutory protection does not apply to the "sanitary works" of a sewerage undertaker and subsidence damage will therefore be actionable only by virtue of the rights of ownership vested in the undertaker.

(d) Support of sewers: removal of coal

Where support is withdrawn from land in connection with the lawful working and getting of coal and/or other minerals worked with coal, causing damage to a public sewer, the responsible

---

[58] This expression is defined in s.2 of the 1883 Act and includes a great many other things besides sewers (in spite of the title of the Act), such as water pipes, street lighting, etc.

[59] The Water Authorities (Transfer of Functions) (Appointed Day) Order 1989 (S.I. 1989 No. 1530).

[60] See the Water Act 1989, Sch. 25, para. 3, as amended by the Water Consolidation (Consequential Provisions) Act 1991; 1991 Act, s.97(6).

person[61] will be liable to make a payment to the sewerage undertaker in which the sewer concerned is vested for the subsidence damage.[62]

THE USE OF PUBLIC SEWERS

Not all liquids and substances may be permitted to flow into a public sewer, certain restrictions being imposed by both statute and common law.

(a) Prohibition upon polluting emissions from public sewers

The detail of pollution control is considered below.[63] However, in the present context it must be said that it is a criminal offence under section 85 of the Water Resources Act 1991 for any person to cause or knowingly permit any matter, other than trade or sewage effluent, to enter "controlled waters"[64] by discharge from a drain or sewer in contravention of a prohibition imposed under section 86;[65] or to cause or knowingly permit any trade or sewage effluent to be discharged into any controlled waters or, from land in England and Wales, through a pipe, into the sea outside the seaward limits of controlled waters;[66] or to cause or knowlingly permit trade or sewerage effluent to be discharged, in contravention of a section 86 prohibition, from a building or any fixed plant on to or into any land or into any waters of a lake

---

[61]   i.e. the licensed operator or, if there is no such operator with responsibility for the area in question, the Coal Authority.

[62]   See the Coal Mining Subsidence Act 1991, as amended by the Coal Industry Act 1994, ss.42-48 and Sch. 9, para. 41. In most cases a "damage notice" must be served under s.3 of the Act in accordance with the Coal Mining Subsidence (Notices and Claims) Regulations 1991 (S.I. 1991 No. 2509).

[63]   See Chapter 8, *post*.

[64]   See *post*, pp.148-157.

[65]   Section 85(2). A relevant "prohibition" for these purposes is one contained in a notice issued by the National Rivers Authority prohibiting a person from making or continuing a discharge or imposing conditions upon its continuation or a proscription by regulation of particular substances or concentrations thereof (s.86(1), (2)).

[66]   Section 85(3).

or pond which are not inland freshwaters.[67] Discharges of sewage effluent into "controlled waters"[68] which a sewerage undertaker did not knowingly cause or permit but which it was bound (unconditionally or otherwise) to receive into the sewer or works matter included in the discharge, will be deemed to have "caused the discharge".[69] Upon summary conviction the offence will carry a penalty of imprisonment for a term not exceeding three months or to a fine not exceeding £20,000 or both; or upon conviction on indictment, to imprisonment not exceeding two years or to a fine or both.[70]

(b) Other material not to be passed into public sewers

It is a criminal offence under section 111 of the Water Industry Act 1991 to "throw, empty or turn, or suffer to permit to be thrown or emptied or to pass, into any public sewer, or into any drain or sewer communicating with a public sewer" any of the following:

"(a) any matter likely to injure the sewer or drain or to interfere with the free flow of its contents, or to affect prejudicially the treatment and disposal of its contents;[71] or

(b) any chemical refuse or waste steam, or any liquid of a temperature higher than one hundred and ten degrees Fahrenheit, being refuse or steam which, or a liquid which when so heated, is, either alone or in combination with the contents of the sewer or drain, dangerous or the cause of a nuisance, or prejudicial to health; or

---

[67] Section 85(4).
[68] Specifically discharges under s.85(3), (4).
[69] Section 87(1).
[70] Section 85(6). As to defences by way of authorities for discharges, see s.88.
[71] See *Liverpool Corporation v Coghill (H) & Son Ltd.* [1918] 1 Ch. 307 where the particular effluent had a deleterious effect on the land on which the sewage matter was eventually deposited. In this case also it was suggested *obiter*, by Eve J., that an authority could not grant a right to a person to cause effluent to flow into public sewers in such a manner as to cause a public nuisance.

(c) any petroleum spirit,[72] or carbide of calcium."

(c) Trade effluent

Under Chapter III of Part IV of the Water Industry Act 1991[73] which is further considered below,[74] no trade effluent (unless it is of a type which may lawfully be discharged into a public sewer) may be discharged from trade premises into a public sewer otherwise than in accordance with a Trade Effluent Notice.

(d) Common law

In addition to the above statutory provisions, the sewerage undertaker may sue for damages or an injunction if it can be shown that an injury is being caused as a consequence of any effluent, etc. being permitted to flow into a public sewer vested in it. Liability will not however arise if the person responsible has a prescriptive right therefor. Moreover, if the injury is sufficiently serious, proceedings may be brought in respect of public nuisance. Normally the statutory remedies should prove adequate, but it seems that the courts would grant an injunction to prevent any contravention in a proper case where the penalties could be shown not to be an adequate deterrent.[75]

---

[72] Defined by s.111(5) as meaning "any such (a) crude petroleum; (b) oil made from petroleum, or from coal, shale, peat or other bituminous substances; or (c) product of petroleum or mixture containing petroleum, as, when tested in the manner prescribed by or under the Petroleum (Consolidation) Act 1928, gives off an inflammable vapour at a temperature of less than seventy-three degrees Fahrenheit." In addition to the above control, it is customary to insert in a licence to store petroleum spirit under s.1 of the Petroleum (Consolidation) Act 1928 (which licence is issued by the county council: 1928 Act, s.2, as amended by the Local Government Act 1972, Sch. 29, para. 32) a condition to the effect that no spirit or vapour shall be allowed to escape into any drain or sewer.

[73] Sections 118-141.

[74] See Chapter 9, *post*, pp.202-212.

[75] See *Att.-Gen. v Sharp* [1931] 1 Ch. 121, and *Att.-Gen. v Bastow* [1957] 1 Q.B. 514.

Chapter 6

HIGHWAY DRAINS

HIGHWAY DRAINS AS PUBLIC SEWERS

In this chapter the expression "highway drain" is used as meaning any conduit or ditch (artificial or natural) which takes off or conveys the surface water from a highway[1] maintainable at the public expense.[2] Since, in this context, there are no legal consequences attaching to the distinction, it is unnecessary to distinguish between a sewer and a drain.

The drains which take off the surface water from a highway – which "belong" to the highway in question[3] – and which serve no other purpose will normally be vested in the highway authority[4] as such, and there will in most cases be no question of them being vested in the sewerage undertaker as public sewers under section 179 of the Water Industry Act 1991. Where, however, a highway drain also conveys foul or surface water from premises in the vicinity of the highway, or where it is desired to connect the drains of such premises to a highway drain, the status of the latter may well be very important; in particular it will have to be ascertained whether or not the drain is a public sewer.

Highway drains constructed subsequent to 1st October 1937, by the highway authority, will be public sewers if they have been constructed under some statutory provision relating to the

---

[1] This term is used in its widest sense as comprising "all portions of land over which every subject of the Crown may lawfully pass" (Pratt and Mackenzie's *Law of Highways*, 21st edn., p.1).

[2] Private streets are considered below, p.132.

[3] The expression used in s.264(1) of the Highways Act 1980.

[4] By s.263 (as amended) of the Highways Act 1980, every highway maintainable at the public expense vests in the highway authority. All such highways are now vested in the county (in Wales, from 1st April 1996, county or county borough) and metropolitan district councils, outside London under ss.1 and 265 of the 1980 Act, although in England urban roads, footpaths and bridleways may be maintained by the district council. The main exceptions are trunk and special roads, vested in the Secretary of State (1980 Act, s.1).

sewering of private streets.[5] They will also be public sewers if they were constructed before 1st April 1974 by a highway authority which was at that time also the local sanitary authority and provided they then drained other property not belonging to the local authority.[6]

If such drains drained the highway alone, or if they were constructed, whether before or after the 1st April 1974, by a highway authority which was not the local sanitary authority, they will not be public sewers, unless the former water authority made a declaration of vesting,[7] on the application of the highway authority or, since 1st September 1989, such a declaration has been made by the sewerage undertaker.[8] On the other hand a statute transferring liability for a highway from one local authority to another only affected "functions with respect to highways", and therefore did not transfer responsibility for a land drain to the new highway authority.[9]

A highway drain constructed prior to 1st October 1937, which belonged to a highway, in respect of which the highway authority was not the local sanitary authority,[10] was excluded from the definition of "sewer" contained in section 4 of the 1875 Act,[11] and any such drain did not, therefore, vest in the local authority

---

5   Successively, the 1936 Act, s.20(1)(c) (original form); 1936 Act, s.20(1)(b), as inserted by the Water Act 1973, Sch. 8, para. 33, and amended by the Highways Act 1980, Sch. 24, para. 4(a); Water Act 1989, s.153(3)(b); Water Industry Act 1991, s.179(2)(b).

6   1936 Act, s.20(1)(b), and proviso to s.20(2), in their original form, before the amendment effected by the Water Act 1973.

7   Or unless such a declaration had been made by the sanitary authority before 1st April 1974.

8   Successively, the 1936 Act, s.17(9); s.17(9), as amended by the London Government Act 1963, Sch. 18, Pt. II, and the Water Act 1973, s.14(2); and the 1991 Act, s.103(3).

9   *Att.-Gen. v St. Ives R.D.C.* [1961] 1 Q.B. 366.

10   Apparently a drain "belonging to" a main road which was formerly vested in the county council, and which was transferred to the district council, which was also the local sanitary authority, would not thereby become a public sewer: *Williamson v Durham R.D.C.* [1906] 2 K.B. 65. This position is preserved by s.264 of the Highways Act 1980.

11   See Chapter 2, *ante*, pp.43-44.

or (now) the sewerage undertaker as a public sewer under section 20 of the 1936 Act.[12] If the highway of which the drain formed part was vested in or under the control of a highway authority which was also the local sanitary authority, the drain would have been a sewer vested in the local authority (and therefore a public sewer under the 1936 Act) under the 1875 Act in accordance with the normal principles applicable to other drains.[13]

The fact that surface water from a highway was caused to flow into a public sewer would not affect its status,[14] and under section 115(1)(b) of the 1991 Act, a "relevant authority"[15] is entitled to use any public sewer vested in the sewerage undertaker for the conveyance of surface water from roads repairable by the authority.[16] Similarly any highway drain or sewer[17] may be used by the sewerage undertaker for the purpose of conveying surface water from premises or streets.[18] Further, the fact that a certain amount of water flowed off a highway into a land drain, would not affect the status of that drain or make it part of the highway.[19] The unauthorised connection of a house drain to a highway drain which is not a public sewer does not affect the status of the highway drain or cause it to become a public sewer.[20] A private individual has no right to cause his drains or sewers to be connected to a highway drain and he would be liable in respect of any nuisance arising as a consequence of any such connection.[21]

A "walkway" in, through or under a building created by agreement

---

[12] See Chapter 2, *ante*, pp.54-55 and *Irving v Carlisle R.D.C.* (1907) 71 J.P. 212.
[13] Chapter 2, *ante*, pp.47-49.
[14] *Wilkinson v Llandaff and Dinas Powis R.D.C.* [1903] 2 Ch. 695.
[15] i.e. a county council or any local authority except a non-metropolitan district council: 1991 Act, s.115(9).
[16] Subject to such terms as may be agreed between the authorities. In default of agreement, the matter may be referred to the Secretary of State, whose decision in the matter is to be final (s.115(4), (5)).
[17] Vested in a "relevant authority".
[18] 1991 Act, s.115(1)(a).
[19] *Att.-Gen. v St. Ives R.D.C.* [1961] 1 Q.B. 366.
[20] *Rickarby v New Forest R.D.C.* (1910) 26 T.L.R. 586.
[21] See e.g. *Wincanton R.D.C. v Parsons* [1905] 2 K.B. 34.

under section 35 of the Highways Act 1980 (as amended) or its predecessor in the Act of 1971, has some of the characteristics of a highway. The agreement made between the local authority and the owner(s) of the building should make provision for the drainage of the building (see s.35(3)(a)), and it is suggested that it should be made clear in the agreement that any such drains should remain in private ownership.

MEANING OF "HIGHWAY DRAIN"

The term "highway drain" is not a term of art, and yet, for the purpose of deciding questions of liability for the cleansing thereof, or in respect of accidents occasioned by such drains, it is important to decide what forms part of a highway drain and what does not. As between the highway authority and the sewerage undertaker, a drain in a highway will be the responsibility of the former only if it is not a public sewer as above explained, and if it forms part of the road or highway, or is vested in the highway authority as such.

Whether or not a particular drain forms part of the highway, and whether such objects as gullies, gratings and manhole covers in the highway are part of a drain belonging to the highway, are questions of fact.[22] Generally speaking, a manhole cover of a

---

[22] See e.g. *Papworth v Battersea Corporation (No. 2)* [1961] 1 K.B. 583. The question may also arise in connection with private streets not maintainable at the public expense. If the gully forms part of the street, its cleansing will not be the responsibility of the sewerage undertaker, but if the gully is to be regarded as part of the sewer to which it drains, and that sewer is a public one, the sewerage undertaker will be responsible for the cleansing of the gully. References to a drain or sewer include references to any "accessories", which include manholes, ventilating shafts, pumps and other machinery or apparatus designed or adapted for use in connection with the maintenance of the sewer or other pipe, for the purposes of the 1991 Act, but it is not clear that this expression includes gullies (see s.219(1), (2) of the 1991 Act). Again, alterations to the sewerage system of a private street may be included in private street works expenses chargeable to the frontagers, but the cost of construction of new gullies leading to an existing sewer necessitated by the widening of the street was held not to be so recoverable from the frontagers in *East Barnet U.D.C. v Stacey* [1939] 2 K.B. 861.

public sewer laid under the highway will be treated as part of the sewer and not part of the highway,[23] unless the drain or sewer itself is a highway drain originally constructed solely for the purpose of draining the highway. Gullies and gratings leading to a public sewer will form part of that sewer,[24] unless they were provided solely for the purpose of draining the highway, in which event they will normally be treated as forming part of the highway.[25]

In a case decided by the Court of Appeal in New Zealand,[26] based on English decisions, it was said that a sewer authority "is not liable in nuisance for the dangerous state of sewers or drains in a highway unless (1) it constructed them, or (2) it is the owner of them, or (3) it has the control or management of them."

CLEANSING OF HIGHWAY DRAINS

Under section 100(1) of the Highways Act 1980, the highway authority for a highway may, for the purpose of draining it or of otherwise preventing surface water from flowing on to it, "scour, cleanse and keep open all drains situated in the highway" or in land adjoining[27] or lying near to the highway. The same section

---

23   See s.219(1), (2) (cited in the preceding note), and *Winslow v Bushey U.D.C.* (1908) 72 J.P. 259, where the local sanitary authority was held liable in respect of an accident which occured in the highway and was caused by a defective manhole cover forming part of their sewer; but in *Thompson v Brighton Corporation* [1894] 1 Q.B. 332, the highway authority was held not liable (in accordance with the principle of non-feasance) nor was the sewer authority, where the cause of the accident was the defective state of the highway surrounding the manhole; and see Chapter 3, *ante*, p.64. Under s.58 of the Highways Act 1980, the highway authority can no longer plead non-feasance as a defence, but the special defences in s.58(2) of that Act will be relevant.

24   *White v Hindley Local Board* (1875) L.R. 10 Q.B. 219.

25   *Papworth v Battersea Corporation, supra.* This distinction is, however, by no means clearly drawn in the cases, and the question is essentially one of fact.

26   See *Patone Borough v Daubney* [1954] N.Z.L.R. 305, *per* Cooke J. at p.325.

27   This includes abutting on: Highways Act 1980, s.329(1). Strict physical contact is not essential and land may adjoin and abut if it is in "close proximity"; however the court may not enlarge the meaning to include all deriving benefit from the drain: *Buckinghamshire C.C. v Trigg* [1963] 1 W.L.R. 155; *Cobstone Investments Ltd. v Maxim* [1985] Q.B. 140, C.A.

gives the highway authority power to construct or lay such drains as it considers necessary and to erect barriers to divert surface water into or through any existing drain. Any surface water may be discharged into or through the drain and into any inland waters, whether natural or artificial, or any tidal waters. If any owner or occupier of land suffers damage, the authority must pay compensation, to be assessed, if the parties agree, by arbitration or, in case of dispute, by the County Court.[28]

This useful section confers a power, not a duty. Accordingly the highway authority could not be compelled, whether by an application for judicial review seeking *mandamus* or otherwise, to keep their drains clean. Before the Highways (Miscellaneous Provisions) Act 1961, the highway authority were not liable for damage caused by their failure to keep their drains clean because such amounted to acts of non-feasance and the authority were only liable for acts of misfeasance.[29] The defence of non-feasance is now no longer available to highway authorities,[30] and they are now under an express duty to maintain any highway maintainable at the public expense which is vested in them,[31] and this duty must include, it is submitted, the maintenance of any drains which are part of the highway. It would therefore seem that an action for damages would lie at the suit of a person injured by a failure to maintain a highway drain, unless the authority could use one of the defences in section 58 of the 1980 Act.[32]

The power given by section 100 in no way overrides or displaces the common law duty of the owner or occupier of land adjoining

---

[28] Act of 1980, s.308.

[29] See *Irving v Carlisle R.D.C.* (1907) 71 J.P. 212, where the highway authority failed to clean out a ditch and as a result an adjoining occupier sustained damage; and *Masters v Hampshire C.C.* (1915) 84 L.J.K.B. 2194, where road gullies not connected to any sewer were allowed to become overgrown with grass. In both of these cases, the defendant highway authority was held not liable, the burden of the complaint being in each case based on non-feasance.

[30] Highways Act 1980, ss.41 and 58.

[31] *Ibid.*

[32] Following *Griffiths v Liverpool Corporation* [1967] 1 Q.B. 374, it seems that the authority should institute a proper system of inspection of all highways vested in it, including drains forming part of such highways.

the highway so to cleanse and scour any ditches on his land as not to permit them to cause a nuisance on the highway.[33] It is, moreover, an offence to alter, obstruct or interfere with any highway drain without the consent of the highway authority.[34]

In cleansing their highway drains, or in causing the surface water to flow off the highway, the highway authority may not cause a nuisance,[35] for here it would be doing positive acts of misfeasance;[36] further, it may not cause or permit any polluted water to flow into a natural stream or watercourse contrary to the Water Resources Act 1991.[37]

The expression "drains" used in this section is defined to include[38] a ditch, gutter, watercourse, soak-away, bridge, culvert, tunnel and pipe. It has been decided, giving a wide definition to the word drain, that a pipe need not be connected to any defined channel for it to be within the section.[39] However a "dumb well" (or "swallow hole", as such a feature is termed in some parts of the country), into which waste water is allowed to flow and there to penetrate into the surrounding soil,[40] or a disused gravel pit or stagnant pond,[41] or the overflow pipe from a catchpit,[42] is not a

---

33   *Attorney-General v Waring* (1899) 63 J.P. 789.
34   Highways Act 1980, s.100(4).
35   *Pemberton v Bright* [1960] 1 W.L.R. 436, and contrast *Burton v West Suffolk C.C.* [1960] 1 Q.B. 72. See also s.117(5)(b) of the 1991 Act, which does not, however, strictly apply in the present context.
36   *Pearce v Croydon R.D.C.* (1910) 74 J.P. 429; it will be an actionable nuisance if the surface water off the highway is caused to flow over private land otherwise than in accordance with the existing rights. See also *Thomas v Gower R.D.C.* [1922] 2 K.B. 76.
37   Water fouled by tar from the surface of the highway was held to be polluted water within this meaning: *Dell v Chesham U.D.C.* [1921] 3 K.B. 427. Pure water, or surface water carrying sand or silt, etc. may be discharged into a natural stream: *Durrant v Branksome U.D.C.* [1897] 2 Ch. 291. See also *post*, Chapter 8, pp.148-157.
38   Highways Act 1980, s.100(9). Note the use of the word "include" rather than "mean"; the definition is therefore not exhaustive.
39   *Attorney-General v Copeland* [1902] 1 K.B. 690.
40   *Croft v Rickmansworth Highway Board* (1888) 39 Ch. D. 272.
41   *Croysdale v Sunbury-on-Thames U.D.C.* [1898] 2 Ch. 515.
42   *Ballard v Leek Urban Council* (1917) 87 L.J. Ch. 146.

drain within the section.[43]

THE SEWERING OF PRIVATE STREETS

Under the private street works code and advance payments code contained in Part XI of the Highways Act 1980,[44] the "street works authority"[45] may execute a variety of works in any street which is not a highway maintainable at the public expense. Provided the procedure of the code is correctly followed, the cost of such work may be charged to the frontagers to the street.[46] It is customary for a number of these works to be done at one and the same time, but this is not an essential feature of the procedure, and any one or more of the works mentioned in the section may be done at one time.[47] One of these works is the "sewering" of the street, where the same is not already sewered to the satisfaction of the authority. There is now no indication as to how "sewer" is to be defined for the purposes of the private street works code contained in the Highways Act 1980, as the expression is not defined in that Act. Formerly the definitions of section 4 of the 1875 Act applied to private street works generally. In practice "sewering" is never regarded as being confined to the provision

---

[43] Therefore the highway authority is not entitled to use such features for the reception of drainage off the highway, except by agreement with the landowners and occupiers concerned. "Unless the pond can be treated as part of the drainage system under the control of the [highway authority], these sections do not empower [the authority] to discharge the surface water into the plaintiff's pond": *per* Stirling J. in *Croysdale v Sunbury-on-Thames U.D.C.* [1898] 2 Ch. 515 at p.520.

[44] The private street works code means the Highways Act 1980, ss.205-218, and the advance payments code means ss.219-225 of the 1980 Act: *ibid.,* s.203(1). The code of 1892 was formerly an adoptive Act, which could originally be applied only in urban areas (boroughs and urban districts), but which came to be applied in all counties, the powers being vested in the county councils: see Highways Act 1980, Part XI, replacing earlier legislation.

[45] i.e. the county (or, in Wales from 1st April 1996, county borough council) or metropolitan district council for streets outside London; the London borough council or the Common Council for streets in London: Highways Act 1980, ss.203(3), 329(2A).

[46] "Street" is defined in s.331(1) of the 1980 Act, and see also definition of "private street" in s.203(2), *ibid.*

[47] This is clear from the wording of the sections.

of a proper system of road drainage for the highway,[48] but includes the provision of a sewer for the drainage from the premises fronting on the street[49] and the expression may include both foul water and surface water conduits.[50] Any sewer constructed under either of these provisions becomes a public sewer on completion, unless it belongs to a road maintained by the highway authority.[51] If these provisions are to be invoked it must be proved that the street has at no time been sewered to the satisfaction of the authority.[52]

Under the similar, but now repealed, provisions of the Public Health Act 1875, a failure to express dissatisfaction with the sewer at, or within a reasonable time of, its construction prevented the authority from subsequently operating these provisions to require the provision of a new sewer at the expense of the

---

[48] A conduit provided for carrying off surface water from roads was held to be a sewer within s.4 of the 1875 Act, in *Durrant v Branksome U.D.C.* [1897] 2 Ch. 291. It might even be arguable that, in view of the absence of any definition of "sewer", the provision of road drainage is not included in the term "sewering"; the term "channelling" would, however, appear to be adequate for this purpose. The provision of separate sewers for the reception of sewage and of surface water respectively, is provided for in s.206 of the 1980 Act.

[49] The authority may, by s.209(2) of the 1980 Act, decide to apportion the expenses according to the "degree of benefit" principle, and include premises which do not strictly front on the street, but to which access is obtained from the street.

[50] In *Bognor Regis U.D.C. v Boldero* [1962] 2 Q.B. 448, it was held that the magistrates were entitled to determine that the local authority was not acting reasonably where it was proposed to construct two sewers at different times, instead of laying both sewers at the same operation.

[51] 1991 Act, s.179(2)(b). See Chapter 2, *ante*.

[52] It is a question of fact whether or not the authority had in fact been so satisfied, but such will be implied by the court if a reasonable time after the sewer had become vested in the authority it took no action to secure its alteration or re-construction: *Bonella v Twickenham Local Board* (1887) 20 Q.B.D. 63, and *Wilmslow U.D.C. v Sidebottom* (1906) 70 J.P. 537. These cases were followed in *Poole Corporation v Blake* [1956] 1 Q.B. 206, when the court held that s.9 of the 1892 Act, empowering the local authority to do incidental works as well as those covered by s.6, *ibid.*, did not have the effect of overruling *Bonella's Case*. In its resolution to sewer the street, the local authority should include a statement to the effect that it was not "satisfied": *Ware U.D.C. v Gaunt* [1960] 1 W.L.R. 1364.

frontagers.[53] This is not to say that an expression of satisfaction with the foul sewers of a street later precludes an authority's resolution dealing with the separate surface water drainage of the streets.[54]

It is perhaps somewhat anomalous that it is the street works authority as highway authority who should be able to decide whether or not a street has been sewered to its satisfaction, as the effect of a positive decision to that effect is to vest the sewer not in itself, but in the sewerage undertaker. Moreover, in non-metropolitan counties, the anomaly is compounded if arrangements have been made under section 97 of the Water Industry Act 1991, for administration may then be undertaken on behalf of the sewerage undertaker not by the county council, but by the district council. Close co-operation between the authorities will clearly be desirable.

---

[53]   *Fulham District Board of Works v Goodwin* (1876) 1 Ex. D. 400; *Bonella v Twickenham Local Board* (1887) 20 Q.B.D. 63; *Bloor v Beckenham U.D.C.* [1908] 2 K.B. 671. This has been held to be the case even where the sewer never became a working sewer, because it had no outfall: *Hornsey Local Board v Davis* [1893] 1 Q.B. 756.

[54]   *Poole Corporation v Blake* [1956] 1 Q.B. 206.

Chapter 7

SEWAGE DISPOSAL AND SEWAGE DISPOSAL WORKS

INTRODUCTORY

By virtue of section 94 of the Water Industry Act 1991, a sewerage undertaker is under a duty not only to drain its area, but also "to make provision for the emptying of [its public] . . . sewers and such further provision (whether inside its area or elsewhere) as is necessary from time to time for effectually dealing, by means of sewage disposal works or otherwise, with the contents of those sewers."[1] In performing this duty a sewerage undertaker must have regard to its existing and likely future obligations to allow for the discharge of trade effluent into its public sewers and to the need to provide for disposal of trade effluent so discharged.[2] This provision is the successor of section 14 of the Water Act 1973.

The remedies by which the duty under section 94 may be enforced have been considered above.[3] It must, however, also be remembered that the functions given by this section may not be exercised by the sewerage undertaker in such a manner as might cause a nuisance.[4] The only practicable methods of dealing with the contents of public sewers are by providing a proper outfall to a river or the sea (without contravening the anti-pollution provisions of the Water Resources Act 1991),[5] or by the provision

---

[1] Section 94(1)(b).
[2] Section 94(2). "Trade effluent" has the same meaning as in Chapter III of Pt. IV of the Water Industry Act 1991: s.94(5).
[3] i.e. ss.18, 23 and 24 of the 1991 Act, see *ante*, pp.17-21.
[4] For examples of a nuisance arising out of a sewage farm see *Bainbridge v Chertsey U.D.C.* (1914) 84 L.J. Ch. 626, and *Cornford v Havant and Waterloo U.D.C.* (1933) 31 L.G.R. 142.
[5] There is no common law right to cause the contents of sewers to flow into the sea, if a nuisance is thereby caused: *Foster v Warblington U.D.C.* [1906] 1 K.B. 648 and *Hobart v Southend-on-Sea Corporation* (1906) 75 L.J.K.B. 305. As to the general prevention see *post,* Chapter 8. As to river prevention in particular see *George Legge & Son v Wenlock Corporation* [1938] A.C. 204.

of disposal works of one type or another.

A Report by the National Rivers Authority[6] notes that discharges of sewage may arise from a number of different sources, including

- treated effluent and storm discharges from urban sewage treatment works operated by the sewerage undertakers;

- effluent from sewage treatment plants serving small populations ("package plants");

- combined sewer overflows and emergency overflows from sewerage systems;

- septic tanks; and

- crude sewerage discharges at some estuaries and coastal locations.

The quality of sewage discharged from *sewage treatment works* depends on the level of treatment accorded. The normal classification is as follows: *preliminary treatment* involves the removal of rags, grit, gross solids, etc.; *primary treatment*, the settlement of solids in suspension; *secondary treatment*, biological treatment to remove organic material; and *tertiary treatment*, treatment to decrease any remaining solids or organic material or to provide disinfection or nutrient removal.[7] Few plants in England and Wales need to proceed beyond the secondary treatment stage; some, mainly in coastal or estuarine locations, only perform primary treatment on sewage received, or discharge preliminary treated effluent direct to sea via a long (offshore) outfall.[8]

Package plants are used for small housing developments and

---

6   *Discharge Consents and Compliance: The NRA's Approach to Control of Discharges of Water* (H.M.S.O., 1994), p.14.

7   *Ibid.* The terms "primary treatment" and "secondary treatment" are the subject of particular definitions in the Urban Waste Water Treatment (England and Wales) Regulations 1994: see *post*, pp.138, 139.

8   NRA Report, *op. cit.*, n.6, p.14.

commercial and industrial premises where connection to a main sewer is not practical or economic; they provide secondary treatment.

Intermittent discharges from *emergency, combined sewer and storm tank overflows*, although infrequent, can result in significant volumes of sewage being discharged to receiving watercourses.[9]

Septic tanks, which normally serve individual domestic premises, provide primary settlement of sewage together with some anaerobic digestion of the collected sludge; most septic tank effluents are discharged to underground strata by means of a soakaway.[10]

Some sewage outfalls, mostly in coastal or estuarine areas, discharge untreated effluent (or effluent which has only received preliminary treatment) close to shore; others, constructed more recently, are much longer and make use of natural dilution and dispersion for preliminary treated effluent.[11] Many of these discharges will cease on implementation of the Urban Waste Water Treatment Directive;[12] some of the outfalls will be retained as discharge points for treated sewage, or for storm or emergency overflows.[13]

The duty under section 94 of the Water Industry Act 1991 is supplemented by the Urban Waste Water Treatment (England and Wales) Regulations 1994,[14] which provide that the duty under section 94(1)(b) shall include a duty to ensure that urban waste water is, before discharge, subject to treatment provided in accordance with Regulation 5, and to ensure that

(a) plants built in order to comply with Regulation 5 are designed (account being taken of seasonal variations of the load),

---

9   NRA Report, *op. cit.*, n.6, p.15.
10   *Ibid.*
11   *Ibid.*, pp.15-16.
12   See *post.*
13   NRA Report, *op cit.*, n.6, p.16.
14   S.I. 1994 No. 2841, Reg. 4(4). See Appendix.

constructed, operated and maintained to ensure sufficient performance under all normal local climatic conditions;

(b) treated waste water and sludge arising from treatment are reused whenever appropriate; and

(c) disposal routes for treated waste water and sludge minimise the adverse effects on the environment.

The requirements of Regulation 5 are that treatment plants which provide secondary treatment[15] or an equivalent treatment are provided

(a) by 31st December 2000 (or, exceptionally, a later date not later than 31st December 2005, agreed with the Commission), in respect of all discharges from agglomerations with a population equivalent of more than 15,000;

(b) by 31st December 2005, in respect of all discharges from agglomerations with a population equivalent of between 10,000 and 15,000;

(c) by 31st December 2005, in respect of all discharges to freshwater and estuaries from agglomerations with a population equivalent of between 2,000 and 10,000.[16]

Treatment plants which provide more stringent treatment than this must be provided by 31st December 1998, in respect of all discharges from agglomerations with a population equivalent of more than 10,000 into sensitive areas, or into the relevant catchment areas of sensitive areas where the discharges contribute to the pollution of these areas.[17] This duty does not, however, apply where the National Rivers Authority certifies that it is satisfied as a result of monitoring, that the minimum percentage

---

[15] i.e. "treatment of urban waste water by a process generally involving biological treatment with a secondary settlement or other process in which the requirements established in Table 1 in Schedule 3 are respected": Reg. 2(1).

[16] Reg. 5(1). For definitions of "agglomeration" and "population equivalent" see *ante*, p.36.

[17] Reg. 5(2). For the definition of "sensitive area" see *ante*, p.35.

of reduction of the overall load entering all treatment plants in that area (and in the catchment area the discharges from which contribute to the pollution of that area) is at least 65% for total phosphorous and 75% for total nitrogen.[18] If an area is reclassified from "high natural dispersion area" or to "sensitive area" the target dates become the seventh anniversary of the change of identification or, if specified, a later date.[19]

Less stringent treatments may be provided in respect of discharges of urban waste water from agglomerations with a population equivalent between 10,000 and 150,000 (or, exceptionally, with the agreement of the Commission, more than 150,000) to coastal waters in high natural dispersion areas, and from agglomerations with a population equivalent between 2,000 and 10,000 into estuaries which are in such areas. This is so, provided that the discharges receive at least primary treatment[20] in conformity with the control procedures set out in Schedule 3, Part II to the Regulations, and the National Rivers Authority certifies that it is satisfied that comprehensive studies have indicated that such discharges will not adversely affect the environment.[21]

Appropriate treatment[22] of urban waste water entering collecting systems must be provided by 31st December 2005 in respect of

(a) discharges to freshwaters and estuaries from agglomerations with a population equivalent of less than 2,000; and

(b) discharges to coastal waters from agglomerations with a

---

[18] 1994 Regulations, Reg. 5(3).

[19] *Ibid.*, Reg. 5(4).

[20] i.e. treatment by a physical and/or chemical process involving settlement of suspended solids, or other processes in which the BOD5 of the incoming waste water is reduced by at least 20% before discharge and the total suspended solids are reduced by at least 50%: Reg. 5(8)(b).

[21] Reg. 5(5). For definitions of "urban waste water", "agglomerations", "population equivalent", "coastal waters", "sensitive areas", "high natural dispersion area", see *ante*, pp.34-37.

[22] i.e. treatment by any process and/or disposal system which after discharge allows the receiving waters to meet the relevant quality objectives and relevant provisions of EC directives: Reg. 5(8)(a).

population equivalent of less than 10,000.[23]

Discharges from treatment plants provided under Regulation 5, including plants provided other than by sewerage undertakers, must satisfy the relevant detailed requirements of Schedule 3, Part I of the Regulations.[24]

TRUNK SEWERS

The provision of a trunk or main sewer is in general governed by the same law as that regulating the provision of all types of public sewers.[25] However, in rural localities the sewerage undertaker may be able to obtain financial assistance by virtue of section 151 of the Water Industry Act 1991 (replacing the Rural Water Supplies and Sewerage Acts 1944 to 1971). Section 151 does not specify any rate of contribution, nor does it define the expression "rural locality". These matters were dealt with in Ministry of Housing and Local Government Circular 75/67. Although the circular provided a contribution formula for sewerage schemes, in exceptional circumstances, the Minister may override the formula. The same circular stated that rural localities are not confined to areas of former rural district councils; and, conversely, for the purpose of the Act, not all localities within the area of a former rural district council will be accepted as a rural locality.

The Secretary of State may make a contribution in such a case only upon such conditions as might be set by the Treasury and he must also be satisfied that the works are actually "necessary". He may also withhold or reduce the amount of the contribution

---

[23]   Reg. 5(7). For definitions of "urban waste water", "collecting systems", "estuaries", "agglomerations", "population equivalent" and "coastal waters", see *ante*, pp.34-37.

[24]   Reg. 6(1). The National Rivers Authority, in exercising its functions under Chapter II of Part III of the Water Resources Act 1991, must secure compliance with the requirements of Reg. 5 (Reg. 6(2)), as well as the limitation of pollution of rising waters due to storm overflows with respect to discharges from a collecting system or treatment plant. See *post*, pp.151-152.

[25]   A main sewer is thus as much a public sewer as is any other sewer constructed by the sewerage undertaker or its predecessor(s).

if it appears that the works have been executed in an unsatisfactory manner or have not proved satisfactory.

A Consultation Paper has proposed that these grants should be abolished, on the ground that they offer poor value for money to taxpayers as there is no national system to allocate priorities.[26] Accordingly, section 151 is to be repealed by the Environment Act 1995.[27]

SEWAGE DISPOSAL WORKS

The power to construct sewage disposal works is conferred by implication upon sewerage undertakers by section 94(1)(b) of the Water Industry Act 1991. Such works may be constructed only upon land already owned by the sewerage undertaker or acquired or lawfully appropriated for that purpose. The distinction between "sewers" and "sewage disposal works" was a source of some difficulty in cases decided under the 1875 Act but these were largely resolved by section 90(4) of the 1936 Act (now section 219(2)(b) of the 1991 Act), according to which a "sewage disposal works" includes "the machinery and equipment of those works and any necessary pumping stations and outfall pipes", and these issues are not presently problematic.

(a) Acquisition of land

Acquisition of land for the purpose of constructing a sewage disposal works may be by agreement or by means of a compulsory purchase order made in accordance with the Acquisition of Land Act 1981. The authority for compulsory acquisition of land *inter alia* for such a purpose is given by section 155 of the Water Industry Act 1991, which empowers a sewerage undertaker, upon authorisation by the Secretary of State, "to purchase compulsorily any land anywhere in England and Wales which is

---

[26] *Review of Rural Water and Sewerage* (DoE, 1994). See *ENDS Report* 235, pp.34-35.
[27] Sch. 22, para. 116. In force from a day to be appointed.

required . . . for the purposes of, or in connection with, the carrying out of its functions." The power of compulsory purchase includes power compulsorily to acquire land required for the purpose of being given in exchange for, or for a right over, other land which under the Acquisition of Land Act 1981 forms part of a common, open space or a fuel or field garden allotment.[28] Alternatively, a sewerage undertaker may by agreement acquire by purchase, lease or otherwise, an existing sewage disposal works or rights of usage in such works in performance of its general functions under section 94.

Express planning permission will have to be obtained in respect of any development for the purposes of sewage disposal works, etc. above ground level.[29] In the case of applications for development relating to the retention, treatment or disposal of sewage,[30] other than the laying of sewers, the construction of pumphouses in a line of sewers and the construction of certain septic tanks and cesspools,[31] and ancillary works, the local planning authority must consult the National Rivers Authority.[32] Furthermore, proposals for "waste water treatment plants" and "sites for depositing sludge" which would be likely to have significant effects on the environment must be accompanied by an "environmental statement", in accordance with the requirements of the Town and Country Planning (Assessment of Environmental Effects) Regulations 1988.[33] On the other hand, local planning authorities have been encouraged by the Secretary of State to give sympathetic consideration to development proposals aimed at enhancing the treatment of sewage. Local plans and Part II of unitary developments plans under the Town and Country Planning Act 1990 should include policies and

---

[28] 1991 Act, s.155(3).

[29] See *ante*, pp.88-89.

[30] Or trade-waste, slurry or sludge.

[31] i.e. those serving single dwelling houses or single caravans or single buildings in which not more than ten people will normally reside, work or congregate.

[32] Town and Country Planning (General Development Procedure) Order 1995 (S.I. 1995 No. 419), Art. 10 and Table, para. (s).

[33] S.I. 1988 No. 1199, as amended.

proposals for treatment works, and the sites should be identified.[34]

(b) General provisions

Sewage disposal works, like public sewers[35] may be constructed outside the sewerage undertaker's area by virtue of section 94(1)(b) of the 1991 Act. A sewerage undertaker could also have taken over from a former water authority privately owned sewage disposal works the construction of which had not been completed prior to 1st October 1937 and which had been adopted by the authority. The Public Health Act 1875 (Support of Sewers) Amendment Act 1883,[36] applies to sewage disposal works, such works being included in the definition of "sanitary work" contained in that Act.

(c) Ownership

Sewage disposal works constructed *de novo* by a sewerage undertaker will automatically vest in that undertaker.[37] In addition, sewage disposal works which were vested in a former water authority on 1st September 1989 (the "Transfer Date")[38] automatically became vested in the successor sewerage undertaker and this necessitates an examination of the former provisions under which disposal works became so vested. The following classes of sewage disposal works would have vested in a water authority:

(a) Those which vested in a local authority under the 1875 Act. Although the term "sewer" under that Act did not include an engine house or pumping station,[39] buildings and works of that nature would have vested in the local sanitary authority

---

[34] DoE Circular 17/91, Welsh Office Circular 62/91, *Water Industry Investment: Planning Considerations.*

[35] See Chapter 3, *ante*, p.62.

[36] *Ante*, p.121.

[37] 1991 Act, s.179(1)(b).

[38] The Water Authorities (Transfer of Functions) (Appointed Day) Order 1989 (S.I. 1989 No. 1530).

[39] *King's College, Cambridge v Uxbridge R.D.C.* [1901] 2 Ch. 768.

under section 13 of the 1875 Act which operated to vest in the authority all sewers "together with all buildings, works, materials and things belonging thereto."[40]

(b) Those actually constructed by the water authority or a predecessor local authority, or acquired by them.[41]

(c) Those in respect of which a vesting declaration was made by a water authority or their predecessor local authority under section 17 of the 1936 Act.

In present circumstances questions of ownership are perhaps relatively unlikely, but may arise where a sewerage undertaker wishes to use a disposal works as an outfall for a new sewer,[42] or where there arises a question as to responsibility for maintenance.[43]

(d) Maintenance

Having constructed, acquired or otherwise provided, sewage disposal works, it will be the duty of the sewerage undertaker to maintain them in such a manner as not to cause a nuisance. There is no express statutory duty relating to the cleansing, etc. of sewage disposal works parallel to that imposed in respect of public sewers by section 94(1)(a) of the 1991 Act. None the less the duty effectually to drain its area under section 94 will clearly require the efficient maintenance of its sewerage disposal works by a sewerage undertaker.

(e) Methods of disposal

Apart from discharges of treated (or untreated) sewage mentioned

---

[40] A septic tank and outfall privately constructed was held to fall within this expanded definition and to vest in the authority, together with the sewer leading thereto, in *Clark v Epsom R.D.C.* [1929] 1 Ch. 287.

[41] See the expanded definition of "sewage disposal works" in s.90(4) of the 1936 Act.

[42] In connection with earlier provisions see *Solihull R.D.C. v Ford* (1932) 30 L.G.R. 385.

[43] *Willoughby v Chapman*, unreported, but see article at (1955) 119 J.P.N. 442.

above,[44] sewage sludge (i.e. the residue left after sewage has been treated) may be dumped at sea from a ship, incinerated or disposed of on land, normally by depositing it for agricultural purposes. Sludge dumping at sea is to be ended by 1998 with, until then, progressive reductions in the total amount of toxic, persistent or bioaccumulable materials in sludge so disposed of.[45] Incineration works that are capable of incinerating one tonne or more of sewage sludge per hour must be authorised by Her Majesty's Inspectorate of Pollution under Part I of the Environmental Protection Act 1990; incinerators with less capacity must be authorised by the local authority.[46] The deposit of sewage or sewage sludge on land is subject to control under Part II of the Environmental Protection Act 1990[47] or, in the case of deposits directly on land for agricultural purposes, the Sludge (Use in Agriculture) Regulations 1989.[48] The National Rivers Authority seeks to liaise with sewerage undertakers and farmers in relation to the disposal of sewage sludge to land, and influence the location, quantity and timing of applications in order to prevent pollution of water resources.[49]

---

44 pp.136-137.
45 Urban Waste Water Treatment (England and Wales) Regulations 1994 (S.I. 1994 No. 2841), Reg. 9. This activity is licensed under Part II of the Food and Environmental Protection Act 1985.
46 See the Environmental Protection (Prescribed Processes and Substances) Regulations 1991 (S.I. 1991 No. 472, as amended, Sch. 1, section 5.1, Parts A, B). A waste management licence may be required: see the Environmental Protection Act 1990, Part II; the Controlled Waste Regulations 1992 (S.I. 1992 No. 588), Reg. 7(1); and the Waste Management Licensing Regulations 1994 (S.I. 1994 No. 1056), Sch. 3, para. 10.
47 Controlled Waste Regulations 1992 (S.I. 1992 No. 558), Reg. 5(1), Sch. 3, para. 7.
48 S.I. 1989 No. 1263, as amended by S.I. 1990 No. 880, implementing the EC Directive on the protection of the environment, and in particular of the soil, when sewage sludge is used in agriculture, Dir. 86/278/EEC. For an example of a prosecution where the conduct fell outside the 1989 Regulations, see *ENDS Report* 230, March 1994, pp.46-47.
49 NRA, *Policy and Practice for the Protection of Groundwater* (H.M.S.O., 1992), section E.

AGREEMENTS WITH OTHER SEWERAGE UNDERTAKERS

Besides providing sewage disposal works itself, or causing the contents of its sewers to flow into the sea or some other natural outfall, a sewerage undertaker might agree with a neighbouring undertaker for the disposal of its sewage through the sewage system of that other undertaker. In view of the extensive areas now served by sewerage undertakers, the likely need for such an agreement must seem slight. The statutory provisions regulating such agreements in respect of the former water authorities contained in section 28 of the 1936 Act were repealed by the Water Act 1973.

At common law the "sending" sewerage undertaker would be in the same position as the owner of a dominant tenement in respect of an easement, and could, therefore, only use the sewer and/or sewage disposal works of the "receiving" undertaker by agreement or in pursuance of a prescriptive right so to do.[50]

CONSERVANCY SERVICES

In addition to the disposal of sewage through a sewerage system, the sewerage undertaker has duties under the Control of Pollution Act 1974 (replacing the 1936 Act) to arrange for the disposal of waste from privies[51] serving private dwellings, which is collected by a "waste collection authority"[52] and duly delivered to it.[53] The

---

[50] See *Attorney-General v Acton Local Board* (1882) 22 Ch. D. 221.

[51] A "privy" is defined to mean a latrine which has a moveable receptacle: Environmental Protection Act 1990, s.45(12).

[52] i.e. district and London borough councils, the Common Council of the City of London, the Sub-Treasurer of the Inner Temple and the Under Treasurer of the Middle Temple: 1990 Act, s.30(3).

[53] Control of Pollution Act 1974, s.14(9), (10), as amended by the Water Act 1989, Sch. 25, para. 48(5). These provisions were generally repealed by the Environmental Protection Act 1990, Sch. 16, Pt. II, but not in respect of "industrial waste" (see the Environmental Protection Act 1990 (Commencement No. 11) Order 1992, S.I. 1992 No. 266, Art. 3). The Controlled Waste Regulations 1992 (S.I. 1992 No. 588), Sch. 3, para. 7, provides that sewage which has been removed from a privy or cesspool is to be treated as "industrial waste".

"waste collection authority" must make such arrangements for the emptying without charge of privies serving one or more private dwellings in its area as it considers appropriate.[54] It must also upon request arrange for the emptying of a cesspool[55] in its area which serves only private dwellings. The authority may make a reasonable charge for the emptying of cesspools, or any other privies which it may agree to empty.[56]

Although the emptying of cesspools, and privies not serving private dwellings, is a matter for arrangement as to financial terms between the authority and the occupier requesting the service, it seems that the amount of the charge must not only be reasonable *per se*, but also comparable with charges made for similar services to similar premises.[57]

---

[54] 1990 Act, s.45(5)(a).

[55] "Cesspool" includes for this purpose a settlement tank or other tank for the reception or disposal of foul matter from buildings.

[56] 1990 Act, s.45(5)(b), (6). The service may be performed by the authority itself or by a contractor. Where a contractor caused a nuisance through the manner of emptying cesspools, the employing local authority was held liable therefor: *Robinson v Beaconsfield U.D.C.* [1911] 2 Ch. 188.

[57] If authority is needed for this rather obvious principle, see the reasoning in *Pegg & Jones Ltd. v Derby Corporation* [1909] 2 K.B. 311.

Chapter 8

THE DISCHARGE OF SEWAGE EFFLUENTS

INTRODUCTORY

In this chapter it is intended to deal with the discharge of sewage effluents (treated or untreated) from public sewers or sewage disposal works vested in a sewerage undertaker; discharge of effluents from private premises into public sewers is discussed elsewhere in this book, but discharges from private premises otherwise than into public sewers are considered here. In the nature of things, sewage effluent can only be discharged to a watercourse or the sea. Discharge from public sewers to a watercourse does not now give rise to any very complicated problems, in view of the modern statutory provisions now found in Part III of the Water Resources Act 1991. The position is also now affected by the provisions of the Urban Waste Water Treatment (England and Wales) Regulations 1994.[1]

THE DEFINITION OF "CONTROLLED WATERS"

The control of pollution provisions of the Water Resources Act 1991 are applicable to a range of waters defined as "controlled" for the purposes of the Act. These are defined by section 104(1) and fall into four broad divisions:

(a) territorial waters extending three miles out from the territorial waters baseline of England and Wales;

(b) coastal waters within the territorial waters baseline as far inland as the limit of the highest tide or, in the case of rivers and watercourses, as far as the fresh-water limit, including the waters of any adjoining enclosed docks;

---

[1] S.I. 1994 No. 2841.

(c) inland freshwaters, i.e. so much of any relevant river or watercourse[2] as is above the fresh-water limit and any relevant lake or pond;[3]

(d) ground waters contained in underground strata or in a well or borehole, including similar or associated works, sunk into such strata or any excavation in which the water level depends wholly or mainly upon supply from such strata.

The fresh-water limits of such rivers as fall within category (c) will be indicated upon maps deposited by the Secretary of State with the National Rivers Authority. Any changes which require to be made in such indications can be made through the deposit of revised maps.[4] Such maps must be made available by the National Rivers Authority for inspection by the public free of charge at all reasonable times.[5]

In addition to those stated waters the Secretary of State may provide by order[6] that other territorial waters, lakes or ponds which would otherwise be "controlled" shall not be so.[7]

The Secretary of State may by regulations prescribe a system for classifying the quality of any description of controlled waters.[8] The criteria so specified are to consist of some or all of:

---

[2] Defined as meaning "any river or watercourse (including an underground river or watercourse and an artificial river or watercourse) which is neither a public sewer nor a sewer or drain which drains into a public sewer": 1991 Act, s.104(3). It includes a watercourse which overflows or which dries up: *R. v Dovermoss Ltd.* (1995) 159 J.P. 448, C.A. (Cr.D.).

[3] Defined as meaning "any lake or pond which (whether it is natural or artificial or above or below ground) discharges into a relevant river or watercourse or into another lake or pond which is itself a relevant lake or pond"; "lake or pond" includes a reservoir of any description: 1991 Act, s.104(3).

[4] 1991 Act, s.192(1).

[5] *Ibid.,* s.192(2).

[6] *Ibid.,* s.104(4).

[7] *Ibid.* And vice versa. All lakes and ponds are to be treated as "controlled waters" in so far as s.85 relates to the discharge of waste water from urban waste water treatment plants: Urban Waste Water Treatment (England and Wales) Regulations 1994 (S.I. 1994 No. 2841), Reg. 6(5).

[8] *Ibid.,* s.82.

(a) general requirements as to the purposes for which the specified waters are suitable;

(b) specifications as to substances or the concentrations thereof which are permissible or impermissible in given waters; and

(c) other specific requirements.

The Secretary of State may then serve a notice on the National Rivers Authority specifying one or more of the prescribed classifications, and a date in relation to each specified classification; this notice establishes the "water quality objectives" for any waters which are, or are included in, waters of a prescribed description.[9] Such objectives may be reviewed by the Secretary of State after five years or at any time upon the request of the National Rivers Authority, a water undertaker or "other person",[10] the latter general category presumably including sewerage undertakers. The Secretary of State must give notice of any proposed variation of water quality objectives and consider any representations or objections made in respect of it and not withdrawn.

It is the general duty of the Secretary of State and the National Rivers Authority to utilise their powers to ensure, so far as is practicable, the achievement of the water quality objectives established under the Water Resources Act 1991.[11] The National Rivers Authority is also under a duty to monitor pollution in controlled waters and to consult where it seems appropriate with the River Purification Authorities in Scotland.[12]

The Secretary of State has established statutory water quality objectives in respect of (1) the quality of inland surface water for abstraction of drinking water;[13] (2) the presence of dangerous

---

9   1991 Act, s.83, as modified by S.I. 1989 No. 2286 and S.I. 1991 No. 1597.
10   *Ibid.,* s.83(3).
11   *Ibid.,* s.84(1). On the significance of this duty, see *ENDS Report* 241, February 1995, p.9.
12   *Ibid.,* s.84(2).
13   Based on the Surface Waters (Classification) Regulations 1989 (S.I. 1989 No. 1148), implementing the Drinking Water Directive, Dir. 75/440/EEC.

substances;[14] and (3) the quality of bathing waters.[15]

The Secretary of State is also in the course of developing statutory water quality objectives under these provisions which will replace formally-agreed but non-statutory river quality objectives which have been in place since the 1970s.[16]

Finally, it is the Authority's duty in exercising its functions under Chapter II of Part III of the Water Resources Act 1991

---

[14] Based on the Surface Waters (Dangerous Substances) (Classification) Regulations 1989 (S.I. 1989 No. 2286) and 1992 (S.I. 1992 No. 337), implementing the framework directive on Pollution caused by Certain Dangerous Substances Discharge into the Aquatic Environment of the Community, Dir. 76/464/EEC and further (daughter) directives. See DoE Circular 7/89, *Water and the Environment.*

[15] Based on the Bathing Waters (Classification) Regulations 1991 (S.I. 1991 No. 1597), implementing the Bathing Water Directive 1976, Dir. 76/160/EEC. "Bathing waters" are as defined in Article 1.2 of the Directive: i.e. "all running or still fresh waters or parts thereof and sea water", in which bathing is "explicitly authorised by the competent authorities of each Member State" or is "not prohibited and is traditionally practised by a large number of bathers". 419 bathing waters have been identified in England and Wales for the purposes of the Directive. The extent of compliance is monitored by the National Rivers Authority: see annual reports on *Bathing Water Quality* published by H.M.S.O.

See also the *ENDS Report* 229, February 1994, p.10, noting research that found a significantly greater risk of falling ill after bathing in waters that breach EC standards; it is a matter of controversy whether compliance with the existing standards is sufficient to ensure that bathers do not fall ill: *ENDS Report* 239, December 1994, pp.29-31, summarising the First Report of the House of Lords Select Committee on the European Communities, *Bathing Water* (1994-95 H.L. 6). See also the Committee's Seventh Report, *Bathing Water Revisited* (1994-95 H.L. 41), summarised in *ENDS Report* 243, p.36. The U.K. has been found by the European Court of Justice to have breached its duty to implement the directive (*Commission v U.K.* (C56/90), 14th July 1993), in respect of bathing areas in Blackpool and adjacant to Formby and Southport. It is government policy that "virtually all bathing waters will meet the Directive standards by the end of 1995" (*This Common Inheritance, Third Year Report* (Cm.2549, 1994), p.100).

[16] See *Discharge Consents and Compliance: The NRA's Approach to Control of Discharges to Water: Report of the National Rivers Authority* (H.M.S.O., 1994), p.9. Objectives will be set on a pilot basis, based on the Surface Waters (River Ecosystems) (Classification) Regulations 1994 (S.I. 1994 No. 1057). The programme has, however, been delayed and reduced in scope: see *ENDS Report* 241, February 1995, pp.34-35 and 36.

(broadly) to secure compliance with Regulation 5 of the Urban Waste Water Treatment (England and Wales) Regulations 1994; the limitation of pollution of receiving waters due to storm water overflows from collecting systems and urban waste water treatment plants; and the phasing out of the discharge of sludge to surface waters by 31st December 1998.[17]

POLLUTION OFFENCES IN RESPECT OF "CONTROLLED WATERS"

(a) Offences

Under section 85 of the Water Resources Act 1991 it is a criminal offence for any person to "cause" or "knowingly permit",[18]

---

17 S.I. 1994 No. 2841, Reg. 6. See pp.137-140 *ante*. For definitions of "collecting systems" and "urban waste water", see *ante*, p.34.

18 "Cause" and "knowingly permit" are distinct concepts. Whether a person has "caused" a discharge is a question of fact, and it is not necessary to show that he had acted intentionally or negligently; *Alphacell Ltd. v Woodward* [1972] A.C. 824, H.L. ("cause" to be used in its ordinary sense); *National Rivers Authority v Yorkshire Water Services Ltd.* [1995] 1 A.C. 444, H.L. (possible to conclude that sewerage undertaker had "caused" the entry of polluting matter into controlled waters where the matter had been discharged into a sewer in secret by an unknown third party, and it then passed with other effluent through the undertaker's works into controlled waters; there was, however, a good defence under what is now section 87(2), see *post*, pp.155-156); *R. v CPC (UK) Ltd.*, *The Times*, 4th August 1994 (jury entitled to find that defendant caused polluting liquid to enter a river where it escaped from pipe with latent defects); *Attorney-General's Reference (No. 1 of 1994)*, *The Times*, 26th January 1995, C.A. (Cr.D.) (jury entitled to find that defendants "caused" pollution where (a) the effluent passed through their pumping system or (b) they ran the pumping system in an unmaintained state). *Cf. Wychavon District Council v National Rivers Authority* [1993] 1 W.L.R. 125 ("causing" requires some positive act involving some active operation or chain of operations bringing about the pollution and not merely passive inactivity; failure of council (as agent) to remedy a blockage in the sewer did not "cause" polluting matter to enter a river); *National Rivers Authority v Welsh Development Agency* [1993] Env. L.R. 407 (defendant responsible for drainage system did not "cause" trade effluent to be discharged into controlled water) (the latter two cases are difficult to reconcile with the *Yorkshire Water Services* case); *National Rivers Authority v Wright Engineering Co.* [1994] 4 All E.R. 281 (justices entitled to conclude that an escape of oil had been "caused" by vandals and not by the company).

(a) any poisonous, noxious or polluting[19] matter or solid waste to enter "controlled waters";

(b) matter, other than trade or sewage effluent,[20] to be discharged into "controlled waters" from a drain or sewer in contravention of a prohibition under section 86 of the Water Resources Act 1991;[21]

(c) any trade or sewage effluent to be discharged into "controlled waters" or, from land in England and Wales, through a pipe, into the sea outside the seaward limits of controlled waters;

(d) any trade or sewage effluent[20] to be discharged, contrary to a section 86 prohibition, from a building or fixed plant on to or into land or into a lake or pond which does not comprise inland freshwaters; or

(e) any matter to enter inland freshwaters which, directly or indirectly or in combination with other factors, tends to impede the proper flow of waters substantially aggravating pollution otherwise caused or its consequences.

It is also an offence to contravene the conditions of a consent.[22]

These offences carry a penalty, upon summary conviction, of imprisonment for a term not exceeding three months and/or a fine not exceeding £20,000 and, upon conviction on indictment, of imprisonment for a term not exceeding two years and/or a fine.[23]

---

[19] "Polluting" is an ordinary English word, and intended to be different from "poisonous" or "noxious"; the relevant OED definition is "to make physically impure, foul or filthy; to dirty, stain, taint, befoul": *R. v Dovermoss Ltd.* (1995) 159 J.P. 448, C.A. (Cr.D.).

[20] Defined in the Water Resources Act, s.221(1).

[21] 1991 Act, s.85(2).

[22] Contravention of a condition can be an offence even where the defendant has not made a discharge into controlled waters: *Taylor Woodrow Property Management Ltd. v National Rivers Authority* [1995] Env. L.R. 52, D.C.; holder of discharge consent liable for failing to ensure that what was discharged "shall not contain any oil or grease". A challenge may not be made collaterally to the validity of a condition: *R. v Etterick Trout Co. and Baxter* [1994] Env. L.R. 165.

[23] 1991 Act, s.85(6).

It is a defence, however, to charges brought under section 85 to show that an authority has been obtained for the discharge(s) concerned. Such authority might be obtained through:

(a) a consent under section 88 and Schedule 10 to the 1991 Act;

(b) an authorisation for a prescribed process designated for central control granted under Part I of the Environmental Protection Act 1990;

(c) a waste management or disposal licence;[24]

(d) a licence under Part II of the Food and Environment Protection Act 1985;

(e) section 163 of the Water Resources Act 1991 or section 165 of the Water Industry Act 1991 (discharges for works purposes);

(f) any relevant express local statutory provision or statutory order; and

(g) any other enactment which may be prescribed.[25]

It is also a defence to such charges to show that the entry or discharge concerned was caused or permitted in an emergency to avert danger to life or health taking all reasonably practicable steps[26] in the circumstances for the minimisation of the entry and its polluting effects and that particulars of the incident were furnished to the National Rivers Authority as soon as reasonably practicable.[27] It is not an offence for a person to permit discharge of trade or sewage effluent from a vessel[28] or to permit water

---

[24] A "disposal licence" is a licence granted under s.5 of the Control of Pollution Act 1974. Nothing in such a licence may authorise any entry or discharge under heads (b)-(d) of section 85: *ante*, p.153.

[25] 1991 Act, s.88(1).

[26] "Reasonably practicable" turns upon questions of fact and degree in each relevant situation.

[27] 1991 Act, s.89(1).

[28] *Ibid.*, s.89(2).

from an abandoned mine to enter controlled waters.[29] Similarly, no offence is constituted by storage of solid waste, not being poisonous, noxious or polluting, from a mine or quarry which then falls or is carried into inland freshwaters so long as the prior consent of the National Rivers Authority was obtained for the storage, no other reasonable site was available and all practicable steps for the avoidance of such entry had been taken.[30] A highway authority will not commit an offence where a drain is kept open by virtue of section 100 of the Highways Act 1980 and a discharge occurs therefrom, unless it be in contravention of a section 86 prohibition.[31]

Where there is a discharge of sewage effluent under heads (c) or (d) of section 85[32] from any sewer or works vested in a sewerage undertaker, if that undertaker did not cause or knowingly permit the discharge, it is nevertheless deemed to have caused it if

(a) matter included in the discharge was received by it into the discharging sewer or any other sewer or works vested in it;

(b) it was bound (either unconditionally or subject to conditions which were observed) to receive that matter into that sewer or works.

However, this does not apply if the sewage effluent was previously discharged into the undertaker's system by another sewerage undertaker by virtue of an agreement under section 110A;[33] in this case, the sending undertaker is deemed to have caused the discharge on an analogous basis.[34]

Furthermore, a sewerage undertaker will not commit an offence under section 85 solely by reason of a discharge from one of its

---

[29] 1991 Act, s.89(3).
[30] *Ibid.*, s.89(4).
[31] *Ibid.*, s.89(5).
[32] As set out at p.153, *ante*.
[33] p.92, *ante*.
[34] Water Resources Act 1991, s.87(1)-(1C), substituted by the Competition and Service (Utilities) Act 1992, s.46.

sewers or works in contravention of conditions of a consent relating to such discharge if the contravention is attributable to a discharge made by some other person into the sewer or works which the undertaker was either not bound to receive or was only so bound subject to conditions which were not met and it could not reasonably have been expected to prevent the discharge into the sewer or works.[35] By the same token a person who makes or permits a discharge into a sewer or works vested in a sewerage undertaker will not thereby commit an offence under section 85 of the 1991 Act if such discharge was one which the undertaker was bound to receive either unconditionally or subject to conditions which were in the given case met.[36]

In addition to these statutory provisions, the Secretary of State has power under section 92 of the 1991 Act to make regulations prohibiting the possession or control of poisonous, noxious or polluting matter unless prescribed anti-pollution precautions or other steps have been carried out. Such precautions and steps may also be required of persons who prior to the making of such regulations already have possession or control of such materials. Such regulations may empower the National Rivers Authority to determine circumstances of application and to impose relevant requirements upon any person. Provision may also be made for appeals to the Secretary of State and for the maximum penalties in cases of contravention, these not exceeding on summary conviction three months' imprisonment and/or a fine not exceeding £20,000 or, upon conviction on indictment, imprisonment for two years or a fine or both.[37]

The Authority's prosecution policy in cases of non-compliance is set out in Section 11 of *Discharge Consents and Compliance:*

---

[35] Water Resources Act 1991, s.87(2). This defence is available in respect of any offence under s.85 and not just where the prosecution alleges contravention of the conditions of a consent: *National Rivers Authority v Yorkshire Water Services Ltd.* [1995] 1 A.C. 444, H.L.

[36] *Ibid.*, s.87(3).

[37] *Ibid.*, s.92(2).

the NRA's Approach to the Control of Discharges to Water.[38] In the cases where the plant is inadequate to achieve consent requirements, but there is an existing programme of remedial works agreed with the Authority, the Authority will not normally prosecute where the non-compliance does not result from poor management or from problems unconnected with the proposed works; and every effort is being made in the interim to comply; and the breach is not of such magnitude so as to cause persistent pollution or to justify criminal proceedings in the public interest. If there is no existing programme, the discharger will be given the opportunity to produce an acceptable action plan. In cases where there is a management failure to operate the plant correctly, a decision to prosecute depends on the impact of the discharge on the environment and the attitude of the discharger to improving plant management.

(b) Consents

The procedure for obtaining a discharge consent is set out in Schedule 10 to the Water Resources Act 1991.[39] Consents are granted by the National Rivers Authority; applications must normally be publicised; conditions may be attached;[40] applications may be called-in by the Secretary of State, who may hold an inquiry; consents may be revoked or modified by the Authority.[41] Appeals lie to the Secretary of State.[42] The policies of the

---

[38] H.M.S.O., 1994 (Water Quality Series No. 17).

[39] A new Schedule 10 is to be substituted by the Environment Act 1995, Sch. 22, para. 183, which removes some of the requirements in respect of publicity: see *ENDS Report* 239, December 1994, p.22.

[40] Conditions appropriate to the nature of the industry concerned must be attached to a consent in relation to discharges of biodegradable industrial waste water from plants representing 4,000 p.e. or more belonging to specified industrial sectors: Urban Waste Water Treatment (England and Wales) Regulations 1994 (S.I. 1994 No 284), Reg. 8. For definitions, see *ante*, p.34*ff*.

[41] Consents must be reviewed and if necessary modified or revoked to comply with Reg. 6 of the 1994 Regulations, see *ante*, pp.137-140.

[42] Water Resources Act 1991, s.91. Appeals lie against, *inter alia*, a refusal, grant subject to conditions or revocation of a consent. By virtue of the Environment Act 1995, Sch. 22, para. 143, an appeal will also lie in respect of variations to a consent and enforcement notices (see *post*, p.162).

National Rivers Authority in granting consents are set out in *Discharge Consents and Compliance: the NRA's Approach to Control of Discharges to Water: A Report of the National Rivers Authority*.[43] Its general approach is to set discharge limits which are individually based on local circumstances, tailored to the needs of the receiving water and to key end uses, rather than uniform emission standards applicable to all discharges of a particular type.[44] Consents must be framed so as to secure compliance with statutory water objectives.[45]

A significant number of consents have been carried over from previous legislation. Thus consents granted under earlier legislation continue to have effect.[46] In addition, the National Rivers Authority Report, *Discharge Consents and Compliance: The NRA's Approach to Control of Discharges to Water*,[47] identifies three "transitional types of consent."

First, there are *deemed consents*. These cover (1) consent applications under the Rivers (Prevention of Pollution) Act 1961 outstanding on the implementation of the Control of Pollution Act 1974 in 1985;[48] and (2) consent applications in respect of discharges which prior to 1987 were outside the scope of consent controls, notably discharges to coastal waters and pre-1960

---

43   Water Quality Series No. 17, H.M.S.O., 1994.
44   *Ibid.*, pp.8-9.
45   See *ante*, pp.150-151.
46   See the Control of Pollution (Consents: Transitional Provisions) Regulations 1985 (S.I. 1985 No. 5) (preserving consents under the Rivers (Prevention of Pollution) Acts 1951 to 1961); the Water Act 1989, Sch. 26, para. 21 (preserving consents in force immediately before the transfer date for the purposes of Part II of the Control of Pollution Act 1974); and the Water Consolidation (Consequential Provisions) Act 1991, Sch. 2, para. 1 (preserving consents in force for the purposes of the Water Act 1989).
47   H.M.S.O., 1994, p.39.
48   Control of Pollution Act 1974, s.40(4); preserved by the Water Act 1989, Sch. 26, para. 24(2) and the Water Resources Act 1991, Sch. 13, para. 3(1). Consents deemed to have been granted to water authorities by the Secretary of State under s. 55 of the 1974 Act were preserved by the 1989 Act, Sch. 26, para. 25(6), (7).

discharges to estuaries.[49] Most such discharges are of sewage.

Secondly, there are *time limited consents* in respect of 800 sewage works found in the build-up to privatisation to be operating in breach of their consents. Here, the existing consents were varied to set temporary limits at the then current levels of performance. The majority had elapsed by 1994, but some had been extended by the NRA because of unforeseen scheme development problems.

Thirdly, there were *temporary (schedule) consents* granted under the Water Act 1989[50] in respect of combined sewer overflows and emergency overflows found in the run-up to privatisation not to be subject to consent conditions; these temporary consents are due to be replaced by individual consents in due course. Such consents were also granted in respect of a number of sewage treatment works.

In 1985, consents in respect of sewage discharges were relaxed to a requirement that the proportion of samples meeting the limits for sanitary determinants (BOD, suspended solids and ammonia) should not be significantly lower than 95%.[51] Following the Kinnersley Report,[52] the NRA adopted a policy that where consents are reviewed, absolute limits are imposed in addition to 95 percentile limits; the undertakers have appealed against these limits to the Secretary of State.[53] The DoE has

---

[49] See the Control of Pollution (Exemption of Certain Discharges from Control) (Variation) Order 1986 (S.I. 1986 No. 1623), Art. 4 (inserted by the Control of Pollution (Exemption of Certain Discharges from Control) (Variation) Order 1987 (S.I. 1987 No. 1782)) made under the Control of Pollution Act 1974, s.32(3). These deemed consents were preserved by the Water Act 1989, Sch. 26, para. 22(1), and now the Water Resources Act 1991, Sch. 13, para. 2(1).

[50] Sch. 26, para. 25; and see the Water Resources Act 1991, Sch. 13, para. 4.

[51] This replaced a tacit assumption that while consents were expressed as requiring 100% compliance, in practice it was acceptable if more than 95% of the samples met the limit.

[52] *Discharge Consents and Compliance Policy: A Blueprint for the Future* (NRA: Water Quality Series No.1, H.M.S.O., 1990).

[53] *Ibid.*, at pp.38, 42-43.

issued policy guidance that absolute limits should not apply to sewage works with a population equivalent of less than 2,000, and that they should generally only be introduced for other works as part of the implementation programme for the Urban Waste Water Treatment Directive.[54]

Notwithstanding these various steps to accommodate the position of sewerage undertakers, a proportion of discharges breach the terms of consent; this in some, but not all, cases leads to prosecutions.[55] The overall rate of compliance is, however, improving.[56] Prosecutions may also arise out of particular pollution incidents.[57]

(c) Samples

Provision is made for the evidential status of samples by section 209 of the Water Resources Act 1991, which states that the result of the analysis of any sample is not admissible in any legal proceedings in respect of any effluent passing from any land, unless the person who took the sample[58]

(a) on taking the sample,[59] notified the owner of the land of his intention to have it analysed;

(b) there and then[60] divided the sample into three parts and caused each part to be placed in a sealed and marked container; and

---

54 *Discharge Consents and Compliance Policy: A Blueprint for the Future* (NRA: Water Quality Series No.1, H.M.S.O., 1990), p.43.

55 See *ENDS Report* 230, March 1994, p.11.

56 *Discharge Consents and Compliance* (*op.cit.* n.43), pp.50-51, noting an improvement from 90% in 1990 to 95% in 1992.

57 See e.g. *ENDS Report* 230, March 1994, p.47.

58 The provisions apply to a sample of a river affected by a discharge and not just to samples of effluent: *National Rivers Authority v Harcros Timber and Building Supplies Ltd.* (1992) 156 J.P. 743.

59 i.e. on the occasion of taking the sample, not necessarily the exact moment or in advance: *Attorney-General's Reference (No. 2 of 1994)* [1994] 1 W.L.R. 1579.

60 i.e. at or proximate to the site where the sample was taken and on the occasion of taking the sample: *ibid.*

(c) delivered one part to the landowner, and retained one part, apart from the one submitted for analysis, for future comparison.[61]

If it is not reasonably practicable for him to comply with these requirements on taking the sample, they must be complied with as soon as reasonably practicable after the sample was taken.[62] In the case of proceedings in respect of effluent passing from a public sewer or other outfall owned by a sewerage undertaker into any water, references to the occupier of the land are to be treated as references to the undertaker in which the sewer or outfall is vested.[63]

The tripartite sampling requirement is to be repealed by the Environment Act 1995[64] and replaced by a provision that information provided or obtained pursuant to or by virtue of a condition of a "relevant licence"[65] (including information so provided or obtained, or recorded, by means of any apparatus[66]) shall be admissible in evidence in any proceedings, whether against the person subject to the condition or any other person. For this purpose, apparatus shall be presumed in any proceedings to register or record accurately, unless the contrary is shown or the relevant licence otherwise provides. Where by virtue of a condition of a relevant licence, an entry is required to be made in any record as to the observance of any condition of the licence,

---

[61] Section 209(1).

[62] Section 209(2).

[63] Section 209(4).

[64] Section 111.

[65] i.e. an "environmental licence" (defined in s.56 to cover various licences, including discharge consents under ss.88(1)(a), 89(4)(a) or 90 of the Water Resources Act 1991); any consent under Chapter III of Part IV of the Water Industry Act 1991 to make discharges of special category effluent; and any section 129 agreement (see *post*, p.211). The reference to a condition includes any requirement to which a person is subject under, by virtue of or in consequence of a relevant licence: s.111(5).

[66] This term includes "any meter or other device for measuring, assessing, determining, recording or enabling to be recorded, the volume, temperature, radioactivity, rate, nature, origin, composition or effect of any substance, flow, discharge, emission, deposit or abstraction": s.111(5).

the fact that the entry has not been made is admissible as evidence that the condition has not been observed. The abolition of tripartite sampling brings the position of the Authority into line with that of other authorities, such as H.M. Inspectorate of Pollution; and will facilitate the installation of automatic effluent and water sampling devices and the self-monitoring by dischargers.[67] In any event, the tripartite system did not apply to private prosecutors.

(d) Enforcement notices

By virtue of the Environment Act 1995,[68] the new Environment Agency is to be given power to serve enforcement notices if it is of the opinion that the holder of a discharge consent is contravening, or likely to contravene, any condition of the consent. Non-compliance is an offence.

(e) Charges

Section 131 of the Water Resources Act 1991 enables the Authority to make a scheme of charges in respect of discharge consents, subject to the approval of the Secretary of State under section 132. A scheme was introduced in July 1991 and was the subject of minor amendments in April 1994. There is an application charge payable when a new consent is applied for or an application is made for an existing one to be revised; there is also an annual charge based on volume, content and the receiving water together with a financial factor set annually. The aim is to enable the Authority to recover its costs.[69] The powers of the new Environment Agency to make charging schemes are set out in sections 41 and 42 of the Environment Act 1995; sections 131 and 132 of the 1991 Act are to be repealed.

---

67 *ENDS Report* 239, December 1994, p.19.
68 Sch. 22, para. 142, inserting a new section 90B in the Water Resources Act 1991.
69 See NRA, *Discharge Consents and Compliance, ante*, p.158, n.43, section 10; NRA, *Annual Charges – Discharges to Controlled Water.*

(f) Integrated pollution control authorisations[70]

Certain activities are subject to regulation under Part I of the Environmental Protection Act 1990, which establishes a system of integrated pollution control enforced by H.M. Inspectorate of Pollution, rather than under the system of discharge consents under the Water Resources Act 1991. IPC applies to the processes and substances prescribed by regulations.[71] After a date determined in accordance with Schedule 3 to the regulations, no person may carry on a prescribed process except under an authorisation granted by HMIP under section 6 of the 1990 Act and in accordance with the conditions attached under section 7 of the Act. Implied in every authorisation is a general condition that the person carrying on the process must use the best available techniques not entailing excessive cost (BATNEEC),

(a) for preventing the release of substances prescribed for any environmental medium into that medium or, where that is not practicable by such means, for reducing the release of such substances to a minimum and for rendering harmless any such substances which are released; and

(b) for rendering harmless any other substances which might cause harm if released into any environmental medium.

Other conditions must be imposed to ensure such matters as compliance with EC directives and statutory water quality objectives. Accordingly, control may be exercised by virtue of

---

[70] See generally S. Ball and S. Bell, *Environmental Law* (2nd edn., 1994), Chap. 11.

[71] 1990 Act, s.2; the Environmental Protection (Prescribed Processes and Substances) Regulations 1991 (S.I. 1991 No. 472), as amended by S.I. 1991 No. 836, S.I. 1992 No. 614, S.I. 1993 Nos. 1749 and 2405, S.I. 1994 Nos. 1271 and 1329. Schedule 1 to the Regulations lists the prescribed processes, Part A processes being designated for central control and Part B for local control (in relation to releases to air). However, a process is not a "prescribed process" (*inter alia*) if it cannot result in the release of a "prescribed substance" to water except in a concentration no greater than the background concentration or the amounts prescribed in Sch. 5 column 2: Reg. 4(1). Sch. 5 sets out the "prescribed substances" for release to water: these are the "Red list" substances: see *post*, p.209.

IPC in respect of certain releases to water,[72] and for this purpose any release into a sewer is treated as a release into water.[73]

Applications for authorisations are made under Schedule 1 to the 1990 Act.[74] Where the activities comprising a prescribed process include the release of any substances into controlled waters,[75] HMIP must not grant an authorisation if the National Rivers Authority certifies that the release will result in or contribute to a failure to achieve any water quality objective in force under the Water Resources Act 1991,[76] and any authorisation that is granted must include such conditions as appear to the Authority to be appropriate and it requires by notice in writing given to HMIP.[77] The Authority may also require HMIP to vary an authorisation.[78] These provisions are to be repealed by the Environment Act 1995[79] when HMIP, the Authority and the waste regulation authorities are merged to form the new Environment Agency.

There are also powers for HMIP to set fees and charges, for authorisations to be transferred, varied or revoked, for the service by HMIP of enforcement and prohibition notices, for appeals as respects authorisations and against variation, enforcement and prohibition notices, for the appointment of inspectors and the conferment of investigatory powers, for the Secretary of State to obtain information from HMIP, for the

---

[72] By the 1990 Act, s.1(11)(a), any release into (i) the sea or the surface of the seabed; (ii) any river, watercourse, lake, loch or pond (whether natural or artificial or above or below ground) or reservoir or the surface of the river bed or of other land supporting such waters; or (iii) groundwaters, is a release into water.

[73] 1990 Act, s.1(11)(c).

[74] See the Environmental Protection (Applications, Appeals and Registers) Regulations 1991 (S.I. 1991 No. 507).

[75] See *ante*, p.148.

[76] See *ante*, pp.150-151.

[77] 1990 Act, s.28(3).

[78] *Ibid.*, s.28(4). Responsibility for monitoring waters remains with the NRA. There is a Memorandum of Understanding between NRA and HMIP on their respective roles.

[79] Sch. 18, para. 38(2).

maintenance of public registers of information, and as regards offences.[80]

DECLARATION OF SPECIAL ZONES UNDER THE WATER RESOURCES ACT 1991

The Water Resources Act 1991 gives power for the creation of various special zones with a view to restriction or prevention of pollution. Two in particular are of significance, *Water Protection Zones* and *Nitrate Sensitive Areas.*

(a) Water protection zones

The Secretary of State after consultation, as regards matters wholly or partly affecting areas in England, with the Minister of Agriculture, Fisheries and Food may where he considers it appropriate for the prevention or control of entry into controlled waters[81] of poisonous, noxious or polluting materials by order designate an area a "water protection zone". Within such a zone activities may be prohibited or restricted by order with a view to the achievement of the informing purpose of the designation of the zone. An order so made may, *inter alia*, confer supervisory and determinative powers upon the National Rivers Authority in connection with the zone.[82] The purpose of such designations clearly extends far beyond pollution by discharges of sewage effluents but, equally, such discharges would obviously fall within their intended limit. The Authority has proposed that a zone should be designated covering the River Dee catchment; a public inquiry has been held, following the receipt of objections by the Secretary of State and a decision is expected in 1996.[83]

---

[80] 1990 Act, ss.8-27.

[81] *Ibid.,* s.104.

[82] *Ibid.,* s.93.

[83] *Freshwater Quality: Government Response to the 16th Report of the Royal Commission on Environmental Pollution* (DoE, February 1995), p.41; *ENDS Report* 243, p.9.

(b) Nitrate sensitive areas

Under section 94 of the Water Resources Act 1991, the Minister of Agriculture, Fisheries and Food and the Secretary of State (in England) or the Secretary of State (in Wales) may by order designate "nitrate sensitive areas" in which agricultural activities may be restricted with a view to the prevention or control of the entry of nitrates into controlled waters.[84] Arrangements may be entered into under section 95 with affected landowners for agreements, including payments from the relevant Ministers, for the achievements of the purpose(s) of the designation. Alternatively, requirements may be imposed by order, for which compensation may be payable. The procedures for making orders are set out in Schedule 12, with more onerous requirements where mandatory orders are to be made. Further requirements are imposed by the EC Nitrates directive,[85] which requires member states to designate "nitrate vulnerable zones" and to draw up action programmes for each NVZ. The Ministry of Agriculture, Fisheries and Food has proposed 72 NVZs in England and Wales.[86] These requirements will affect the sewage sludge disposal sites of some sewerage undertakers.[87]

The Secretary of State and the Minister of Agriculture, Fisheries and Food may jointly by order made by statutory instrument promulgate codes of good agricultural practice with a view to avoiding or minimising the pollution of inland waters.[88] The code makes specific reference to, *inter alia*, the disposal of sewage sludge on agricultural land.

---

[84]   The Nitrate Sensitive Areas (Designation) Order 1990 (S.I. 1990 No. 1013), as amended by S.I. 1990 No. 1187 and S.I. 1993 No. 3198, designates 10 trial areas. See also the Nitrate Sensitive Areas Regulations 1994 (S.I. 1994 No. 1729), as amended by S.I. 1995 Nos. 1708 and 2095.

[85]   Dir. 91/676/EEC.

[86]   *Designation of vulnerable zones in England and Wales under the EC Nitrate Directive* (MAFF, 1994). See *ENDS Report* 232, May 1994, pp.34-35.

[87]   See *ENDS Report* 233, June 1994, p.11.

[88]   Water Resources Act 1991, s.97. See the *Code of Good Agricultural Practice for the Protection of Water* (approved by the Water (Prevention of Pollution) (Code of Practice) Order 1991 (S.I. 1991 No. 2285)).

REGISTRATION AND SUPPLY OF INFORMATION UNDER THE WATER RESOURCES ACT 1991

Under section 190 of the Water Resources Act 1991, the National Rivers Authority is under a duty to maintain registers containing particulars as prescribed by order of:

(a) notices served respecting water quality objectives;

(b) applications for consents in respect of discharges;

(c) consents granted, including any conditions to which they have been made subject;

(d) certificates issued under Schedule 10 paragraph 1(7) of the Act excusing disclosure of information in public in connection with such an application upon grounds of public interest or trade secrecy;

(e) samples of effluent taken for the purposes of the Act and conclusions derived therefrom;

(f) any matter about which particulars are required to be kept in any register under section 20 of the Environmental Protection Act 1990 (particulars about authorisations for prescribed processes, etc.) by the Chief Inspector under Part I of that Act.[89]

It is further the duty of the National Rivers Authority under the section to make such registers available for free public inspection at all reasonable times[90] and to afford members of the public reasonable facility at reasonable cost for taking copies of entries upon the register.

It is also the duty of the National Rivers Authority and water

---

[89] (d) and (f) are to be repealed by the Environment Act 1995, Sch. 22, para. 169, which also adds further items ((g) to (r)) to be recorded, including applications for the variation of discharge consents, enforcement notices, revocations of discharge consents, appeals under s.91, convictions under Part III of persons who have the benefit of discharge consents, and other matters.

[90] Water Resources Act 1991, s.190(2).

undertakers to supply information *inter se* for the purpose of the performance of their respective statutory duties. These duties do not appear to extend expressly to sewerage undertakers.[91] Other persons may be required by notice to supply information in this connection to the Secretary of State, the Minister for Agriculture Fisheries and Food or the National Rivers Authority and failure of compliance without reasonable excuse will be a criminal offence with liability upon summary conviction to a fine not exceeding level 5 on the standard scale.[92]

CIVIL AND CRIMINAL LIABILITIES UNDER THE WATER RESOURCES ACT 1991

Apart from the specific provisions upon given liabilities considered above, where an offence under the control of pollution provisions of the Water Resources Act 1991 is due to the act or default of some person other than the apparent principal, such other person may be prosecuted whether or not the principal is also charged. In a sewerage connection this will be of obvious relevance where in the circumstances considered above a discharge from a sewer results from the discharge into a sewerage undertaker's sewer of materials which it was not bound to receive or in breach of the conditions imposed upon such receipt.[93] A Magistrates' Court may try any summary offence in this connection upon information laid not more than 12 months after the commission of the offence despite the provision upon time limits for summary proceedings made by section 127 of the Magistrates' Courts Act 1980.[94]

Where a body corporate, including *ex hypothesi*, a sewerage undertaker, is guilty of an offence under the 1991 Act and that offence is proved to have been committed with the consent or connivance, or to be attributable to the neglect, of any director, manager, secretary or similar officer of the body or any person

---

91   Water Resources Act 1991, s.203.
92   *Ibid.*, s.202.
93   *Ibid.*, s.217(3).
94   *Ibid.*, s.101.

purporting to act in such or a similar capacity, that person will also be liable to prosecution and punishment in respect of the offence.[95] For this purpose the member of a body corporate who directly manages the affairs of the body will be considered to be in the position of the "directors" of the body concerned.[96]

So far as civil liability is concerned, except in so far as it might otherwise be provided, no contravention of the control of pollution provisions of the 1991 Act will confer a civil right of action, other than proceedings for the recovery of a fine, derogate from any right of action or other remedy (civil or criminal) arising from other provisions or compromise any restriction which might be imposed by other, public, local or private, enactment.[97]

RADIOACTIVE SUBSTANCES

The control of pollution provisions of the Water Resources Act 1991 apply to radioactive substances only in so far as might be expressly stated or provided by regulations.[98] The Control of Pollution (Radioactive Waste) Regulations 1989[99] now provide that sections 82, 84, 85, 86, 87(1), 88(2), 92, 99, 161, 190, 202, 203 and 213 of the Act do apply to radioactive waste as they apply to non-radioactive waste, except that no account is to be taken under the 1991 Act of the radioactivity. For this purpose "radioactive waste" has the same meaning as under the Radioactive Substances Act 1993.

ANTI-POLLUTION WORKS AND OPERATIONS UNDER THE WATER RESOURCES ACT 1991

Under section 161 of the Water Resources Act 1991, the National

---

[95] Water Resources Act 1991, s.217(1). The company itself will be vicariously liable under s.85 (see *ante*, p.152) for the acts or omissions of its employees acting within the course of employment: *National Rivers Authority v Alfred McAlpine Homes East Ltd.* [1994] 4 All E.R. 286, D.C.

[96] *Ibid.*, s.217(2).

[97] *Ibid.*, s.100.

[98] *Ibid.*, s.98.

[99] S.I. 1989 No. 1158.

Rivers Authority has power where any noxious, poisonous or polluting matter seems likely to enter or has entered controlled waters to undertake certain works and operations. These are works for the prevention of likely entry of such materials or works and operations for the removal and disposal of materials already having entered, mitigation of resulting pollution and, so far as might be practical, restoration of the aquatic environment to its state immediately prior to the incident, including flora and fauna dependent upon the state of the waters concerned. The Environment Act 1995[100] is to add new provisions to the 1991 Act (sections 161A-161D) enabling the new Environment Agency to serve works notices requiring persons to carry out anti-pollution works and operations. An appeal against a notice lies to the Secretary of State; non-compliance is an offence.

Section 4 of the Salmon and Freshwater Fisheries Act 1975[101] also prohibits putting into any waters or tributaries of waters containing fish, any liquid or solid matter so as to cause the waters to be poisonous or injurious to the fish or the spawning grounds, spawn or food for fish.[102] However, a person is not guilty of an offence in respect of the entry of matter into controlled waters under and in accordance with a consent under Chapter II of Part III of the Water Resources Act 1991.[103]

DISCHARGES TO A WATERCOURSE AT COMMON LAW

Quite apart from statutory provisions, the discharge of sewage effluent or other polluting matter into any stream may amount to a nuisance in respect of which a riparian owner may take proceedings at common law for an injunction and/or for damages. The pollution need not be so bad as to amount to a public

---

[100] Sch. 22, para. 162.
[101] As amended by the Water Act 1989, Sch. 27, Pt. I.
[102] As to the Authority's bye-law making powers, see the Water Resources Act 1991, Sch. 25, para. 6(4).
[103] Water Consolidation (Consequential Provisions) Act 1991, Sch. 1, para. 30(1).

nuisance, as any riparian owner is entitled to have a flow of water in any natural stream which is in all respects in its natural state; a similar right may attach to an artificial stream, if the right has be acquired by grant or by prescription. At common law pollution means the addition of something to water which changes its natural qualities, such as the addition of hard water to soft water, the raising of the temperature of the water, or the addition of something which on meeting some other substance already in the water, each in themselves harmless, causes pollution.[104] In this context the rule in *Rylands v Fletcher*[105] applies whereby liability will arise where "dangerous" materials are stored upon land and in fact escape therefrom causing foreseeable damage.

Compliance with the provisions of the Water Resources Act 1991 will be no defence in common law proceedings. The standards of the common law are higher than those so far imposed by Parliament; seemingly harmless extraneous matter is none the less capable of being treated as pollution at common law. On the other hand an injunction is a discretionary remedy, and it would not be granted by a court where no prejudice whatever can be shown to the plaintiff's interests.[106]

The discharge of effluent into a watercourse by an undertaker may amount to a nuisance;[107] indeed, an undertaker is expressly prohibited from causing a nuisance in the exercise of its

---

[104] See *Coulson & Forbes on Waters and Land Drainage*, 6th edn., at p.198, and *Crossley v Lightowler* (1866) L.R. 2 Ch. 476, and other cases there cited. In *Young & Co. v Bankier Distillery Co.* [1893] A.C. 691, Lord Macnaghten said (at p.698), "A riparian owner is entitled to have the water of the stream, on the banks of which his property lies, flow down as it has been accustomed to flow down to his property, subject to the ordinary use of the flowing water by upper proprietors, and to such further use, if any, on their part in connection with their property as may be reasonable in the circumstances. Every riparian proprietor is thus entitled to the water of his stream, in its natural flow, without sensible diminution or increase and without sensible alterations in its character or quality."

[105] (1866) L.R. 1 Ex. 265.

[106] *Kensit v G.E. Rlwy. Co.* (1884) 27 Ch. D. 122.

[107] *Pride of Derby and Derbyshire Angling Assn. v British Celanese Ltd.* [1953] Ch. 149.

functions[108] by section 117(6) of the Water Industry Act 1991. The fact that the particular watercourse was already polluted from some other source would also be no defence in such proceedings.[109]

It used to be said that at common law a right to pollute a watercourse could be acquired by prescription or by grant as an easement as against a riparian proprietor lower down the watercourse[110] but where such pollution would constitute an offence against the 1991 Act (and a similar principle applied under the earlier statutes), it seems that such a right would not now be upheld by the courts.

STATUTORY NUISANCES

In addition to the above restrictions, statutory or common law, on pollution of watercourses and streams, certain matters are expressly dealt with by section 259 of the 1936 Act.[111] These provisions are enforceable not by an undertaker under the 1991 Act but by the local authority.[112] The section provides that the following are statutory nuisances for the purposes of Part III of the Environmental Protection Act 1990:

"(a) any pond, pool, ditch, gutter or watercourse which is so foul or in such a state as to be prejudicial to health or a nuisance;[113]

(b) any part of a watercourse, not being a part ordinarily navigated by vessels, employed in the carriage of goods by water, which is so choked or silted up as to obstruct or

---

[108] Under ss.102-105, 112, 115 and 116 of the 1991 Act.

[109] *Pride of Derby, supra.*

[110] See *Wright v Williams* (1836) 1 M.&W. 77.

[111] As amended by the Environmental Protection Act 1990, Sch. 15, para. 4.

[112] i.e. district and London borough councils, the Common Council of the City of London, the Sub-Treasurer of the Inner Temple and the Under Treasurer of the Middle Temple and the Council of the Isles of Scilly and, after 1st April 1996, county and county borough councils in Wales: 1990 Act, s.79(7), as amended.

[113] *Att.-Gen. v Leeds Corporation* (1870) 5 Ch. App. 583.

impede the proper flow of water and thereby to cause a
nuisance, or give rise to conditions prejudicial to health;[114]

Provided that in the case of an alleged nuisance under para.
(b), nothing in this subsection shall be deemed to impose any
liability on any person other than the person by whose act or
default the nuisance arises or continues."

In order therefore, for a local authority to act in such a situation,
the actual offender must be discovered, either *flagrante delicto*,
or by establishing that he has failed to perform a legal duty
already imposed on him to clear out the watercourse in question.
A riparian owner may be under a limited common law duty to
clear out a natural stream,[115] and in practice it may well be
difficult to prove a sufficient act or default to bring a defendant
within the proviso to the present section.

Ancillary powers with regard to watercourses, ditches, etc. are
given to the local authority by sections 260 to 266 of the 1936
Act, and these are not affected by the 1989 or 1991 Acts.

DISCHARGE TO THE SEA AT COMMON LAW

At common law there is no right for a local authority, or any
person, to discharge sewage or any polluting matter into the sea,
and an injunction may be granted if a nuisance is caused by any

---

[114] "Prejudicial to health" is defined by s.343(1) of the 1936 Act to mean
"injurious, or likely to cause injury to health". It is not necessary to prove that
a particular state of affairs is *both* a nuisance and injurious to health: *Betts v
Penge U.D.C.* [1942] 2 All E.R. 61.

[115] *Leakey v National Trust for Places of Historic Interest or Natural Beauty*
[1980] 1 Q.B. 485, *per* Megaw L.J. at pp.526-527, impliedly disapproving the
decision of the Divisional Court in *Neath R.D.C. v Wllliams* [1951] 1 K.B. 115.
The test is what it is reasonable to expect of the occupier given the relevant
resources, taken on a broad basis, of the parties. See further *Goldman v
Hargrave* [1967] 1 A.C. 645, P.C. Very different considerations apply if the
defendant creates an artificial watercourse or does anything to make artificial
that which was previously natural: *Sedleigh-Denfield v O'Callaghan* [1940]
A.C. 880. See now, however, the Water Resources Act 1991, s.90, with
specific reference to "deposits and vegetation in rivers".

such discharge, at the instance of the person injured.[116] On the other hand, if the discharge is effected in such a manner as to obviate any nuisance, no legal proceedings can be taken.

Every accretion from the sea, whether natural or artificial, and any part of the sea-shore to the low-water mark, forms part of the district of the local authority whose area it adjoins,[117] but section 187 of the Water Industry Act 1991 provides that a sewerage undertaker may not execute any works below high water mark without the approval of the Secretary of State.

The discharge of oil[118] or any mixture containing oil into UK territorial waters or navigable internal waters, from a "place" on land (which would presumably include a sewer), constitutes an offence against section 2 of the Prevention of Oil Pollution Act 1971.[119]

---

[116] *Hobart v Southend-on-Sea Corporation* (1906) 75 L.J.K.B. 305, and *Foster v Warblington U.D.C.* [1906] 1 K.B. 648. A local authority may itself be in the position of plaintiff where its property has been injured as the consequence of pollution of the sea or tidal waters: *Esso Petroleum Co. Ltd. v Southport Corporation* [1956] A.C. 218.

[117] Local Government Act 1972, s.72.

[118] "Oil" is defined, somewhat loosely, in s.29(1) of the 1971 Act as meaning "oil of any description" and including "spirit produced from oil of any description and coal tar".

[119] As amended by the Prevention of Oil Pollution Act 1986, s.1.

Chapter 9

DRAINAGE OF PREMISES

INTRODUCTORY

In this chapter it is proposed to deal mainly with drains, as distinct from sewers, and in particular with the drainage of individual buildings and other premises.

In practice, care has to be exercised to consider whether the particular statutory function in question is exercisable by the sewerage undertaker or by the local authority. In general, matters related to a public sewer are the concern of the sewerage undertaker, while matters relating exclusively to drains are the concern of the local authority.

Drains are not vested in the sewerage undertaker or local authority (except where they are owners of property served thereby), but it is the concern of the local authority to ensure that proper means of drainage are provided for new buildings, and that the drains of existing buildings do not cause a nuisance, and also that their contents do not injure the public sewers into which the drains – mediately or immediately – discharge. It is also necessary to consider the circumstances in which the owner or occupier of a building may cause his drains or sewers to be connected to the public sewer vested in the sewerage undertaker, and the use that may be made of any drains so connected.

RIGHTS TO CONNECT DRAINS TO PUBLIC SEWERS

(a) The nature of the rights

Under section 106 of the Water Industry Act 1991,[1] the owner[2] or occupier of any premises or the owner of any private sewer

---

[1]   As amended by the Competition and Service (Utilities) Act 1992, s.43(2).
[2]   Defined in s.219(1) of the 1991 Act.

draining premises[3] is entitled to have his drains or sewer communicate with the public sewers of any sewerage undertaker, provided he has the right (by virtue of ownership or easements) to cause his drain or sewer to pass through the intervening land, and he may thereby discharge foul and surface water from those premises or that private sewer; the right does not, however, apply to a sewer vested in the undertaker which has not become a public sewer. Subject to the restrictions mentioned below, and to the prescribed procedure being observed, this right is absolute (the owner or occupier exercising the right must act, however, at his expense) and the person exercising such right will not be responsible if the public sewer is not properly maintained or has an inadequate outfall, or connects with a stream in such a manner as to offend against the control of pollution provisions of the Water Resources Act 1991.[4] Under the 1875 Act, it was held that once a communication had been lawfully made under the statutory power which was the predecessor of the present section,[5] any type of effluent (not injurious to health) could be discharged into the public sewer.[6] On the other hand, in two cases[7] in both of which no notice had been given to the local authority pursuant to section 21 of the 1875 Act,[8] a right claimed to connect a foul water drain with a highway (public) sewer, or to change the nature of the effluent to such a sewer from slops to faecal matter, was denied by the court. It is not clear that the decisions would have been the same if the statutory procedure had been followed,

---

3   This is also defined in s.219(1), as any sewer which is not a public sewer.

4   See *ante*, Chapter 8, p.152. This does not mean, however, that a particular effluent which would offend against the Act when it reached the stream may be discharged into the sewer (see proviso (a)(ii) to the present section, below), but that if the effluent from the sewer already pollutes that stream, a particular owner or occupier of premises discharging into the sewer will not be held responsible. On the general principle, see *Ainley & Sons Ltd. v Kirkheaton L.B.* (1881) 60 L.J. Ch. 734, and *Brown v Dunstable Corporation* [1899] 2 Ch. 378.

5   Act of 1875, s.21.

6   See the judgment of Charles J. in *Peebles v Oswaldtwistle U.D.C.* [1897] 1 Q.B. 384, at p.392.

7   *Kinson Pottery Co. v Poole Corporation* [1899] 2 Q.B. 41, and *Graham v Wroughton* [1901] 2 Ch. 451.

8   The predecessor to s.34(3) of the 1936 Act.

but it may be possible to argue that a sewer designed (e.g.) for slop water only cannot be used for other purposes.

Under the 1991 Act, there are a number of specific restrictions as to what may be discharged to a public sewer, and some public sewers may be reserved for foul, or for surface, water[9] respectively. Subject to the restrictions, it seems that any effluent coming within this expression may be discharged into the public sewer without the consent of the sewerage undertaker.

Section 106 provides that this right shall not entitle any person:

"(a) to discharge directly or indirectly into any public sewer–

   (i) any liquid from a factory,[10] other than domestic sewage or surface water or storm water, or any liquid from a manufacturing process,[11] or

   (ii) any liquid or other matter the discharge of which into public sewers is prohibited by or under any enactment; or

(b) where separate public sewers are provided for foul water and for surface water,[12] to discharge directly or indirectly–

   (i) foul water into a sewer provided for surface water, or

   (ii) except with the approval of the sewerage undertaker, surface water into a sewer provided for foul water; or

(c) to have his drains or sewer made to communicate directly with a storm-water overflow sewer."[13]

---

[9] "Surface water" is defined by s.219(1) of the 1991 Act for the present purpose as including "water from roofs".

[10] This term is to be understood as defined by s.175 of the Factories Act 1961; see s.106(9) of the 1991 Act and s.184(l) of the Factories Act 1961.

[11] But see below, pp.203-204 and, in particular, the definition therein of "trade effluent".

[12] Under s.116 of the 1991 Act, the undertaker may prohibit the use of any public sewer vested in it, either entirely, or for the purpose of foul water drainage, or for the purpose of surface water drainage (and see Chapter 5, *ante*, p.118).

[13] 1991 Act, s.106(2). This expression is not defined in the Act.

It should also be noted that the right relates only to communications to be made from a drain or sewer as defined in the 1991 Act, which would exclude land or agricultural drains, and any person making a communication with a public sewer must comply with the provisions of the section (see section 109).

(b) How the rights may be exercised

In order that a person may exercise the rights given by this section, he must give the sewerage undertaker prior written notice[14] of the proposals, and at any time within 21 days of the receipt of such notice, the undertaker may by notice[15] refuse to permit the communication to be made "if it appears to the undertaker that the mode of construction or condition of the drain or sewer is such that the making of the communication would be prejudicial to the undertaker's sewerage system"[16] and for the purpose of examining the mode of construction and condition of the drain or sewer it may, if necessary, require it to be laid open for inspection.[17]

Any question as to the reasonableness of any refusal of the undertaker to permit a communication to be made is to be determined by the Director General of Water Services. The

---

[14] The notice must be in writing (s.219(1) (definition of "notice")) and duly served in accordance with s.216. The form need not follow any particular wording, but Shaw's Form PH58 is appropriate.

[15] This also must be in writing and duly signed and served (see preceding note); Shaw's Form PN12 is appropriate.

[16] Section 106(4). There is no explanation of this expression afforded by the Act. Clearly the subsection could be invoked to prevent (for example) a 12-inch private sewer being connected to a 4-inch public sewer, but it is doubtful, especially in view of *Smeaton v Ilford Corporation* [1954] Ch. 450, whether the power could be used where it is alleged that the effluent to be discharged into the sewer would surcharge the sewer or otherwise cause a nuisance. The same result as an exercise of the power under s.106(4) may be achieved by a planning agreement under s.106 of the Town and Country Planning Act 1990: *R. v Canterbury City Council, ex p. Springimage Ltd.* (1993) 68 P.&C.R. 171.

[17] 1991 Act, s.106(5). The requirements of the undertaker should, it is submitted (although this is not expressly stipulated in the statute), be notified in writing; Shaw's Form PN13 is appropriate.

undertaker will then have to justify its contention that the communication would prejudice its system or (as the case may be) that the person concerned is not entitled to use the section as one or the other of the above restrictions applies. Similarly, any question arising as to the reasonableness of the requirements of the undertaker regarding the opening of the drain or sewer in question may also be determined by the Director.[18]

If the communication is made without prior notice having been given to the sewerage undertaker, the person responsible will be liable to a fine, and the undertaker will be entitled to close the communication and recover its expenses from the person responsible.[19]

(c) The making of the communication

The physical work of making the communication with the public sewer may be executed by the owner or occupier concerned unless, within 14 days of the notice of his proposals having been served on the sewerage undertaker,[20] the undertaker has given notice[21] to such person to the effect that it intends to make the communication[22] itself.

Whichever party actually executes the works, the provisions of section 158 of the 1991 Act relating to the breaking-up of streets will apply.[23] Section 106 does not give the owner or occupier the right to enter or lay pipes on intervening land not owned by him and not forming part of a private street. He will have to negotiate

---

[18] 1991 Act, s.106(6), as amended by the Competition and Service (Utilities) Act 1992, s.35(8). On the powers of the Director to determine questions, see the 1991 Act, s.30A, *ante*, p.23.

[19] *Ibid.*, s.109.

[20] Or within 14 days of the determination of any question by the Director.

[21] This notice must be in writing and duly served (1991 Act, ss.216 and 219(1)). See also *Epping Forest District Council v Essex Rendering* [1983] 1 W.L.R. 158.

[22] 1991 Act, s.107, as amended by the Competition and Service (Utilities) Act 1992, s.35(9).

[23] *Ibid.*, s.108.

for such rights in the form of easements or wayleaves. A sewerage undertaker making the communication is subject to the same limitation, for in the context of section 107 it has no greater rights than a private individual.[24]

Where the owner or occupier decides to execute the work of communication himself, he must, before commencing the work, give reasonable notice[25] to any person directed by the undertaker to superintend the execution of the work and afford him all reasonable facilities for superintending the carrying out of the work.[26]

Where the sewerage undertaker has given notice to the effect that it intends to execute the work of making the communication, it has "all such rights in respect of the making of the communication as the person desiring it to be made would have".[27] Before starting the work it is entitled to ask for payment of such sum, not exceeding the undertaker's estimate of all the cost of the work, as the undertaker may require to be paid to it, or for reasonable security to be given for payment of the cost of the work.[28] Where any advance payment exceeds the expenses reasonably incurred[29] in the execution of the work, the sewerage undertaker must repay the excess, and if its expenses[30] are not covered by any payment, it may recover the balance from the

---

[24] See *Wood v Ealing Tenants Ltd.* [1907] 2 K.B. 390.

[25] This notice must be in writing and duly served: 1991 Act, ss.216 and 219(1).

[26] 1991 Act, s.108(1).

[27] Section 107(3)(a). This would include e.g. the right to enter on private land without payment of compensation, but only where that right is vested in the person in whose place they are acting: see *Wood v Ealing Tenants Ltd.* [1907] 2 K.B. 390, decided under the earlier legislation. The powers of s.171 of the 1991 Act would not apply to such a case. If the private owner has no right to cause his drain to run through land belonging to some other person but lying between the premises to be drained and the public sewer, the communication cannot be made. A similar position obtains if the sewerage undertaker acts by agreement under s.160 of the Act.

[28] 1991 Act, s.107(3)(b). Having given such notice, it seems that it could be compelled by *mandamus* to do the work.

[29] A reasonable sum by way of establishment expenses may be included: Local Government Act 1974, s.36.

[30] i.e. its reasonable expenses, plus establishment expenses.

person for whom the work was done.[31] Any dispute between a sewerage undertaker and any other person as to the reasonableness of the estimate, any requirement of security or whether an excess is payable or expenses recoverable, or the amount of any such expenses, may be referred to the Director for determination under section 30A of the 1991 Act.[32]

(d) Offences

It is expressly made an offence to cause a drain or sewer to communicate with a public sewer without complying with the procedure of section 106 of the 1991 Act, or before the expiration of 21 days after the receipt by the undertaker of the notice of proposals under section 106(3).[33] It is also an offence to proceed to make such a communication after a notice has been given to the effect that the authority intends to make the communication itself.[34]

(e) Rights, not duties

The power to communicate with a public sewer is a right, and not a duty. The sewerage undertaker (or the local authority) cannot, therefore, require the owner or occupier of premises to cause his drains to communicate with a public sewer, unless it can be said that "satisfactory provision has not been made for drainage" of the building, and that the only means of so providing would be by making such communication,[35] and in such an event action would have to be taken by the local authority, not the sewerage

---

[31] 1991 Act, s.107(4). The means of recovery will be as a simple contract debt under s.293 of the 1936 Act, or by simple action in the local County Court or the High Court.

[32] 1991 Act, s.107(4A), inserted by the Competition and Service (Utilities) Act 1992, s.35(9).

[33] Section 109(1). If a person fails to serve proper notice as required by the section, he will not be able to plead the section as a defence in nuisance proceedings brought as a consequence of the connection of his drains to the sewer: *Graham v Wroughton* [1901] 2 Ch. 451.

[34] 1991 Act, s.107(2).

[35] See Building Act 1984, s.59.

undertaker. Thus, where premises are drained to a cesspit, which is in good order and adequate for the purpose, neither the authority nor the undertaker can, except by offering to pay the cost thereof,[36] require the cesspit to be abolished and main drainage substituted therefor. The local authority would also not be entitled to refuse to cleanse a cesspool or empty a privy, as a means of putting pressure on the owner of the premises to cause them to be communicated with the public sewer.[37]

THE DRAINAGE OF NEW BUILDINGS

The Building Act 1984 gives an effective means of control over the type of drainage proposed for a new building, but as this is exercised by the local authority (and *not* the sewerage undertaker) through the medium of the Building Regulations 1991,[38] it is first important to appreciate the types of work to which, and the circumstances in which, this control is applicable.

(a) When the control is effective

In the first place, the control over the drainage of new buildings herein discussed depends on the terms of the Regulations, which apply only with respect to the design and construction of buildings,[39] and alterations and extensions of buildings, and also to the provision of services, fittings or equipment in or in connection with buildings.[40] Control in practice is most effective where plans are required to be submitted before the work is

---

[36] See s.113 of the 1991 Act.

[37] Under s.45(5)(a) of the Environmental Protection Act 1990, *ante*, p.147.

[38] S.I. 1991 No. 2768, as amended by S.I. 1992 No. 1180.

[39] Section 121 of the Building Act 1984 provides that "building" for the purposes of Part I of the 1984 Act and any other enactment relating to building regulations "means any permanent or temporary building, and, unless the context otherwise requires, it includes any other structure or erection of whatever kind or nature (whether permanent or temporary)". "Structure or erection" includes a "vehicle, vessel, hovercraft, aircraft or other movable object of any kind in such circumstances as may be prescribed" by building regulations. Note that this definition does not apply to powers under Part III of the 1984 Act (ss.59-90).

[40] Building Act 1984, s.1 and Sch. 1.

commenced, but these have to be submitted only where the Building Regulations so provide.[41] Where a building is totally exempt from this control,[42] this section also is inoperative.

(b) Drainage provisions

Apart from specific breaches of the express requirements of the Regulations, it is also an offence to fail to submit plans (where these are required) before commencing the work and, where the plans provide for the drainage of a building, the local authority has power to order the demolition of works executed prior to the submission of plans, even if such work does not in fact contravene the section.[43]

When plans are received by the local authority, they must be considered, and if they contravene the provisions of the Building Regulations the authority must reject the plans, and give notice of such rejection to the building owner.[44] If such notice of rejection is not served within the prescribed period,[45] the plans cannot subsequently be rejected, but failure to serve notice of rejection does not of itself legalise any contravening work, but merely destroys the right of the authority to require the building owner to remove the contravening work.[46] Similarly, approval of work which contravenes the Building Regulations does not legalise such work, but the authority again lose their powers to order removal.[47]

---

[41] Building Act 1984, Sch. 1, para. 2.
[42] *Ibid.*, s.4(1), exempting educational buildings and the buildings of statutory undertakers.
[43] *Ibid.*, s.36(2).
[44] *Ibid.*, s.16. The notice must be in writing, and duly signed and served, in accordance with ss.92 to 94; Shaw's Form BR7 is appropriate.
[45] Five weeks, or such extended period (not more than two months from the deposit of the plans) as may be agreed: Building Act 1984, s.16(12).
[46] Building Act 1984, s.36(2).
[47] In either case, the authority may still prosecute for an offence against the Regulations. They may also take proceedings for an injunction in the High Court, but in the circumstances the court may order the authority to pay compensation to the building owner: Building Act 1984, s.36(6).

The authority has no discretion, as has a local planning authority acting under the Town and Country Planning Act 1990, whether to pass or reject plans;[48] if the Regulations or the Act are contravened, the plans must be rejected; however, if the provisions of the Regulations would be unreasonable in relation to a particular case, they may be dispensed with or relaxed by direction made by the Secretary of State or the local authority.[49] Further, plans of a building or of an extension of a building must be rejected "unless

(a) the plans show that satisfactory provision will be made for the drainage of the building[50] or of the extension, as the case may be, or

(b) the local authority are satisfied that in the case of the particular building or extension they may properly dispense with any provision for drainage."[51]

This provision merits more detailed consideration.

(i) "Satisfactory provision"
The local authority must be satisfied that satisfactory provision has been made and, subject to compliance with the section, it seems that the Magistrates' Court (on appeal to them under the section) is not entitled to substitute its decision for that of the authority, provided there were grounds on which the latter could reasonably have come to its decision. The provision referred to is only for the drainage of the particular building and the authority cannot reject the plans because the sewerage system

---

[48] It seems that the Secretary of State will not support a decision under the Town and Country Planning Act 1990, refusing planning permission for the erection of a single dwelling solely on the ground that satisfactory provision is not proposed to be made for the drainage thereof; this is a matter to be controlled under the public health legislation and not under the Planning Act: see article at [1959] J.P.L. 236.

[49] Building Act 1984, s.8.

[50] "Drainage" for the purposes of the section is defined to include "the conveyance, by means of a sink and any other necessary appliance, of refuse water and the conveyance of rain-water from roofs": Building Act 1984, s.21(2).

[51] Building Act 1984, s.21(1).

into which the drains (otherwise satisfactory) are to discharge, is unsatisfactory.[52]

Section 21(4) of the 1984 Act provides that a proposed drain is not to be deemed to be satisfactory for the purposes of this section, unless it is proposed to be made, as the local authority[53] may require, "either to connect with a sewer,[54] or to discharge into a cesspool[55] or some other place".

The authority may not[56] require a drain to be made to connect to a sewer[57] *unless*:

"(a) that sewer is within one hundred feet[58] of the site of the building or, in the case of an extension, the site either of the extension or of the original building, and is at a level that makes it reasonably practicable to construct a drain to communicate with it, and, if it is not a public sewer, is a sewer that the person constructing the drain is entitled to use;[59] *and*

---

52   *Chesterton R.D.C. v Ralph Thompson Ltd.* [1947] K.B. 300; "I think, therefore, the court of quarter sessions were right in coming to the conclusion that the only matter they had to consider was the suitability of the particular drain which does connect with the sewer, and they are not concerned with what happens to the drainage of the houses once it passes into the sewer, or whether the sewer itself is satisfactory": *per* Lord Goddard C.J. at p.306.

53   Or the Magistrates' Court on appeal to them under the section.

54   Not necessarily a public sewer.

55   "Cesspool" is defined for the purposes of the 1984 Act by s.126 thereof, as including "a settlement tank or other tank for the reception or disposal of foul matter from buildings", but the term is not, it seems, thereby confined to receptacles for foul matter.

56   Subject to their agreeing to pay the extra cost as mentioned below.

57   Not necessarily a public sewer.

58   The measurements must be taken "in a straight line on a horizontal plane": Interpretation Act 1978, s.8. The hundred feet is to be measured, not from the curtilege, but the site of the building drained: *Meyrick v Pembroke Corporation* (1912) 76 J.P. 365.

59   In the case of a private sewer, the person draining thereto must have a right, acquired by grant or prescription, to drain thereto. Because a particular sewer is a public sewer, it does not follow that a particular person must have a right to drain into it, if he can only get access thereto through private land, and this point is therefore covered by the ensuing words of the section: see Building Act 1984, s.21(4).

(b) the intervening land is land through which that person is entitled to construct a drain."

On the other hand, if the authority requires a connection to be made to a sewer which is not within the distance of one hundred feet above-mentioned, the authority must then undertake to "bear so much of the expenses reasonably incurred in constructing, and in maintaining and repairing, the drain as may be attributable to the fact that the distance of the sewer exceeds" that distance.[60] Such a requirement and undertaking are not matters of routine administration, and therefore they must be embodied in a formal resolution of the council if they are to be effective.[61]

(ii) Combined drains
The above provision, like its predecessor in the 1875 Act,[62] enables the authority to insist on a separate drain being provided for each building (or each separate premises), and to reject plans providing for drainage in combination, at least where there is an existing sewer available. This is not provided for in as many words in section 21(4), but it seems to follow from the wording of section 22(1),[63] and the authority is, under section 21(4), apparently entitled only to insist on the drain being made to "connect with a sewer" (which, it is submitted, must mean "connect directly"), or to "discharge into a cesspool"; plans providing for combined drainage terminating in a cesspool, if otherwise unexceptional, would therefore, it seems comply with section 21(4).[64]

Whenever separate drainage could be insisted upon for each of two or more buildings, to be made to communicate with an

---

[60] Building Act 1984, s.21(5).
[61] *Princes Investments Ltd. v Frimley and Camberley U.D.C.* [1962] 1 Q.B. 681.
[62] i.e. s.25 of the 1875 Act: see *Woodford U.D.C. v Stark* (1902) 66 J.P. 536.
[63] "Where a local authority might under the last preceding section require each of two or more buildings to be drained separately into an existing sewer . . . ."
[64] The drain may also be made to discharge into "some other place", such as a soakaway.

existing sewer,[65] the authority may as an alternative require the buildings to be drained in combination into the existing sewer, by means of a private sewer (which under the Public Health Acts Amendment Act 1890, s.19, would have been described as a "single private drain"), to be constructed by the owners to the directions of the authority, or (at the option of the authority), by the authority on behalf of the owners.[66]

This power may be exercised subject to the following:

(1) It must appear to the authority that the buildings in question may be drained more economically or advantageously in combination.

(2) Combined drainage cannot be insisted upon, except by agreement with the owners of the buildings concerned, in respect of "any building for the drainage of which plans have been previously passed by the authority".

(3) Combined drainage cannot be insisted upon otherwise than "when the drains of the buildings are first laid".

(4) The proportions in which the expenses of constructing, maintaining and repairing the communicating private sewer are to be borne by the owners concerned, must be fixed by the authority. The authority must give notice of its decision on such a matter to each owner affected,[67] and any owner aggrieved may appeal to the local Magistrates' Court. [68]

(5) Any sewer constructed by the local authority under this

---

65 If the sewer was constructed before 1937, this must be a public sewer. If it is a private sewer, there must be an easement or some other right to connect to it, as the authority's requirement cannot here override private rights: see e.g. *Wood v Ealing Tenants Ltd.* [1907] 2 K.B. 390.

66 Building Act 1984, s.22(1).

67 The notice must be in writing, signed by the authorised officer of the authority, and duly served, in accordance with ss.92 to 94 of the 1984 Act. The requirement of writing is mandatory, see *Epping Forest District Council v Essex Rendering* [1983] 1 W.L.R. 158.

68 1984 Act, s.22(4).

provision is not to be deemed to have become a public sewer as a consequence of such construction.[69]

(iii) Appeals

Provision is made by sections 21(3), 21(4), 21(6) and 22(4) of the 1984 Act for a person aggrieved by a decision of the local authority under the provisions hereinbefore discussed to appeal to the Magistrates' Court. Appeal in each such case will be by way of complaint for an order,[70] and the normal procedure of the Magistrates' Courts Act 1980 will then apply. From the decision of the magistrates, either party will be able to appeal to the Crown Court, under section 41 of the Building Act 1984. Alternatively, either party may appeal to the Queen's Bench Divisional Court on a case stated on a point of law.[71]

(c) Enforcement of control

This control, effected through the Building Regulations 1991, can be enforced by the following means:

(i) *Criminal penalty.* The execution of work without submission of plans, where such are required, the execution of work otherwise than in accordance with the deposited plans, and the execution of work which contravenes the Building Regulations, are made offences by section 35 of the 1984 Act. On conviction by the Magistrates' Court a fine may be imposed including a fine not exceeding £50 for each day on which the default continues after conviction. Criminal proceedings may be taken irrespective of the local authority's rights to serve a Section 36 notice.

(ii) *Removal or alteration of offending work.* Where work to which the Regulations apply is executed either without

---

[69] 1984 Act, s.22(6), and compare s.179(1) of the 1991 Act, Chapter 2, *ante*, p.40.
[70] 1984 Act, s.103(1); proceedings must be commenced within 21 days: *ibid.,* s.103(2).
[71] Magistrates' Courts Act 1980, s.111; and *post*, Chapter 11, p.242.

plans having been deposited, or notwithstanding the rejection of plans, or otherwise than in accordance with the deposited plans, and also where the work contravenes the Regulations, or it is of the description referred to in section 21 of the 1984 Act,[72] the authority may[73] serve a Section 36 notice[74] to require the building owner to pull down or remove the work or, at his election, to comply with the authority's requirements.[75] The recipient may, within certain time limits,[76] notify[74] the authority of his intention to obtain a written report[77] concerning the work to which the Section 36 notice relates. If having considered the report the authority decides to withdraw the notice it may reimburse any expenses reasonably incurred by the recipient as a result of the notice being served, in particular the cost of the report. On the other hand, if no report is submitted, or the local authority does not withdraw its notice, if the owner fails to comply with a Section 36 notice within 28 days,[78] the authority may itself act in default, and recover its expenses reasonably incurred[79]

---

[72] Or various other sections of the Act, such as s.18 (see Chapter 5, *ante*, p.119), and others not the concern of this book.

[73] See 1984 Act, s.36(2); it has a discretion.

[74] This notice (called a "Section 36 notice" – s.36(4)) must be in writing, signed by the authorised officer of the authority, and duly served (1984 Act, ss.92 to 95). Shaw's Forms BR21 and BR22 are appropriate. The requirement as to writing is mandatory: *Epping Forest District Council v Essex Rendering, supra.*

[75] These must be requirements which the authority might have made under s.16 as a "condition of passing plans". Strictly speaking, there is no provision made in s.16 for "conditional approvals", and s.36(2), here referred to, must be read as contemplating a rejection of the plans, coupled with an intimation to the effect that, if certain amendments are made in the plans, they would be passed under the terms of the section. The burden of showing that the work does not comply with the Regulations is on the authority. Thereafter the appellant against the notice must show he has nonetheless complied with them: *Rickards v Kerrier District Council* (1987) 151 J.P. 625.

[76] 28 days, or such longer period allowed by the magistrates under s.36(3).

[77] "... from a suitably qualified person ...": s.37(1)(a).

[78] Or such longer period as the Magistrates' Court may on his application allow, s.36(3); for the procedure see s.103.

[79] A reasonable sum by way of establishment expenses may be included: Local Government Act 1974, s.36.

from him.[80] No notice may be issued under this section after the expiration of 12 months from the completion of the work in question, or if the plans had been passed by the authority, or not rejected within the "prescribed period".[81] There is a right of appeal to a Magistrates' Court within 28 days from the giving of a Section 36 notice. If the court is satisfied that, although the authority was entitled to give the notice, the purposes of section 36 have been substantially achieved, it may direct the authority to withdraw the notice. Pending final determination, or withdrawal of the appeal, the notice will have no effect. Under section 41 either party may appeal to the Crown Court against the Magistrates' Court decision. Alternatively, on a point of law either party may appeal to the Queen's Bench Division of the High Court by way of case stated.

(iii) An action may be brought for an injunction for the alteration or removal of any work which offends against the Building Regulations. This action may be brought in the High Court, at the suit of the Attorney-General (on the relation of an interested person), or of a person aggrieved. In any such case, the court on granting the injunction may, where the plans had been passed by the local authority, or notice of rejection of plans had not been given within the "prescribed period",[82] order the local authority to pay compensation to the owner of the work.[83]

---

[80] Building Act 1984, s.36(3). The authority's expenses hereunder will be recoverable as a simple contract debt in the local County Court, or the High Court. The expenses will also be a charge on the property, being recoverable from the owner thereof, and should be registered in the local land charges register (see 1984 Act, s.107(1), and Chapter 11, *post*, p.240).

[81] Five weeks or such extended period as may be agreed: 1984 Act, s.16(12).

[82] Or such longer period as the Magistrates' Court may on his application allow, s.36(3); for the procedure see s.103.

[83] 1984 Act, s.36(6). If the court proposes to make an order against the local authority, it must first make the authority a party to the proceedings, if it is not already a party (*ibid*).

THE IMPROVEMENT OF EXISTING DRAINS

Apart altogether from the question of nuisances and "unsatisfactory" drains, considered hereafter,[84] the sewerage undertaker or the local authority may take certain action to secure the improvement of existing private drains – at their expense. Further, where a private individual proposes himself to alter an existing drainage system, the local authority can exercise control over such work.

(a) Water Industry Act 1991, s.113: power to alter drains

Under this section, a sewerage undertaker may close any existing drain or sewer[85] which communicates with a public sewer or a cesspool,[86] and fill up any such cesspool, and do any work necessary for these purposes. Such works are carried out at the expense of the undertaker. This power is exercisable only in the following circumstances:

(i) The drain or sewer in question, though sufficient for the effectual drainage of the premises,[87] must either be "not adapted to the general sewerage system of the area" or, in the opinion of the authority, "otherwise objectionable".

(ii) Before exercising the power to close the existing drain or sewer, the undertaker must first provide in a position "equally convenient to the owner of the premises, a drain or sewer which (a) is equally effectual for the drainage of the premises; and (b) communicates with a public sewer".[88]

---

[84] *Post*, p.193*ff*.

[85] The expression is here clearly intended to refer to private sewers only; the alteration, closure, etc. of public sewers could be effected under s.116 of the 1991 Act.

[86] See definition in s.113(7).

[87] If the drainage is not so sufficient, action could normally be taken under s.59 of the 1984 Act.

[88] Substituted drainage communicating immediately with a cesspool does not, therefore, comply with the section.

(iii) Notice[89] of the undertaker's proposals must be given to the owner of the premises in question and, if he is aggrieved as regards either the position or the sufficiency[90] of the drain or sewer proposed to be provided by the undertaker, he may refer the matter to the Director General of Water Services under section 30A of the 1991 Act.[91]

(b) 1984 Act, section 61: notice of drain repairs, etc.

This section prohibits the repair, reconstruction or alteration of the course of any underground[92] drain that communicates with a sewer,[93] cesspool or other receptacle for drainage, without giving to the local authority[94] at least 24 hours' notice[95] of an intention to do so. This prohibition does not apply to the following:

(i) a case of emergency; but in any such case, the prohibition applies to the covering over of the drain or sewer in question;

(ii) so much of any drain or sewer constructed by, or belonging to, a railway company as runs under, across or along their railway;

(iii) so much of any drain or sewer constructed by, or belonging to, dock undertakers, as is situated in or on land of the undertakers that is held or used by them for the purposes of their undertaking.

---

[89] Such notice must be in writing and duly served (1991 Act, ss.216 and 219(1)); Shaw's Form PH60 is appropriate.

[90] But not on other grounds.

[91] 1991 Act, s.113, as amended by the Competition and Service (Utilities) Act 1992, s.35(1). As to the Director's powers under s.30A, see *ante*, p.23.

[92] Note the limitation of the operation of the section.

[93] Not necessarily a public sewer; but even a private sewer must itself drain into a public sewer or a receptacle for drainage.

[94] *Not* the sewerage undertaker in this case.

[95] This must be in writing and duly served (see 1984 Act, ss.92 to 94).

(c) 1984 Act, sections 62 and 81: controls over disconnecting of drains

Where the use of a drain is being discontinued, the local authority may require it to be disconnected and sealed at such points as they may reasonably specify.[96] Disputes as to the reasonableness of such specifications may be determined by the Magistrates' Court.[97] In particular no person can be required to perform work on land in respect of which he has no right so to do.[98] Knowingly to fail to comply with a local authority requirement and failing to give a minimum of 48 hours' notice to the local authority before such compliance are offences punishable by a fine.[99]

The local authority may serve a notice[100] requiring persons engaged in the demolition of a building to disconnect and seal any sewer or drain in or under the building, at such points as it may reasonably require and/or to remove such a conduit and seal any connecting sewer or drain.[101] At least 48 hours' notice of compliance of such a requirement must be given[100] and default is an offence punishable by a fine. Work may not be required beyond the demolition site where the person engaged in the demolition lacks the appropriate rights. In event of non-compliance the local authority may perform the works and recover the expenses of doing so.[102] Where a local authority has power to serve a notice in case of demolition works under section 81, the disconnection powers under section 61 are inapplicable.[103]

UNSATISFACTORY DRAINS

The Public Health Acts 1936 and 1961, and the Building Act

---

[96] 1984 Act, s.62.
[97] *Ibid.,* s.62(2).
[98] *Ibid.,* s.62(3).
[99] *Ibid.,* s.62(4), (5).
[100] In writing and duly served, ss.92 to 94.
[101] 1984 Act, ss.81, 82(1)(e), (f).
[102] *Ibid.,* ss.82(6) and 99.
[103] See *Ibid.,* s.62(6).

1984 vest several distinct powers in local authorities which enable them to deal with drains or private sewers that are unsatisfactory in one respect or another. These powers overlap to some extent, but it seems that the authority has a discretion in selecting which procedure to follow. The most specific of these powers is section 60 of the Building Act 1984, dealing with the condition of certain pipes and appurtenances to drains. Section 59 deals with cases where satisfactory provision has not been made for the drainage of a building, and the nuisance clauses of the 1936 Act, which are not confined in their operation to buildings, provide a residuary control whereby nuisances in drains may be abated. There is also a summary power given by section 17 of the 1961 Act to remedy stopped up drains, which is of great use in practice. In addition, a local authority may act as contractor, on the application of the owner or occupier of premises, to cleanse or repair drains, water-closets, sinks or gullies.[104]

(a) Ventilation, etc. of drains

If it appears to the local authority that on any premises there is a contravention of any requirements contained in section 60 of the Building Act 1984, it may by notice[105] require the owner or the occupier of the premises to execute such work as may be necessary to remedy the matter; in default of compliance therewith, the local authority may do the work itself, and recover the expenses reasonably incurred[106] by it from the person in default.[107]

---

[104] 1961 Act, s.22.

[105] This notice must be in writing, signed by the authorised officer of the authority, and duly served (see 1984 Act, ss.92 to 94). Shaw's Form PH15 is appropriate.

[106] A reasonable sum by way of establishment expenses may be added to these: Local Government Act 1974, s.36.

[107] 1984 Act, s.60(4), (5). The expenses will be recoverable as a simple contract debt in the County Court or the High Court (1984 Act, s.107). If the owner of the premises is the party charged, it seems that the expenses will be a charge on the premises (1984 Act, ss.107(1) and 129) and should, therefore, be registered in the local land charges register. See also Chapter 11, *post,* p.240.

The requirements specified in the section are as follows:

(i) no pipe for conveying rain water from a roof shall be used for the purpose of conveying the soil or drainage from any sanitary convenience;

(ii) the soil pipe from every water-closet[108] shall be properly ventilated;

(iii) no pipe for conveying surface water[109] from any premises shall be permitted to act as a ventilating shaft to any drain or sewer carrying foul water.[110]

(b) Satisfactory provision for drainage

Section 59 of the 1984 Act is a more general section, enabling the local authority to require (*inter alia*) satisfactory provision to be made for the drainage of an existing building. The control is exercised in a manner similar to that applicable to section 60 of the Act, in that the authority must serve a notice,[111] and may then act itself in default of compliance, and recover its expenses in so acting from the party in default. Only the owner[112] of the premises may be required to make satisfactory provision for drainage, but either the owner or the occupier[113] may be required to take the other action referred to in section 60. It should also be noted that the section applies only to buildings,[114] and not to all types of premises.[115]

---

108 Defined in s.126, and see *post*, Chapter 10, pp.213-214.
109 This expression includes "water from roofs": 1984 Act, s.126.
110 This expression is not defined in the Act.
111 Shaw's Form PN23D is appropriate. In the case of a break in a private sewer rendering it prejudicial to health, the notice may be served only on the owners of premises above the break: *Swansea City Council v Jenkins* [1994] C.O.D. 398.
112 As defined by s.126 of the 1984 Act: Chapter 11, *post*, p.248.
113 The local authority has a discretion in selecting the appropriate party, but it must take into consideration the rights and duties as between the owner and the occupier, where appropriate: *Croydon Corporation v Thomas* [1947] K.B. 386.
114 See *ante*, p.182.
115 As defined by s.126 of the 1984 Act (which include buildings, lands, easements and hereditaments of any tenure).

Action may be taken by the local authority under the section whenever the authority considers that in the case of a building:

"(a) satisfactory provision[116] has not been, and ought to be, made for drainage as defined in section 21(2) above;[117]

(b) a cesspool,[118] private sewer, drain, soil pipe, rain water pipe, spout, sink or other necessary appliance provided for the building, is insufficient or, in the case of a private sewer or drain communicating directly or indirectly with a public sewer, is so defective as to admit subsoil water;

(c) a cesspool[118] or other such work or appliance as aforesaid provided for the building is in such a condition as to be prejudicial to health[119] or a nuisance;[120] or

(d) a cesspool,[118] private sewer or drain formerly used for the drainage of the building, but no longer used for it, is prejudicial to health[119] or a nuisance."[120]

Paragraphs (a) and (b) of this subsection cannot be invoked in respect of any building which belongs to a statutory undertaker[121] or the Civil Aviation Authority and which is held or used by them

---

[116] This expression is not expressly defined in the section, except that it is provided in s.59(3) that subsections (4), (5) and (6) of s.21 shall apply to the present section. If the drains are sufficient, the authority cannot use the present section to secure an improvement therein at the expense of the owner of the premises. If the sewerage undertaker decides to alter a private system of drainage, it may do so under s.113 of the 1991 Act, or if it wishes to alter its own sewerage system it may do so under s.116, *ibid.*, but in either case any consequential alterations to private drains or sewers will have to be executed at the expense of the undertaker: see *St. Martin's-in-the-Field Vestry v Ward* [1897] 1 Q.B. 40.

[117] The conveyance of rain water from roofs is included in this expression: *ante*, p.184, n.50.

[118] See definition in s.126 of the 1984 Act, and *post*, p.213.

[119] i.e. "injurious, or likely to cause injury, to health": 1984 Act, s.126.

[120] *Post*, p.199.

[121] See definition in s.126 of the 1984 Act: these include sewerage undertakers under the 1991 Act.

for purposes of their undertaking, other than houses,[122] or buildings used as offices or showrooms which do not form part of a railway station[123] or in the case of the Civil Aviation Authority not being on an aerodrome which it owns.[124]

(c) Power to repair and unblock drains

Section 17(1) of the Public Health Act 1961[125] provides that where it appears to a local authority that a drain or private sewer[126] is not sufficiently maintained and kept in good repair and can be sufficiently repaired at a cost not exceeding £250, the authority may, after giving not less than seven days' notice to the person or persons concerned, cause the drain or sewer to be repaired; the authority may thus take the remedial action itself, without having to follow the more dilatory procedure of section 59 of the Building Act 1984, under which it must first serve a notice and wait for the person on whom the notice is served to default. By section 17(3) the local authority may give notice[127] requiring the owner or occupier of premises whereon it seems that a drain or sewer is blocked up to remedy the situation within 48 hours. If the notice is not complied with, the local authority may carry out the remedial work. For valid service of such a notice it is sufficient that it appears to the local authority that a drain upon the premises is blocked, even if it later transpires that the blockage is not in fact on those premises.[128] In *Rotherham Borough Council v Dodds*[129] the Court of Appeal indicated that in such cases the court might properly use its power under what

---

[122] i.e. "dwelling-houses, whether private dwelling-houses or not": 1984 Act, s.126.

[123] It seems that a house which forms part of a railway station is outside this special exemption, and subject to the control afforded by the section.

[124] 1984 Act, s.59(4), as amended by s.83(9) and Sch. 6 of the Airports Act 1986.

[125] In this Part of the 1961 Act all the definitions of Part II of the 1936 Act apply: 1961 Act, s.1(1). Section 17 was substituted by the Local Government (Miscellaneous Provisions) Act 1982, s.27(1).

[126] Or water-closet, waste pipe or soil pipe.

[127] See Shaw's Form PN75.

[128] *Rotherham Borough Council v Dodds* [1986] 1 W.L.R. 1367.

[129] *Ibid.*

is now section 17(6) to relieve in whole or part any financial liability arising from remedial action. Where powers under section 17(1) are exercised, expenses of the authority incurred under the section are recoverable from the person concerned,[130] to a maximum of £250. Where powers under section 17(3) are exercised, expenses are recoverable from the person on whom the notice was served; these are not subject to the £250 limit. The expenses may be apportioned. If they are not in excess of £10, the authority may remit and not attempt to recover them. In proceedings for recovery of expenses, the court must inquire whether the drain or sewer was in fact not sufficiently maintained and kept in good repair; and if the court considers that the authority was not justified in so concluding, the authority will not be able to recover the expenses.

A notice under section 17(3) may be served only upon the owner or occupier of the premises at which the blockage occurs. Under section 35 of the Local Government (Miscellaneous Provisions) Act 1976,[131] the owner or occupier of premises *served* by a *private sewer* may by notice[132] be required to remove the blockage. Such work may be performed by the local authority in default which may then recover its reasonable expenses from the persons served by the sewer.[133]

(d) The nuisance clauses

A detailed discussion of the provisions of Part III of the Environmental Protection Act 1990 dealing with statutory nuisances (sections 79 to 82 inclusive) would be out of place in the present work,[134] but it should be appreciated that action may

---

[130] i.e. in relation to a water-closet, waste pipe or soil pipe, the owner or occupier of the premises on which it is situated, and, in relation to a drain or private sewer, any person owning any premises drained by means of it and also, in the case of a sewer, the owner of the sewer: s.17(2).

[131] As amended by s.102(2) and Sch. 7 of the Local Government Act 1985.

[132] See s.44 of the 1976 Act ("notice" means "notice in writing"). Shaw's Form ML30 is appropriate.

[133] s.35(2), (3). See Shaw's Form ML30A.

[134] See *Cross on Local Government Law* (8th edn., 1991), paras. 16.40–16.46.

be taken under these provisions in a proper case, to secure the abatement of a nuisance in a private sewer or drain, or a cesspool or any other appliance used in connection with a private drainage system. No action can, however, be taken under these provisions in respect of a public sewer or sewage works vested in the sewerage undertaker.[135]

Statutory nuisances may exist as a consequence of a variety of causes. Those of importance for present purposes include "premises[136] in such a state as to be prejudicial to health or a nuisance", and "any accumulation or deposit which is prejudicial to health or a nuisance".[137]

"Prejudicial to health" and "nuisance" are phrases that have been subject to much litigation. Only the former is defined in section 79(7) of the 1990 Act as meaning "injurious, or likely to cause injury, to health". If this can be established, it is not necessary to establish a nuisance as well.[138] It is now clear that "nuisance" in this context is to be given its ordinary common law meaning as either a *public* nuisance (to Her Majesty's subjects as such) or a *private* nuisance. The latter involves two properties: the defendant's, where the cause arises, and the plaintiff's, which suffers the nuisance, inconvenience, etc.; no statutory nuisance exists where premises are in such a state as to interfere only with the personal comfort of the occupiers.[138] Where a statutory nuisance exists by virtue of premises being prejudicial to health or a nuisance it is irrelevant that the premises are empty.[139]

Where a statutory nuisance is alleged to exist, and the authority is so satisfied, it is its duty to serve an abatement notice[140] on the

---

135   *R. v Parlby* (1889) 22 Q.B.D. 520, and *Fulham Vestry v London C.C.* [1897] 2 Q.B. 76.

136   This expression is defined by s.79(7) of the 1991 Act to include "land".

137   1990 Act, s.79(1)(a), (d) and (e).

138   *Betts v Penge U.D.C.* [1942] 2 K.B. 154, read with *National Coal Board v Thorne* [1976] 1 W.L.R. 543.

139   *Coventry City Council v Doyle* [1981] 1 W.L.R. 1325.

140   As to service of notices under the 1990 Act, see s.160. Shaw's Form EPA30 is appropriate.

"person responsible for the nuisance", which means the person "by whose act, default, or sufferance the nuisance is attributable".[141]

The notice may impose all or any of the following requirements:

"(a) requiring the abatement of the nuisance or prohibiting or restricting its occurrence or recurrence;

(b) requiring the execution of such works, and the taking of such other steps, as may be necessary for any of those purposes."

It must also specify the time or times within which the requirements of the notice are to be complied with.[142] Non-compliance without reasonable excuse is an offence;[143] whether or not it institutes a prosecution, the local authority may itself take action to abate the nuisance,[144] and recover expenses.[145] If the authority is of the opinion that a prosecution would afford an inadequate remedy, it may take proceedings in the High Court.[146] A person served with a notice may appeal to a Magistrates' Court.[147] Under section 82 of the 1990 Act, any "person aggrieved"[148] by the existence of a statutory nuisance may make a complaint to a Magistrates' Court, and a similar procedure and

---

[141] 1990 Act, ss.79(7), 80(2). If the nuisance arises from a defect of a structural character, the notice must instead be served on the owner of the premises (i.e. the premises which are prejudicial to health, even where the structural defect is on other premises: *Pollway Nominees v Havering London Borough Council* (1989) 21 H.L.R. 462, in respect of the Public Health Act 1936); if the person responsible cannot be found or the nuisance has not yet occurred, it must instead be served on the owner or occupier of the premises: *ibid.*

[142] 1990 Act, s.80(1).

[143] *Ibid.*, s.80(4)-(10).

[144] *Ibid.*, s.81(3).

[145] *Ibid.*, s.81(4).

[146] *Ibid.*, s.81(5), (6).

[147] *Ibid.*, s.80(3) and the Statutory Nuisance (Appeals) Regulations 1990 (S.I. 1990 No. 2278).

[148] See Chapter 11, *post*, pp.243-244. It has been held that the occupier of a single flat could not be a "person aggrieved" in relation to the whole block where the statutory nuisance of which he complained related only to his own flat: *Birmingham City Council v McMahon* (1987) 86 L.G.R. 63.

penalties apply as in the case of a local authority but without the prior need to serve an abatement notice or its equivalent.

It will be observed that this procedure is advantageous to the local authority, in that a decision as to the legality of the proceedings is obtained from the court before the authority has acted in default and expended money on a private individual's premises. On the other hand, where proceedings are taken under section 59 of the Building Act 1984, default action will have to be taken first, and the legality of the authority's proceedings will be tested normally only after money has been expended, and in proceedings taken to recover such moneys from the party charged. Action under section 59 will, however, normally be more expeditious than nuisance proceedings.

(e) Improper construction or repair

If a water-closet, drain or soil pipe is so constructed or repaired as to be prejudicial to health[149] or a nuisance,[150] the person who undertook or executed the construction or repair will be liable to prosecution for an offence, unless he can show the prejudice to health or nuisance could not have been avoided by the exercise of reasonable care.[151]

LOAN OF CONVENIENCES

In any case where work is being carried out at premises by a local authority or by the owner or occupier in pursuance of a requirement under section 59 of the 1984 Act,[152] the local authority may supply on loan any temporary sanitary conveniences required in substitution for any water-closet or other sanitary convenience disconnected as a consequence of the work.[153] Such a loan may be made only at the request of the

---

[149] See 1984 Act, s.126.
[150] *Ante*, p.199.
[151] 1984 Act, s.63.
[152] *Ante*, p.195.
[153] 1984 Act, s.67.

occupier of the premises; the request need not be made in writing. The conveniences may be used free of charge for the first seven days, but the authority is entitled to make a charge for supplying, removing and cleansing any conveniences lent for more than seven days. If the works are necessary because of some defect in a public sewer, no charge at all may be made under the section.

PRIVATE IMPROVEMENTS

Where improvements or repairs are required in respect of dwellings in multiple occupation or the common parts of buildings containing one or more flats, or for the provision of dwellings in multiple occupation or the provision of facilities for the disabled, grants towards the cost thereof may be payable under Part VIII of the Local Government and Housing Act 1989. A local housing authority must under section 112 of that Act approve renovation grants in cases where it determines (a) that the dwelling is unfit for human habitation, (b) that the works proposed will remedy the situation and (c) that their completion is the most satisfactory course of action.[154]

THE DRAINAGE OF TRADE PREMISES

The drainage of trade premises is regulated by Chapter III of Part IV of the Water Industry Act 1991, which applies in particular to the discharge of trade effluent into sewers.[155] There is a power, not as yet exercised, to apply Chapter III to other effluents.[156] It

---

[154] The amount of any grant will be determined by reference to s.116(2) of the Act by reference to the amount of the expenses properly incurred, in the view of the authority, in the execution of works eligible for grant.

[155] The discharge of trade effluent direct into "streams" is regulated by the Water Resources Act 1991, discussed *ante*, Chapter 8, pp.148-157. The discharge of such effluent direct into the sea is in part regulated by the 1991 Act, but at common law the person discharging any matter into the sea will be responsible for any nuisance thereby caused: *Hobart v Southend-on-Sea Corporation* (1906) 75 L.J.K.B. 305.

[156] 1991 Act, s.139.

is now the duty of every sewerage undertaker, the Director and the Secretary of State in exercising their functions under this Chapter with respect to any discharge of "industrial waste water"[157] to secure that the specified requirements[158] are met in respect of that discharge.[159] These requirements are that collecting systems and treatment plants for industrial waste water shall be subject to such pre-treatment as is required to protect the health of staff, ensure that the systems, plant and associated equipment are not damaged, ensure that the operation of the plant and the treatment of sludge are not impeded, that discharges do not effect the environment or prevent receiving waters from complying with other EC Directives and ensure that sludge can be disposed of safely in an environmentally acceptable manner. This duty is enforceable under section 18 of the 1991 Act.[160]

(a) Definitions

Trade effluent is defined in section 141(1) of the 1991 Act as meaning "any liquid, either with or without particles of matter in suspension in the liquid, which is wholly or in part produced in the course of any trade or industry carried on at trade premises" and, in relation to any trade premises, means "any such liquid which is so produced in the course of any trade or industry carried on at those premises" but does not include "domestic sewage". "Domestic sewage" is not defined under the 1991 Act, and it is presumably intended to be understood in much the same sense as water supplied for "domestic purposes" in the Waterworks Clauses Act 1847.[161] It seems that neither the character of the effluent nor the nature of the premises producing

---

[157] For the definition, see *ante*, p.34.

[158] S.I. 1994 No. 2841, Sch. 4.

[159] Urban Waste Water Treatment (England and Wales) Regulations 1994 (S.I. 1994 No. 2841), Reg. 7(1).

[160] 1991 Act, s.7(7).

[161] "If the purpose is one for which, according to the ordinary habits of domestic life, people require water in their houses, the purpose is a domestic purpose": *per* Atkinson J. in *Re Willesden Corporation and Municipal Mutual Insurance Ltd.'s Arbitration* [1944] 2 All E.R. 600, at p.602.

the effluent is decisive. The purpose of the activity producing the effluent would be more significant.[162]

To understand the expression "trade effluent" it is also necessary to appreciate the definition of "trade premises". By the same section of the 1991 Act it is provided that "'trade premises' means . . . any premises used or intended to be used for carrying on any trade or industry", but it does not define "trade" or "industry", and these words must therefore be given their ordinary dictionary meanings. However, any land or premises used or intended for use (in whole or part and whether or not for profit) for agricultural or horticultural purposes or for fish farming, or for scientific research or experiment, are deemed to be premises used for trade or industry.

(b) The discharge of trade effluent

Section 118 of the 1991 Act provides that the occupier of any trade premises may discharge into the sewerage undertaker's public sewers any trade effluent proceeding from those premises, with the sewerage undertaker's consent, which may be "deemed" or express. If, in the case of trade premises, any trade effluent is discharged without such consent or an authorisation derived from an agreement under section 129 of the 1991 Act,[163] the occupier of the premises is guilty of an offence.[164]

(i) "Deemed consent"
Trade effluent may not now be discharged without consent, even if the discharge is made pursuant to an agreement made prior to, and still subsisting, at the time of the passing of the Public Health (Drainage of Trade Premises) Act 1937. The exemptions formerly

---

[162] See *Thames Water Authority v Blue and White Laundrettes Ltd.* [1980] 1 W.L.R. 700.

[163] See *post*, p.211.

[164] 1991 Act, s.118(5). Compliance with consents in respect of industrial discharges is less satisfactory than for discharges from sewerage undertakers' sewage works; between 1990 and 1992, only about two-thirds of industrial discharges fully complied: see NRA, *Discharge Consents and Compliance: the NRA's Approach to Control of Discharges to Water* (H.M.S.O., 1994), pp.52-53.

provided for by section 4 of the 1937 Act were all withdrawn as a result of repeals of section 4(4) by the Water Act 1973[165] and of section 4(1), (2) and (3) by section 43 of the Control of Pollution Act 1974. Agreements previously safeguarded by section 7(4) of the 1937 Act were not thereafter exempt from the need to obtain consent to a discharge. However, in cases formerly covered by such exemptions, the owner of premises concerned could obtain a "deemed consent" by serving a notice on the water authority under section 43(2) of the 1974 Act; but this deemed consent may then be cancelled and an actual consent may be substituted therefor.[166]

(ii) Discharge with express consent

Normally the consent of the sewerage undertaker must be obtained under the 1991 Act to the discharge of trade effluent from trade premises into public sewers. The application must be by notice[167] served on the undertaker by the owner or occupier of the premises, stating the nature or composition of the trade effluent; the maximum quantity it is proposed to discharge in any one day; and the highest rate at which it is proposed to discharge the trade effluent.[168]

The undertaker may either give consent unconditionally, or subject to such conditions as it may think fit with respect to any of the following matters:

(a) the sewer or sewers (or any altered drain or sewer[169]) into which the effluent may be discharged, the nature and composition of the effluent, the maximum quantity that may

---

[165] Sch. 8, para. 44.

[166] 1991 Act, s.140 and Sch. 8, and see the Control of Pollution (Discharges into Sewers) Regulations 1976 (S.I. 1976 No. 958), as modified by the Water Act 1989, Sch. 8, paras. 1, 5(1), (2). "Deemed consents" having effect under the Water Act 1989 in relation to any sewerage undertaker have effect as a "deemed consent" for the purposes of Chapter III of Part IV of the 1991 Act: Sch. 8, para. 2(1). "Actual consents" under Sch. 8 are treated similarly to express consents (see *post*).

[167] In writing: s.219(1) (definition of "notice").

[168] 1991 Act, s.119.

[169] *Ibid.,* s.113(6), subject to regulations.

be discharged on any one day, and the highest permissible rate of discharge.[170]

Conditions may also be attached with respect to

(b) the period or periods of the day during which the trade effluent may be discharged from the trade premises into the sewer;

(c) the exclusion from the trade effluent of all condensing water;

(d) the elimination or diminution of any specified constituent of the trade effluent, before it enters the sewer, where the sewerage undertaker is satisfied that the constituent would, either alone or in combination with any other matter with which it is likely to come into contact while passing through any sewers:

(i) injure or obstruct those sewers, or make specially difficult or expensive the treatment or disposal of the sewage from those sewers, or

(ii) (where the trade effluent is to be, or is, discharged into a sewer having an outfall into any harbour or tidal water or into a sewer which connects directly or indirectly with a sewer or sewage disposal works having such an outfall) cause or tend to cause injury or obstruction to the navigation on, or the use of, the said harbour or tidal water;

(e) the temperature of the trade effluent at the time when it is discharged into the sewer, and acidity or alkalinity at that time;

(f) the payment by the occupier of the trade premises to the sewerage undertaker of charges for the reception of the trade effluent into the sewer, and for the disposal thereof, regard being had to the nature and composition and to the volume

---

[170] 1991 Act, s.121(1).

and rate of discharge of the trade effluent so discharged, to any additional expense incurred or likely to be incurred by a sewerage undertaker in connection with the reception or disposal of the trade effluent, and to any revenue likely to be derived by a sewerage authority from the trade effluent;

(g) the provision and maintenance of such an inspection chamber or manhole as will enable a person readily to take at any time samples of what is passing into the sewer from the trade premises;

(h) the provision, testing and maintenance of such meters as may be required to measure the volume and rate of discharge of any trade effluent being discharged from the trade premises into the sewer;

(i) the provision, testing and maintenance of apparatus for determining the nature and composition of any trade effluent being discharged from the premises into the sewer;

(j) the keeping of records of the volume, rate of discharge, nature and composition of any trade effluent being discharged, including the keeping of records of readings of meters and other recording apparatus provided in compliance with a consent condition;

(k) the making of returns and giving of other information to the sewerage undertaker concerning the volume, etc. of trade effluent discharged.[171]

These powers, it will be noted, are wide but conditions may not be imposed outside these provisions. However, nothing in the powers to impose conditions is to be construed as restricting the power of a sewerage undertaker to impose such conditions as are necessary to comply with its duty under the Urban Waste Water Treatment (England and Wales) Regulations 1994.[172]

---

[171] 1991 Act, s.121(2).
[172] S.I. 1994 No. 2841, Reg. 7(2). See *ante*, p.203.

As mentioned above, a discharge without consent or a contravention of a condition is an offence.[173] If a consent is granted on the basis of permitting the discharge of specifically named substances, the discharge of substances not named, other than in a background concentration, constitutes the offence.[174]

An appeal against a refusal of consent lies to the Director General of Water Services, who has wide powers to refuse or grant consent subject to such conditions as he thinks fit.[175]

The sewerage undertaker may give a direction varying the conditions of a consent.[176] This may not be done within two years of the date of the consent or a previous direction without the agreement of the owner and occupier of the trade premises in question;[177] however, a variation may be made within the time limit if the undertaker considers it necessary to do so to provide proper protection for persons likely to be affected by the relevant discharges.[178] In the latter event, compensation is payable unless the undertaker is of the opinion that there has been an unforeseeable change of circumstances since the two-year period in question and otherwise than in consequence of consent given after the beginning of that period.[179] The Secretary of State may make regulations as to the payment of compensation.[180] The owner or occupier may appeal against the direction to the

---

[173] 1991 Act, ss.118(5), 121(5).

[174] Ruling of Judge Crowther Q.C. in *R. v Rechem International Ltd.* (Newport Crown Court, 10th September 1993), discussed in S. Tromans and M. Grant, *Encyclopedia of Environmental Law*, para. D23-094/1.

[175] 1991 Act, s.122. The Director may state a case for the High Court: s.137. See OFWAT Information Note No. 21, *Trade Effluent Appeals*, May 1993.

[176] 1991 Act, s.124(1), (7). Notice must be given of the direction which must include information as to rights of appeal and state the date the decision is to take effect: s.124(5), (6).

[177] *Ibid.,* s.124(2).

[178] *Ibid.,* s.125(1).

[179] *Ibid.,* s.125(2). "Circumstances" includes the information available as to the discharges to which the consent in question relates or as to the interaction of those discharges with other discharges or matter: s.125(4). The undertaker must give reasons for its opinion: s.125(3).

[180] *Ibid.,* s.125(5).

Director,[181] who may annul the direction and substitute another which is more or less favourable to the appellant. An appeal also lies to the Director on the ground that compensation should be paid in consequence of the direction.[182]

Nothing shall, however, restrict the power of a sewerage undertaker or the Secretary of State to vary a consent in pursuance of the duty under Regulation 7 of the Urban Waste Water Treatment (England and Wales) Regulations 1994,[183] or render it or him liable to pay compensation.[184]

Consents must be reviewed and if necessary modified at regular intervals.[185]

(c) Special control of trade effluent functions

Special arrangements apply to trade effluents in which there are prescribed substances or prescribed concentrations thereof which derive from a prescribed process or one involving the use of substances in quantity exceeding prescribed amounts ("special category effluent"[186]). These arrangements implement both the government's own policy of seeking to minimise inputs to water of certain of the most dangerous substances, identified in the "Red List" published in 1988,[187] and the framework EC Directive on Pollution Caused by Certain Dangerous Substances Discharged into the Aquatic Environment of the Community[188] and daughter directives. The relevant regulations are the Trade Effluents (Prescribed Processes and Substances) Regulations

---

[181] 1991 Act, s.126(1)-(4). The Director on an appeal under s.126(1) may state a case for the opinion of the High Court: s.137.

[182] *Ibid.*, s.126(5), (6).

[183] S.I. 1994 No. 2841. See *ante*, p.203.

[184] *Ibid.*, Reg. 7(6).

[185] *Ibid.*, Reg. 7(4).

[186] Defined in s.138 of the 1991 Act.

[187] *Inputs of Dangerous Substances to Water: Proposals for a Unified System of Control – The Government's Consultative Proposals for Tighter Controls over the Most Dangerous Substances Entering the Aquatic Environment* (DoE, 1988).

[188] Dir. 76/464/EEC.

1989[189] and 1992.[190]

Under these provisions it is the duty of a sewerage undertaker to refer an application for consent with respect to discharges of any special category effluent to the Secretary of State for determination of the issue of whether the proposed discharge should be prohibited or made subject to conditions.[191] Such a reference must be made within two months of the day after service of the notice[192] and the references must be in writing.[193] A copy of a reference made under the section must be served upon the applicant by the undertaker.[194] Similar references must be made by the Director General of Water Services where, upon an appeal under section 122 of the 1991 Act, relevant matters appear to him to arise.[195] In any such case the period of two months for the purposes of section 122(2) will not begin to run until the beginning of the day after notice of the Secretary of State's determination upon the matter is served upon the sewerage undertaker.[196] Existing consents to the discharge of special

---

[189] S.I. 1989 No. 1156, as amended by S.I. 1990 No. 1629, listing 24 prescribed substances (List I substances under the Directive) and 5 prescribed processes, mostly involving asbestos or chloroform. The provisions as to prescribed substances apply when they are present in trade effluent in a concentration greater than the "background concentration". This term means such concentration as would, but for anything done on the premises in question, be present in the effluent discharged from those premises, and this includes such concentrations as are present in water supplied to or abstracted for use in the premises, and in precipitation onto the site within which the premises are situated: S.I. 1989 No. 1156, Reg. 2.

[190] S.I. 1992 No. 339, prescribing further processes.

[191] 1991 Act, s.120(1). No reference need be made if the undertaker refuses consent within two months: s.120(3). References are in practice dealt with by H.M. Inspectorate of Pollution and responsibility is to be transferred to the new Environment Agency by the Environment Act 1995, Sch. 22, para. 105, amending the 1991 Act, s.120. The Agency is to have power to require information to be supplied for the purpose of the discharge of its functions in relation to special category effluent: 1991 Act, s.135A, inserted by the 1995 Act, Sch. 22, para. 113.

[192] *Ibid.*, s.120(2).

[193] *Ibid.*, s.120(5).

[194] *Ibid.*, s.120(6).

[195] *Ibid.*, s.123(2), (3).

[196] *Ibid.*, s.123(1).

category effluent are also subject to review by the Secretary of State.[197] The detailed mechanisms of review are set out in sections 132 and 133 of the 1991 Act.[198]

The duties of a sewerage undertaker under section 120 are enforceable under section 18 of the 1991 Act.[199] Rights of entry are conferred by section 132(7).[200]

Trade effluent is not, however, "special category effluent" if it is produced, or to be produced, in any process which is a prescribed process designated for central control under Part I of the Environmental Protection Act 1990,[201] as from the "determination date" for that process.[202] These processes are regulated by H.M. Inspectorate of Pollution under the system of Integrated Pollution Control, and this provision avoids duplication of the control regimes.

(d) Agreements under the 1991 Act

In addition to the provisions above discussed, the Act of 1991 enables sewerage undertakers to enter into agreements with the owner or the occupier of trade premises for the reception and disposal of any trade effluent produced on those premises.[203] Such an agreement may authorise such a discharge as, apart from

---

[197] 1991 Act, s.127. This responsibility is also to be transferred to the Environment Agency by the Environment Act 1995, Sch. 22, para. 107, amending s.127.

[198] Compensation may be payable by the Secretary of State in respect of determinations made for the protection of public health or of flora and fauna dependent on an aquatic environment: s.134.

[199] 1991 Act, s.120(7). By virtue of the Environment Act 1995, Sch. 22, para. 105(4), non-compliance with these duties is to become an offence.

[200] i.e. the same powers as are conferred on a sewerage undertaker under s.171 of the 1991 Act.

[201] 1991 Act, s.138(2). See the Environmental Protection (Prescribed Processes and Substances) Regulations 1991 (S.I. 1991 No. 472), as amended; *ante*, p.163.

[202] i.e. the date on which authorisation is granted or refused by HMIP or, in the case of an appeal against refusal, the refusal is affirmed: 1991 Act, s.138(3).

[203] See s.129 of the 1991 Act (formerly s.7 of the Public Health (Drainage of Trade Premises) Act 1937). For a precedent for such an agreement, see (1961) 25 Conv. N.S. 38 and 662.

the agreement, would require a consent under Chapter III.[204] If the agreement is to relate to special category effluents, it must be referred to the Secretary of State; and existing agreements involving such effluents are subject to review.[205] Nothing in any agreement between an undertaker (or its predecessor) and an owner or occupier of trade premises is to be treated as a consent or authorisation unless the terms are such as will secure compliance with the requirements of Schedule 4 to the Urban Waste Water Treatment (England and Wales) Regulations 1994.[206] Authorisations given by virtue of these agreements must be reviewed and if necessary modified at regular intervals.[207] An undertaker may vary any Section 129 agreement which provides for the discharge of industrial waste water to an urban waste water treatment plant without first entering a public sewer, and any such agreement is not enforceable to the extent that it permits the discharge of industrial waste water where the requirements of Schedule 4 are not met.[208]

(e) Other matters

A section is included enabling the undertaker to obtain certain information,[209] and to take samples of trade effluents.[210] The 1991 Act provides that "nothing in this Chapter shall affect any right with respect to water in a river stream or watercourse, or authorise any infringement of such a right . . ."[211]

---

[204] See ss.118(5) and 129(3) of the 1991 Act. Such agreements "authorise" the discharge without technically constituting a "consent" under Chapter III: see Recommendation No. 2 of the Law Commission's *Report on the Consolidation of Legislation Relating to Water* (Cm. 1483, April 1991).

[205] 1991 Act, ss.130, 131. See ss.132, 133 as to the procedure for review. Under the Environment Act 1995, Sch. 22, paras. 108-111, references are to be to the Environment Agency.

[206] S.I. 1994 No. 2841, Reg. 7(3). As to Sch. 4, see *ante*, p.203.

[207] *Ibid.,* Reg. 7(4).

[208] *Ibid.,* Reg. 7(5).

[209] 1991 Act, s.204.

[210] *Ibid.*, s.121(3)-(6).

[211] *Ibid.*, s.141(4), referring to Chapter III.

Chapter 10

SANITARY CONVENIENCES

INTRODUCTORY

Statutory provisions regulating the installation, maintenance, etc. of sanitary conveniences are to be found in several Acts of Parliament, of which the most important is the Act of 1936, while certain specific classes of buildings are affected in this respect by other statutes. These provisions are enforceable by the local authority, not the sewerage undertaker. In the first place, it is important to appreciate the specialised meanings of particular words, as used by Parliament in both the 1936 Act and the 1984 Act. These definitions apply, to the most part, only for the purposes of Part II of the 1936 Act whereas they apply generally to the 1984 Act.[1]

By section 90(1) of the 1936 Act and section 126 of the 1984 Act, the words listed below have the meanings respectively assigned to them:

"'cesspool' includes a settlement tank or other tank for the reception or disposal of foul matter from buildings;

'closet' includes privy;

'earth-closet' means a closet having a moveable receptacle[2] for the reception of faecal matter and its deodorisation by the use of earth, ashes or chemicals,[3] or by other methods;

'sanitary conveniences' means closets and urinals;

'water-closet' means a closet which has a separate fixed receptacle connected to a drainage system and separate

---

[1]   The Building Act provisions derive from the 1936 Act.
[2]   An earth-closet having a fixed receptacle will, therefore, be a mere privy for the purposes of the statute.
[3]   The usual type of chemical closet is therefore an "earth-closet".

provision for flushing from a supply of clean water[4] either by the operation of mechanism or by automatic action."

The question sometimes arises in practice whether "closet" in these definitions is intended to refer only to the sanitary apparatus itself, or whether it includes the room, shed or outhouse in which the apparatus is housed. This is a question to be determined according to the context in which the term is used; thus, in the phrase "sufficient closet accommodation",[5] a reference to the apparatus alone is presumably intended, but in the reference to closets which are "prejudicial to health or a nuisance",[6] it seems that the shed, etc. in which the apparatus is housed is to be included in the term "closet".[7]

In several places in the pages which follow, we shall have occasion to refer to a requirement of the Acts of 1936 and 1984 to the effect that a building must have a sewer "available". Section 125(2) of the 1984 Act provides that there shall not be deemed to be a sewer available, *unless*:

"(i) there is within 100 feet of the site[8] of the building or proposed building, and at a level that makes it reasonably practicable to construct a drain or communicate with it, a public sewer or other sewer that the owner of the building or proposed building is, or will be, entitled to use, *and*

(ii) the intervening land is land through which he is entitled to construct a drain."

Subsection (3) provides that: "The limit of 100 feet does not

---

4　A slop closet is thus not a "water-closet".

5　See 1984 Act, s.64(1)(a)(b).

6　See 1984 Act, s.64(1)(c) and 1936 Act, s.45(1).

7　It is submitted that the primary meaning of "closet", which is not displaced by any of the statutory definitions set out above, is that of a small room or retiring chamber, and that the word should be used or understood in the more specialised sense as referring to the sanitary apparatus only where the context clearly shows that such was the intention of the legislature.

8　See Chapter 9, *ante*, p.185.

apply, for the purposes of subsection (2) above, if the local authority undertakes to bear so much of the expenses reasonably incurred in –

(a) constructing, and maintaining and repairing, a drain to communicate with a sewer, or

(b) laying, and maintaining and repairing, a pipe for the purpose of obtaining a supply of water,

as the case may be, as is attributable to the fact that the distance of the sewer, or of the point from which a supply of water can be laid on, exceeds 100 feet."

SANITARY ACCOMMODATION FOR NEW BUILDINGS

The local authority's powers to ensure that sufficient and satisfactory closet accommodation is to be provided for a new building[9] are, by virtue of section 26 of the 1984 Act, made dependent on Building Regulations 1991.[10] When plans for a building[11] or an extension of a building are deposited under the Regulations, the local authority *must* reject the plans, unless:

(a) the plans show that "sufficient and satisfactory" closet accommodation consisting of one or more water-closets or earth-closets, as the authority may approve, will be provided, or

(b) the authority is satisfied that in the case of the particular building or extension it may properly dispense with the provision of closet accommodation.

The authority may not reject the plans on the ground that the proposed accommodation consists of or includes an earth-closet or earth-closets unless a sufficient water supply and sewer are available.

---

[9] Note that the section is not confined in its operation to houses.
[10] For a discussion of the extent of this control, see Chapter 5, *ante*, p.119.
[11] See discussion of this term, *ante*, pp.119-120.

The authority must also reject the plans if they show that the proposed building or, as the case may be, extension is likely to be used as a factory or workplace[12] in which persons of both sexes will be employed or will be in attendance,[13] unless:

(i) the plans show that sufficient and satisfactory separate closet accommodation for persons of each sex will be provided; or

(ii) the authority is satisfied that in the circumstances of the particular case it may properly dispense with the provision of such separate accommodation.

An appeal lies, on the application of the person depositing the plans, to the local Magistrates' Court against a decision of the local authority under this section, on any of the following (but no other[14]) questions:

(i) whether the provision of closet accommodation may properly be dispensed with;

(ii) whether the closet accommodation proposed is sufficient and satisfactory; or

(iii) whether the provision of an earth-closet should, in a particular instance, be approved in lieu of a water-closet.

The words "sufficient and satisfactory" are not defined for the purposes of this section, and the question seems to be mainly one of fact. Under a predecessor of the present section, it was held that the provision of a separate closet or privy for every house could not be insisted upon[15] but, at the present day, it is doubtful whether a court would quash a requirement of the local authority under this section for every house to be provided with separate accommodation; on the other hand, the authority could certainly

---

[12] "Factory" is to be defined as used in the Factories Act 1961 (*post*, p.223); "workplace" is defined in s.126 of the 1984 Act, *post*, p.221.

[13] For an example of circumstances in which persons may be "in attendance", but not employed at a place, see *Bennett v Harding* [1900] 2 Q.B. 397.

[14] See 1984 Act, s.26(3).

[15] *Clutton Union v Ponting* (1879) 4 Q.B.D. 340.

not require separate accommodation to be provided for every type of building to which the section applies.[16]

Each case under the section must be considered on its merits, and not in accordance with preconceived general principles for which there is no express statutory justification,[17] and it seems that the local authority cannot require any particular type of sanitary accommodation to be provided, where that proposed is both sufficient and satisfactory.[18]

SANITARY ACCOMMODATION FOR EXISTING BUILDINGS

(a) Buildings other than special[19] buildings

(i) Section 64 of the 1984 Act
Under this section, if it appears to the local authority:

"(a) that a building[20] is without sufficient[21] closet accommodation; or

(b) that a part of a building,[20] being a part that is occupied as a separate dwelling,[22] is without sufficient[21] closet accommodation; or

(c) that any closets provided for or in connection with a building are in such a state as to be prejudicial to health[23] or a nuisance[24] and cannot without reconstruction be put into a satisfactory condition,"

---

16 Such as e.g. a lock-up shop or office in close proximity to public conveniences.
17 *Wood v Widnes Corporation* [1898] 1 Q.B. 463.
18 *Robinson v Sunderland Corporation* (1898) 78 L.T. 19, but compare *Carlton Main Colliery v Hemsworth R.D.C.* [1922] 2 Ch. 609.
19 See para. (b), below, as to the sense in which the term "special buildings" is here used, as referring to shops, factories, workshops and workplaces, etc.
20 Other than a factory, workplace or shop: s.64(6).
21 This term is not defined.
22 It would seem that "separate" in this context means distinct as a dwelling, not necessarily separated physically or partitioned off; see further *Woodfall on Landlord and Tenant* (looseleaf edition, 1994), para. 23.014 *et seq.*
23 i.e. "injurious, or likely to cause injury, to health": 1936 Act, s.343(1).
24 As to the significance of this expression, see *ante*, p.199.

the authority is under a duty to serve a notice[25] on the owner of the building requiring him to provide such closets, additional closets or substituted closets as may be necessary, the closets in any such case to be either earth-closets or water-closets. In the special case of a building consisting of several dwellings, the owner of the building may appeal to a court on the ground that he has a cause of action in respect of the occupation of part of the building as a separate dwelling and that the need for the works to be executed would not arise but for that occupation.[26]

The local authority cannot, under this section, require the abolition of a privy, unless it is either insufficient, prejudicial to health or a nuisance, etc., and a water-closet cannot be required to be provided (except in substitution for an existing water-closet), unless a sufficient water supply and sewer are available.[27] It also seems that the authority cannot require a particular type of water-closet (or earth-closet) to be provided, if that proposed falls within the statutory definition.[28]

It will also be noted that this section can only be used in respect of nuisances, where the closet in question cannot be rendered satisfactory without reconstruction; if the closet[29] is capable of repair, the powers of section 45 of the 1936 Act (discussed below) should be used. It may be important, therefore, in a particular case to decide whether a closet is or is not capable of repair. Unfortunately, there is no rule of thumb or standard to be applied in answering such a question. In the law of landlord and tenant, repair has been said to include the replacement of parts, but not the renewal of the whole. At the same time new work

---

[25] The notice must be in writing, signed by the authorised officer of the authority, and duly served (see ss.92 to 94 of the 1984 Act and *Epping Forest District Council v Essex Rendering* [1983] 1 W.L.R. 158 in which it was held by the House of Lords that the requirement of writing is mandatory). Shaw's Form PH67 is appropriate.

[26] 1984 Act, s.64(4).

[27] See definition of this expression in s.125(2) of the 1984 Act.

[28] See *Robinson v Sunderland Corporation*, p.217, *supra*.

[29] The term here probably includes the shed, etc. in which the sanitary apparatus is housed: see *ante*, p.214.

which is an exact replacement of the old is none the less capable of being "reconstruction", as distinct from repair.[30]

This sub-section also deals with the case of houses occupied as two or more dwellings; in a case where a building is in "multiple occupation" it may be found necessary to use the powers of Part XI of the Housing Act 1985 in order that existing conveniences, etc. may be required to be maintained in a proper condition.[31]

If the notice of the authority is not complied with, the authority may itself execute the work required, and recover its reasonable expenses[32] thereby incurred from the owner of the premises.[33]

(ii) Repair of defective closets
It is provided by section 45 of the 1936 Act that, if it appears to the local authority that any closets provided for or in connection with a building[34] are in such a state as to be prejudicial to health or a nuisance,[35] but they can without reconstruction[36] be put into a satisfactory condition, the authority must[37] serve a notice[38] on the owner or the occupier[39] of the building, requiring him to take such steps[40] or execute such works as may be necessary.

---

[30] See e.g. *Agar v Noakes* (1905) 93 L.T. 605, a case on the meaning of "reconstruction", as used in a local authority's building byelaws.

[31] And see the Housing (Management of Houses in Multiple Occupation) Regulations 1990 (S.I. 1990 No. 830).

[32] A reasonable sum by way of establishment expenses may be included in this sum: Local Goverriment Act 1974, s.36.

[33] 1984 Act, ss.64(3), 99 and 107.

[34] Other than a shop, factory, workshop, or workplace: s.45(4).

[35] See p.199, *supra*.

[36] See the discussion of this expression in para. (i), *supra*.

[37] The authority is under a duty to take such action.

[38] The notice must be in writing, signed by the authorised officer of the authority, and duly served (see ss.283 to 285 of the 1936 Act and *Epping Forest District Council v Essex Rendering* [1983] 1 W.L.R. 158 in which the House of Lords held the requirement of writing to be mandatory). Shaw's From PN20 is appropriate.

[39] The authority must select the person responsible as between the owner and the occupier: see *Croydon Corporation v Thomas* [1947] K.B. 386, decided under s.75 (dustbins).

[40] "By cleansing the closets or otherwise". Presumably "otherwise" must here be construed as being *ejusdem generis* with "cleansing".

In so far as the notice requires work to be executed, in any case of default in compliance therewith, the authority may itself execute the work required and recover its reasonable expenses[41] thereby incurred, from the person in default.[42] In so far as the notice requires steps other than the execution of works to be undertaken, any person required to take such steps is liable to a fine in the event of non-compliance with the terms of the notice.[43]

(b) Special buildings

(i) Houses

The extent to which a particular house may be defective in the matter of sanitary conveniences is a matter to be taken into consideration when deciding whether or not the house is unfit for human habitation for any of the several purposes of the Housing Act 1985.[44] A special application of this principle is also found in the case of houses in "multiple occupation":[45] *ibid.*[46]

---

[41] See note 32 above.

[42] 1936 Act, ss.45(2), and 290, and *post*, Chapter 11, p.238.

[43] *Ibid.*, s.45(3). In any such proceedings the defendant is entitled to question the reasonableness of the requirements of the local authority, or its decision to serve the notice on him and not the owner, or the occupier (as the case may be).

[44] 1985 Act, s.604, as substituted by the Local Government and Housing Act 1989, Sch. 9, Part V, para. 83. Requirement (g) is that the house "has a suitably located water-closet for the exclusive use of the occupants (if any)".

[45] i.e. a house which is occupied by persons who do not form a single household: 1985 Act, s.345, as amended by the Local Government and Housing Act 1989, Sch. 9, Part III, para. 46. For the purposes of this section the term "house" includes any part of a building which would not otherwise be regarded as a house and was originally constructed or subsequently adapted for occupation by a single household: *ibid.*

[46] Section 352, as amended by the Local Government and Housing Act 1989, Sch. 9, Part III, paras. 49, 50. Requirement (b) specified in s.352(1A) is that the house "has an adequate number of suitably located water-closets for the exclusive use of the occupants". Sections 604 and 352 provide power to require works to be carried out to render the premises fit for habitation, or the number of occupants, respectively. For the purposes of s.604, DoE Circular 6/90 contains advice on the application of the requirements which form the fitness standard: see Annex A, para. 11. Similarly, DoE Circular 12/86, Memorandum para. 3.4.2. offers the minimum shared housing standard of, *inter alia*, one water-closet for every five residents as guidance for the purpose of the s.352 power.

(ii) Workplaces

By section 65 of the 1984 Act, every building used as a "workplace"[47] must be provided with sufficient and satisfactory accommodation in the way of sanitary conveniences,[48] and provision must also be made (where necessary) for persons of each sex.[49] In the event of the local authority being satisfied that this requirement is not being complied with in respect to a particular building, it must by notice[50] require the owner or the occupier of the building "to make such alterations in the existing conveniences, and to provide such additional conveniences, as may be necessary".

If the notice of the authority is not complied with, the authority may itself execute the work required, and recover its reasonable expenses[51] thereby incurred from the person in default.[52]

Provision as to sanitary accommodation in workplaces[53] is also contained in the Workplace (Health, Safety and Welfare) Regulations 1992,[54] which implement the EC Workplace Directive[55] and aspects of the EC Temporary Workers Directive.[56]

---

47 This expression is defined in s.126 of the 1984 Act. It "does not include a factory but otherwise it includes any place in which persons are employed otherwise than in domestic service". It will be noticed that the present section applies only to such workplaces as are buildings (and not being shops: s.65(4)), and that the reference to factories and workshops in the original section was deleted by the Factories Act 1937, but see now s.175 of the Factories Act 1961. In *Bennet v Harding* [1900] 2 Q.B. 397, a stable yard for London cabbies was held to be a workplace within the meaning of the predecessor of the present section.

48 This term includes urinals: see definition, *ante*, p.213.

49 Regard must be had to the number of persons employed in, or in attendance at, the building.

50 The notice must be in writing, signed by the authorised officer of the authority and duly served (see ss.92 to 94 of the 1984 Act, and *Epping Forest District Council v Essex Rendering* [1983] 1 W.L.R. 158 in which the House of Lords decided that the requirement as to writing is mandatory). Shaw's Form PH46 is appropriate.

51 See *post*, p.238.

52 See 1984 Act, ss.65(3), 99 and 107, and *post*, Chapter 11, p.238.

53 Not just workplaces in buildings.

54 S.I. 1992 No. 3004.

55 89/654/EEC.

56 91/383/EEC.

These regulations come fully into effect on 1st January 1996. However, as from 1st January 1993, they apply to all new workplaces,[57] and on the completion of the modification, extension or conversion of an existing workplace.

The term "workplace" means

"any premises or part of premises which are not domestic premises and are made available to any person as a place of work, and includes

(a) any place within the premises to which such person has access while at work; and

(b) any room, lobby, corridor, staircase, road or other place used as a means of access to or egress from that place of work or where facilities are provided for use in connection with the place of work other than a public road."

However, it does not include a modification, extension or conversion of any of the above until completed.[58] The regulations apply to every workplace except (*inter alia*) those in or on a ship, or where the only activities being undertaken are building operations or works of engineering construction[59] or for the exploration for or extraction of mineral resources.[60] Every employer must ensure that every workplace, modification, extension or conversion which is under his control and where any of his employees works complies with the regulations.[61] Furthermore, every person who has, to any extent, control of a workplace, etc. in connection with the carrying on by him of a trade, business or other undertaking (whether for profit or not) must ensure that it complies with any requirement which relates

---

[57] i.e. a "workplace used for the first time as a workplace after December 31st, 1992": S.I. 1992 No. 3004, Reg. 2(1).

[58] S.I. 1992 No. 3004, Reg. 2(1).

[59] Within the Factories Act 1961, s.176.

[60] S.I. 1992 No. 3004, Reg. 3

[61] *Ibid.*, Reg. 4(1).

to matters within his control.[62] Finally, every person who is deemed to be the occupier of a factory by virtue of section 175(5) of the Factories Act 1961 must ensure that the premises comply with the regulations.[63]

The regulations cover a series of matters, including ventilation, temperature, lighting and cleanliness. Specific provision is made by Regulation 20 for sanitary conveniences.[64] Thus "suitable and sufficient" sanitary conveniences shall be "provided at readily accessible places". Without prejudice to the generality of this provision, conveniences are not suitable unless:

"(a) the rooms containing them are adequately ventilated and lit;

(b) they and the rooms containing them are kept in a clean and orderly condition; and

(c) separate rooms containing conveniences are provided for men and women except where and so far as each convenience is in a separate room the door of which is capable of being secured from inside."

As regards a workplace which is not a new or modified, etc. workplace, there is sufficient compliance if it was subject to the provisions of the Factories Act 1961 and now complies with Part II of Schedule I to the Regulations. This provides that in workplaces where females work, there shall be at least one water closet for use by females only for every 25 females, and an analogous requirement for males.[65]

---

[62] S.I. 1992 No. 3004, Reg. 4(2), (3). This is not to impose any requirement upon a self-employed person in respect of his or a partner's work: Reg. 4(4).

[63] *Ibid.,* Reg. 4(5). s.175 sets out an extended definition of "factory"; in general, a "factory" means premises where persons are employed in manual labour.

[64] Reg. 20 does not apply to aircraft, locomotives, or rolling stock or vehicles, and only applies so far as is reasonably practicable to temporary work sites and to land forming part of an agricultural undertaking away from the undertaking's main buildings: Reg. 3(2)-(4).

[65] In calculating the numbers, any number not divisible by 25 without fraction or remainder shall be treated as the next number higher that is a multiple of 25.

These regulations revoke and replace the provisions governing factories and workshops, offices and shops and agricultural units set out in the previous edition of this work,[66] and are enforceable under the Health and Safety at Work etc. Act 1974.[67] Contravention of the regulations is an offence.[68] Inspectors appointed by the enforcing authority have powers of entry and to serve improvement and prohibition notices.[69]

(iii) Food premises

Premises of the type discussed in this paragraph may also be workplaces, in which case they will be subject to the provisions discussed in the previous paragraph; otherwise, if they do not fall within the scope of the 1992 Regulations and they form part of a building, they will be subject to the normal provisions of section 64 of the 1984 Act and section 45 of the 1936 Act. Apart from these, there are also requirements imposed to safeguard food hygiene.

The Food Safety (General Food Hygiene) Regulations 1995,[70] made under section 16 of the Food Safety Act 1990, require the proprietor of a "food business"[71] to ensure that specified operations concerning food are carried out in a hygienic way, and that "rules of hygiene" specified in Schedule 1 to the regulations are complied with. These include for "food premises"[72] requirements that "an adequate number of flush lavatories must be available and connected to an effective drainage system. Lavatories must not lead directly into rooms in which food is handled." Furthermore, "all sanitary conveniences within food premises shall be provided with adequate natural or mechanical ventilation."[73]

---

[66] pp.178-181, 183-184.
[67] As "Health and safety regulations" under s.15 of the 1974 Act, they are "relevant statutory provisions" as defined in s.53(1) and so enforceable in accordance with s.18.
[68] 1974 Act, s.33; and see further ss.34-42.
[69] *Ibid.*, ss.19-26.
[70] S.I. 1995 No. 1763.
[71] As defined in Reg. 2(1).
[72] Except moveable or temporary premises, which must just have "hygienic sanitary arrangements".
[73] Sch. 1, paras. 3, 6.

These regulations are enforceable by the "food authority".[74] In an extreme case the court may make a prohibition order under the Food Safety Act 1990.[75] A number of activities are exempted from the General Food Hygiene Regulations and are dealt with under specific regulations,[76] where the enforcement authority may be the Minister of Agriculture or the Secretary of State for Wales rather than the food authority. For example, the Fresh Meat (Hygiene and Inspection) Regulations 1995[77] provide that slaughterhouses must be provided with "sanitary conveniences, separate from any part of the premises which at any time contain fresh meat" and the occupier must cause every sanitary convenience to be kept clean and maintained in efficient working order.[78] The Dairy Products (Hygiene) Regulations 1995[79] require dairy establishments to have changing rooms with flush lavatories either in the room or in the immediate vicinity; the lavatories must not open directly on to work rooms.[80]

(iv) Places of entertainment
Section 20 of the Local Government (Miscellaneous Provisions) Act 1976, replacing section 89 of the 1936 Act, enables a local authority to require the owner or occupier of a "relevant place" to provide sanitary appliances[81] as may be specified by the

---

[74] Food Safety Act 1990, s.6(2); i.e. London borough and district councils, county councils which are unitary authorities, the Common Council of the City of London, and, from 1st April 1996, county and county borough councils in Wales: 1990 Act, s.5, as amended; 1995 Regulations, Reg. 2(1).

[75] Sections 11 and 12.

[76] See the list in the 1995 Regulations, Reg. 3(2).

[77] S.I. 1995 No. 539.

[78] *Ibid.*, Sch. 1, para. 1(k), and Sch. 7, para. 1(m).

[79] S.I. 1995 No. 1086.

[80] *Ibid.*, Sch. 2, para. 1(h).

[81] This means water-closets, other closets, urinals and washbasins: s.20(9). A notice may specify the number and location of the appliances and whether they are to be provided for continuing or occasional use (an occasional notice); in respect of notices requiring continuing rather than occasional provision there is a right of appeal to the County Court under s.21 of the 1976 Act. Under subsection (10) a duty is imposed to bear in mind, so far as is practicable and reasonable, the needs of disabled persons; the notice must alert the owner or occupier to the relevant Regulations and codes of practice; subsections (11)-(13) inserted by the Disabled Persons Act 1981, s.4.

authority, to maintain and clean them to the reasonable satisfaction of the authority, and to make them available for public use, free of charge (if so required). A "relevant place" for this purpose means a betting shop, or any place (including a building) normally used for public entertainment, exhibitions, or sporting events, or for the sale of food or drink to members of the public, or any place occasionally used for any of those purposes. It is an offence to fail to comply with the specifications contained in a notice served by the authority under this section unless there is a reasonable excuse for the non-compliance. It is a defence to prove that the alleged offence is in respect of an unreasonable requirement in an occasional notice, or that it would have been fairer to serve such a notice on some other person whose name and address was supplied by the defendant.

(v) Theatres and cinemas

Licences for the use of premises for the public performance of plays may be granted by the "licensing authority" under the Theatres Act 1968.[82] They may contain restrictions on any topic other than the nature of the plays or the manner of performing plays presented at the premises; therefore, presumably, restrictions could regulate the provision of public conveniences.[83]

By way of contrast it does not seem that councils when acting as licensing authorities under the Cinemas Act 1985 have any powers to impose conditions in cinema licences as to sanitary conveniences.[84]

THE REPLACEMENT OF EXISTING CLOSETS

Under section 66 of the 1984 Act, provided the building has a sufficient water supply and sewer available,[85] the local authority

---

[82] Section 16, as amended by the Local Government Act 1972, s.204. The "licensing authority" is the district or London borough council or the Common Council of the City of London or, from 1st April 1996, county or county borough councils in Wales: s.18(1), as amended.

[83] Theatres Act 1968, s.1(2) and First Schedule.

[84] See Home Office Circular 150/1955.

[85] See definition in s.125 of the 1984 Act, *supra*, pp.214-215.

may[86] by notice[87] require the owner of a building to substitute a water-closet[88] for a closet[89] of any other type. Alternatively, the notice may require the owner to permit the local authority to execute the works of replacement.

This power may be exercised even where the closets are not insufficient in number or prejudicial to health or a nuisance.[90] If the owner executes the work himself he is entitled to recover from the local authority one-half of any expenses he reasonably incurs. Similarly, where the authority itself executes the work, it may recover from the owner an amount not exceeding one-half of its reasonable expenses incurred in doing the work.[91]

In so far as the expenses of the authority are recoverable, they will be recoverable as a civil debt, and will be a charge on the property[92] but, on any appeal under section 102 of the 1984 Act, the necessity of the works cannot be called into question.[93]

SUPPLEMENTARY PROVISIONS

Sections 48 to 52 (inclusive) of the Act of 1936 contain a variety of supplementary provisions designed to promote the main

---

[86] The power is optional, not a mandatory duty similar to those imposed by s.44 of the 1936 Act and s.64 of the 1984 Act. The authority should not issue a notice automatically because of a blanket policy but exercise its discretion in each case: see *Wood v Widnes Corporation* [1898] 1 Q.B. 463.

[87] The notice must be in writing, signed by the authorised officer of the authority, and duly served (see ss.99 to 102 of the 1984 Act). Shaw's Form PH11A is appropriate. The form of notice must state the effect of subsection (3): see s.66(2).

[88] In any such case action should be taken under s.45 of the 1936 Act, *supra*.

[89] ". . . provided for, or in connection with, the building"; and see definition in s.126, *supra*, pp.213-214.

[90] *Ante*, p.199.

[91] See s.66(3). Similarly, where the owner of a building, on his own initiative and without receiving any notice from the local authority, proposes to provide a water-closet for the building in substitution for a closet of some other type, the authority may (if it thinks fit) agree to bear half his expenses incurred in such replacement (see s.66(4)). In this case there need not be a water supply and sewer "available".

[92] Section 66(5) and s.107, and see *post*, Chapter 11, p.240.

[93] Section 66(5)(a).

controls over the conditions of sanitary equipment already discussed in this chapter.

(a) Overflowing and leaking cesspools[94]

If the contents of any cesspool[95] soak away or overflow, the local authority may require[96] the person responsible[97] to execute such works or take such steps[98] as may be necessary for preventing the soakage or overflow.[99]

In so far as the notice requires work to be executed, in any case of default, the authority may execute the work, and recover its reasonable expenses[100] from the person in default.[101] However, in so far as the notice requires other steps to be taken, any person who defaults is liable to a fine.[102]

(b) Offences

The following matters are offences under this part of the 1936 Act:

    (i) The occupation, or the permitting of occupation, of a room, in contravention of section 49(1), after seven days' notice[103] from the local authority prohibiting such occupation.

---

[94] 1936 Act, s.50.

[95] See definition in s.90(1), *supra*, p.213.

[96] By notice: this must be in writing, signed by the authorised officer of the authority, and duly served (see ss.283 to 285 of the 1936 Act). Shaw's Form PN23 is appropriate.

[97] "... the person by whose act, default or sufferance the soakage or overflow occurred or continued ..."

[98] By periodically emptying the cesspool or otherwise.

[99] The subsection does not, however, apply to the effluent from a properly constructed tank for the reception and treatment of sewage, if the effluent is of such a character, and is so carried away and disposed of, as not to be prejudicial to health or a nuisance.

[100] A reasonable sum by way of establishment expenses may be added to this figure: see Local Government Act 1974, s.36.

[101] See ss.50(2) and 290, and *post*, Chapter 11, pp.238-240.

[102] See s.50(3), as amended by the Criminal Justice Act 1982.

[103] This notice must be in writing, signed by the authorised officer of the authority, and duly served (see ss.283 to 285 of the 1936 Act).

This section provides that a "room which or any part of which, is immediately over a closet,[104] other than a water-closet or earth-closet,[104] or immediately over a cesspool,[104] midden or ashpit,[105] shall not be occupied as a living room, sleeping room or workroom."

(ii) Failing to cause the flushing apparatus of a water-closet[106] to be kept supplied with water sufficient for flushing or, where necessary, to be properly protected against frost or, in the case of an earth-closet,[107] failing to cause it to be kept supplied with dry earth or other suitable deodorising material.[108]

The only person who may be charged with an offence under this provision is the occupier of the building[109] in, or in connection with, which the closet in question is provided.

Sometimes the facts of a particular case may fall within both this section and section 45, but it is suggested that in such a case the machinery of this section should be used.

(iii) Where a sanitary convenience is used in common by the members of two or more families,[110] there may be an offence[111] if

---

104 See definition in s.90(1), *supra*, p.213.
105 These expressions are not defined in the Act.
106 See definition in s.90(1), *supra*, p.213.
107 *Ibid.*
108 Section 51.
109 The section applies to all types of buildings: shops, factories, etc. not being excluded.
110 This term is not defined in the Act, but for the purposes of the Rent Acts has been widely construed as a popular rather than a technical term; it does not mean the same as household; nor is it restricted to cases of a *familial nexus* in a strict legal sense though it requires a *de facto familial nexus* recognisable as such by the ordinary man (see e.g. *Price v Gould* (1930) 143 L.T. 333, *Brock v Wollams* [1949] 2 All E.R. 715, and *Carega Properties S.A. v Sharrat* [1979] 1 W.L.R. 928).
111 1936 Act, s.52.

    (a) "any person injures or improperly fouls the convenience, or anything used in connection therewith, or wilfully or by negligence causes an obstruction in the drain[112] therefrom";[113] *or*

    (b) "the convenience, or the approach thereto, is, for want of proper cleansing or attention, in such a condition as to be insanitary"; in any such case such of the persons having the use thereof in common as are in default or, in the absence of satisfactory proof as to which of them is in default, each of them, will be liable.[114]

It seems that action can be taken against any person who acts contrary to the terms of paragraph (a) even if he or she is not a member of the two or more families using the convenience.

(c) Power to examine drains, etc.

Section 48 of the 1936 Act[115] gives the local authority power to examine the condition of a sanitary convenience, drain, private sewer or cesspool.[116] For this purpose the authority may apply a test[117] and, if it deems it necessary, open the ground. However, this power does not extend to a drain or private sewer connecting with a public sewer.[118] A local authority may delegate this function (as in the case of other functions) to one of its officers.[119]

The power may be exercised only in the following

---

[112] Obstruction of a sewer is not, apparently, within this offence.

[113] The fine in respect of such an offence may not exceed level 1 on the standard scale (1936 Act, s.52, as amended by the Criminal Justice Act 1982).

[114] Again the fine may not exceed level 1 on the standard scale, but there is a further fine not exceeding 25p for each day on which the offence continues after conviction (*ibid*).

[115] As amended by the Water Consolidation (Consequential Provisions) Act 1991, Sch. 1, para. 2(1), Sch. 3, Pt. I.

[116] See definition in s.90(1), *supra*, p.213.

[117] Other than a test by water under pressure.

[118] 1991 Act, Sch. 1, para. 2(1).

[119] Section 101 of the Local Government Act 1972.

circumstances:[120]

(i) the sanitary convenience, drain, private sewer or cesspool is in such a condition as to be prejudicial to health or a nuisance; *or*

(ii) a drain or private sewer communicating indirectly with a public sewer is so defective as to admit subsoil water.

The power will be enforceable by use of the right of entry given by section 287 of the Act.[121] However, once on the land the authority must be careful to act within the powers of the section or within the terms of any agreement with the landowner or other interested person.

If the convenience or drain, etc. is found on examination to be in a proper condition, the authority must, as soon as possible, reinstate any ground which has been opened and make good any damage done by it;[122] there is no provision made in the section enabling it to recover its expenses in so doing. Even if the convenience or drain, etc. is found not to be in a proper condition, the expenses incurred in the examination, etc. cannot be recovered.

A power in similar terms is conferred on sewerage undertakers in respect of drains and private sewers connecting with public sewers, by section 114 of the Water Industry Act 1991.

---

[120] And where the authority, or possibly a local authority officer acting under delegated powers, considers there are reasonable grounds for believing these circumstances exist.

[121] See Chapter 11, *post*, pp.236-237.

[122] 1936 Act, s.48(2).

Chapter 11

PROCEDURES

INTRODUCTORY

Whilst it is not the object of this book to provide a commentary on all the many statutory provisions relevant to sewerage services, or to take the place, so far as public health legislation is concerned, of the standard works on the procedure in Magistrates' Courts,[1] it is considered desirable that a brief summary should be included of those procedural provisions which are common to the preceding chapters, and to which reference has been made in the footnotes and the text.

In general, separate procedural regimes apply to (a) local authorities, exercising powers under the Public Health Acts 1936 and 1961 and the Building Act 1984; and (b) sewerage undertakers exercising powers under the Water Industry Act 1991. However, some provisions of the 1936 Act are expressly applied under the 1991 Act.

STATUTORY NOTICES

(a) Under the Public Health Act 1936[2] and the Building Act 1984[3]

Where the local authority is required to give a notice to a person under the 1936 or 1984 Acts, this must be in writing,[4] and it must

---

[1] Such, for example, as *Stone's Justices' Manual*, to which reference should be made in any case of difficulty.

[2] The relevant provisions of the 1936 Act also apply for the purposes of the 1961 Act.

[3] The rules as to the form of, and persons to be served with, abatement notices under the statutory nuisance provisions of Part III of the Environmental Protection Act 1990 are found within those sections: see *ante*, pp.198-201. As to the methods of service, see the 1990 Act, s.160.

[4] See s.283(1) of the 1936 Act and s.92 of the 1984 Act. "Writing" includes other modes of representing or reproducing words in a visible form: Interpretation Act 1978, s.5, Sch. 1.

be signed by an officer of the authority who has been duly authorised (either generally or specifically) by the authority.[5] A local authority may arrange for any of its functions to be discharged by a committee, a sub-committee, one of its officers, or by another local authority.[6]

(i) Person to be served

It is the duty of the authority to select the appropriate person on whom the notice is to be served. If the wrong person is served, he will be entitled to appeal as a "person aggrieved",[7] and the court may quash the notice.[8] Information as to the ownership, etc. of property may be obtained by serving a requisition for information,[9] and it is made an offence for any person on whom such a requisition may be served[10] either to fail to give such information, or knowingly to make a misstatement in respect thereof.[11]

(ii) Methods of service

The methods of service of notices are prescribed by section 285 of the 1936 Act and the similarly although not identically worded section 94 of the 1984 Act,[12] and one or other of the

---

5   See the 1936 Act, s.284(1), and definition in s.343(1) and the 1984 Act, s.93. A printed signature is sufficient (s.284(2) and s.93(3)), and so is a rubber stamp, provided it is affixed by an authorised officer: *Goodman v J. Eban Ltd.* [1954] 1 Q.B. 550, and *Plymouth City Corporation v Hurrell* [1968] 1 Q.B. 455.

6   Local Government Act 1972, s.101, but this does not authorise delegation to a *single* member of the authority.

7   See s.290(3)(e), (f) of the 1936 Act and s.102(e), (f) of the 1984 Act.

8   *Croydon Corporation v Thomas* [1947] K.B. 386. As to the meaning of "owner", see the 1936 Act, s.343(1) and the 1984 Act, s.126(1), and *post*, pp.248-249.

9   Shaw's Form ML33 or ML33A is useful for this purpose.

10 Only the occupier of premises, or any person who either directly or indirectly receives rent in respect of the premises, may be asked to supply the required information, and the only information obtainable by this method is "the nature of his [the informant's] interest therein [the premises] and the name and address of any other person known to him as having an interest therein, whether as freeholder, mortgagee, lessee or otherwise".

11 See Local Government (Miscellaneous Provisions) Act 1976, s.16(2).

12 As to the references in s.94 of the 1984 Act to service by post, see s.7 of the Interpretation Act 1978.

methods there stated must be followed strictly (unless actual service can be proved to have been effected by some other means); however, subject to compliance with the terms of the relevant section,[13] it seems that the authority is not bound to adopt any particular one of these possible methods of service in any specific instance.[14] The methods prescribed in these sections apply equally to a summons, as they do to other "documents" served under the relevant Act.[15]

(iii) Form of notice

Apart from the requirement that the notice must be in writing and duly signed,[16] the notice need not follow any particular form, as the Secretary of State has not used his power to prescribe the forms to be used for these purposes.[17] Nevertheless, the notice should follow as nearly as practicable the wording of the appropriate section, and the notice may be quashed by the court if it is satisfied that there has been some "informality, defect or error in, or in connection with, the notice",[18] unless it is also satisfied that such error, etc. was not a material one.[19] It is also important, where the notice is one requiring the execution of works, that the time within which the works are required to be completed, should be reasonable,[20] and the nature of the works required should be clearly stated.[21] Where there is a right to appeal against the notice this must be stated on the notice.[22]

---

[13] For example, if the notice is to be affixed "to some conspicuous part of the premises", there must be no person there to whom it can be delivered.

[14] See *Woodford U.D.C. v Henwood* (1899) 64 J.P. 148.

[15] See e.g. *R. v Braithwaite* [1918] 2 K.B. 319.

[16] See above, pp.232-233.

[17] See s.283(2) of the 1936 Act; s.93(2) of the 1984 Act.

[18] Section 290(3)(b) of the 1936 Act; s.102(1), (5) of the 1984 Act.

[19] Section 290(4) of the 1936 Act; s.102(2) of the 1984 Act.

[20] Section 290(3)(d).

[21] Section 290(2) of the 1936 Act; s.99(1) of the 1984 Act. *Perry v Garner* [1953] 1 Q.B. 335.

[22] Section 66(2) of the 1984 Act requires the purport of that section also to be set out. On the general principle, see s.300(3), and *Rayner v Stepney Corporation* [1911] 2 Ch. 312, also *Nalder v Ilford Corporation* [1951] 1 K.B. 822.

(b) Under the Water Industry Act 1991

By section 219(1) of the Water Industry Act 1991, the term "notice" in the Act means "notice in writing". The Secretary of State may prescribe the forms of any notice or other documents to be used for the purposes of the "relevant sewerage provisions".[23] Sewerage undertakers are not given powers requiring the execution of works and so there are no general provisions corresponding to section 290 of the Public Health Act 1936.[24] There is also no express provision governing the authentication of documents corresponding to section 284 of the 1936 Act. Service of documents under the 1991 Act is governed by section 216, which, in accordance with a recommendation of the Law Commission,[25] applies to all the provisions in the water legislation consolidation. Any document required or authorised by the 1991 Act to be served on any person may be served

"(a) by delivering it to him or by leaving it at his proper address or by sending it by post to him at that address; or

(b) if the person is a body corporate, by serving it in accordance with paragraph (a) above on the secretary or clerk of that body; or

(c) if the person is a partnership, by serving it in accordance with paragraph (a) above on a partner or a person having the control of management of the partnership business."

For the purposes of this section, and section 7 of the Interpretation Act 1978 (which relates to the service of documents by post) in its application to this section, the proper address of any person on whom a document is to be served is his last known address. However, in the case of (b) and (c) above, it is, respectively, the address of the registered or principal office of the body corporate

---

23   1991 Act, s.214. This power has not been exercised.
24   *Ante*, pp.232, 233.
25   *Report on the Consolidation of the Legislation relating to Water*, Cm. 1483, 1991, Recommendation No. 14.

or the principal office of the partnership.[26] A person may specify another address as the proper address. Where any document is to be served on the owner, or a lessee or on the occupier of any premises, then if that person's name and address cannot be ascertained after reasonable enquiry or, in the case of service on the occupier, if the premises appear to be or are unoccupied, the document may be served either by leaving it in the hands of a person who is or appears to be resident or employed on the land, or by leaving it conspicuously affixed to some building or object on the land.

POWERS OF ENTRY

(a) Under the Public Health Act 1936 and the Building Act 1984

A local authority may authorise in writing any of its officers[27] to exercise the power of entry on premises given by section 287 of the 1936 Act and sections 95 and 96 of the 1984 Act. 24 hours' notice[28] – at least – must be given of the intention to exercise this power, and it may be exercised only at reasonable hours. The power is exercisable only for the purposes listed in the section,[29] and the officer exercising the power must, if required, produce a duly authenticated document showing his authority.

If the authorised officer is obstructed in endeavouring to exercise this power of entry, he may not use force, but must (if necessary) apply for a warrant to a justice of the peace and, if this warrant is issued, force, but only the minimum

---

[26] The principal office in the UK of a company registered or a partnership carrying on business outside the UK.

[27] See definition of "authorised officer" in s.343(1), which in an amended form is found in s.126 of the 1984 Act. See also s.127 of the 1984 Act.

[28] Except in the case of a factory or workplace: s.287(1), proviso. The notice must be in writing, signed and duly served: Shaw's Forms PH70A (for the 1936 Act) or PH70 (for the 1984 Act) are appropriate.

[29] See s.287(1) of the 1936 Act; s.95(1) of the 1984 Act; see, in particular, the power to enter "for the purpose of the performance by the council of their functions under this Act", or any byelaws made under the 1936 Act.

necessary, may then be used.[30]

(b) By sewerage undertakers

A sewerage undertaker may under the Water Industries Act 1991 authorise a person in writing to enter premises for a number of purposes:

(a) to carry out any survey or tests to determine whether it is appropriate and practicable for the undertaker to exercise any "relevant works power",[31] or how any such power should be exercised, or to exercise any such power;[32]

(b) to ascertain whether there is or has been, on or in connection with the premises, any contravention of the "relevant sewerage provisions"[33] which it is the undertaker's function to enforce; or to ascertain whether circumstances exist which would authorise or require the undertaker to take any action or carry out any works under the relevant sewerage provisions; or to take action or carry out works authorised by or under the relevant sewerage provisions to be taken or carried out by the undertaker; or "generally for the purpose of carrying out the undertaker's functions under the relevant sewerage provisions";[34]

---

[30] See s.287(2); he must be able to show that the statutory procedure has been strictly observed: *Stroud v Bradbury* [1952] 2 All E.R. 76. It is an offence wilfully to obstruct an officer in the exercising of his powers: 1936 Act, s.298; 1984 Act, s.112.

[31] i.e. any powers conferred by ss.158 (power to lay pipes in streets), 159 (power to lay pipes in other land), 161 (power to deal with foul water and pollution), 163 (water undertaker's power to fit stopcocks) and 165 (discharge for works purposes by water undertakers).

[32] 1991 Act, s.168.

[33] i.e. (a) Chapters II and III of Part IV (except ss.98 to 101 and 110 and so much of Chapter III as provides for regulations under s.138 or has effect by virtue of any such regulations); (b) ss.160, 171, 172(4), 178, 184, 189, 196 and 204 and Sch. 12, para. 4; and (c) the other provisions of the Act so far as they have effect for the purposes of (a) and (b): s.219(1).

[34] 1991 Act, s.171(1). There is an associated power to take samples of trade effluent: s.171(3)-(6).

(c) to carry out surveys, tests, works or inspections in relation to metering, where the conditions in section $162(1)^{35}$ are satisfied.[36]

The impersonation of persons entitled to entry is an offence.[37] The detailed provisions regulating the rights of entry under (b) above are set out in Schedule 6, Part I; those regulating rights of entry under (a) and (c) are found in Schedule 6, Part II. Generally speaking, under Part I, 24 hours' notice of intended entry to any premises which are not business premises must be given to the occupier; a warrant to enter, if need be by force, may be obtained from a JP in defined circumstances (e.g. if entry is refused or if the case is one of urgency); obstruction of persons exercising a right of entry is an offence. Under Part II, no entry can be made except in an emergency, or at a reasonable time and after the required notice[38] of intended entry has been given to the occupier; and there are similar provisions governing warrants and offences of obstruction.

THE ENFORCEMENT OF STATUTORY NOTICES

In most cases, notices served under the Public Health Act 1936 and the Building Act 1984 are enforceable by the authority, which is empowered to act itself in default of compliance with the terms of the notice by the person on whom the notice is served; in a few cases,[39] the notice is enforceable only by means of proceedings taken against the person in default.[40]

(a) Recovery of expenses

Where the local authority is authorised by either of the Acts of 1936[41] or 1984 to execute works in default of compliance with

---

35 *Ante*, p.115.
36 1991 Act, s.172.
37 *Ibid.*, s.173.
38 Seven days' notice, in respect of sewerage undertakers.
39 e.g. ss.49, 51 and 52 of the 1936 Act.
40 See *post*, p.240.
41 Or the Public Health Act 1961.

the terms of a statutory notice, it is provided[42] that the authority may recover the expenses from the party in default.[43] These expenses must, however, have been reasonably incurred, and the work executed must not exceed that specified in the statutory notice. The expenses actually incurred may, however, be increased by a reasonable sum by way of establishment expenses.[44]

The expenses are recoverable by serving a demand,[45] and interest on the sum demanded will run as from the date of the demand.[46] The authority may also declare any sum so due to them to be repayable by instalments (with interest[47]), over a period not exceeding thirty years.[47]

Any sum which a local authority is entitled to recover under either Act may be recovered as a simple contract debt in any court of competent jurisdiction.[48] The ordinary six years' time limit for actions in contract applies,[49] the period running from the date of demand. There is no time limit within which the demand must be served, and it seems that there is no reason why a fresh demand should not be served at any time; certainly this is so where there has been a change of owner.[50]

In cases where the person responsible for the payment of the authority's expenses is the owner of the premises, those expenses

---

42 This applies to notices served under ss.45 and 50 of the 1936 Act and ss.18, 59, 60, 64 and 65 of the 1984 Act (and other provisions with which this book is not concerned).
43 See 1936 Act, s.290(6); 1984 Act, s.99(2)(a). The liability of a mere agent or trustee is limited to the total amount of money he has in his hands on behalf of his principal: s.294 of the 1936 Act; s.110 of the 1984 Act.
44 Local Government Act 1974, s.36.
45 This must be in writing, signed by the authorised officer of the authority, and duly served, in accordance with ss.283 to 285 of the 1936 Act; ss.92 to 94 of the 1984 Act.
46 1936 Act, s.291(1), (3); 1984 Act. s.107(1), (3).
47 1936 Act, s.291(2); 1984 Act, s.108.
48 1936 Act, s.293; 1984 Act, s.107(4).
49 Limitation Act 1980, s.5.
50 *Dennerley v Prestwich U.D.C.* [1930] 1 K.B. 334.

become a charge on the property,[51] and the authority has all the powers and remedies given by section 121 of the Law of Property Act 1925 (including a power of sale) for the enforcement of such charge.[52] The charge should be registered in the local land charges register[53] but, if the same is not so registered, or if a charge is not disclosed on an official certificate of the result of search, the charge will still be enforceable against a purchaser of the land affected. Any person who can prove he has suffered loss in consequence will be able to claim compensation from the registration authority.[54] In any case the local authority could always demand payment of the expenses from the "owner for the time being" of the premises.[55]

(b) Prosecutions

In addition to specific offences created in the various sections of any of the relevant Acts, the failure to comply with a statutory notice to which section 290 of the Public Health Act 1936 or sections 99 and 102 of the Building Act 1984 applies, is itself made an offence,[56] and in addition to its right to execute works in default, the authority may prosecute for an offence under the section.

All offences under these statutes may be prosecuted summarily,[57] but proceedings may be commenced only by the local authority concerned, or by a "party aggrieved";[58] any other person who

---

51   1936 Act, s.291(1); 1984 Act, s.107(1).
52   1936 Act, s.291(4); 1984 Act, s.107(2). The charge must be enforced within 12 years (Limitation Act 1980, s.20) of the date when the works were completed (see *Hornsey Local Board v Monarch Investment Building Society* (1889) 24 Q.B.D. 1).
53   Maintained under the Local Land Charges Act 1975 (as amended). This charge should be registered in Part II of the register (see the Local Land Charges Rules 1977 (S.I. 1977 No. 985), as amended).
54   Local Land Charges Act 1975, s.10.
55   See e.g. s.291(2).
56   By s.290(6) of the 1936 Act and s.99 of the 1984 Act.
57   1936 Act, s.296; 1984 Act, ss.35, 61(3), 62(4)(5), 63(1), 68(2), 96(3), 112.
58   1936 Act, s.298; 1984 Act, s.113. For an illustration of the use of the term "party aggrieved" in this context, see e.g. *Sheffield Corporation v Kitson* [1929] 2 K.B. 322.

wishes to commence proceedings may do so only with the written consent of the Attorney-General.[59] Where a local authority is taking proceedings, it must be shown that the officer (or possibly, the member) who lays the information in its name has been authorised so to do either generally or specially.[60]

It may be considered appropriate in some prosecutions to use the summary trial procedure of the Magistrates' Courts Act 1980, which enables the accused to plead guilty by post, thereby saving him time and (much more important) making it possible for the prosecution to dispense in advance with the attendance of witnesses in court. Where it is decided to use this procedure, special documents, giving notice of the effect of section 12 of the 1980 Act, and summarising the facts relating to the charge, in the prescribed forms, have to be served upon the accused with the summons. As none of the offences here considered are triable on indictment, and usually are not punishable with a term of imprisonment exceeding three months, the 1980 Act procedure may be applied in any such case (see section 12(1) thereof). However, the authority may on occasion consider that the additional publicity that may result from an oral hearing is to be preferred to the saving of time which results from the 1980 Act procedure; moreover, even when this procedure is used, the accused may not wish to plead guilty, or if he does he may prefer to attend court and explain his conduct in person.

The maximum fine under section 290(6) of the 1936 Act and section 99(2) of the Building Act 1984 is at level 4 on the standard scale 4 (currently £2,500) with a further fine not exceeding £2 for each day on which the default continues after conviction. Where provision is made for the imposition of a daily penalty in respect of a continuing offence, the court may fix a reasonable period for compliance, after which the daily penalty is to come into effect.[61]

---

[59] As to the proof of any such consent having been given, see s.26 of the Prosecution of Offences Act 1985.

[60] *Bob Keats Ltd. v Farrant* [1951] 1 All E.R. 899.

[61] 1936 Act, s.297; 1984 Act, s.114.

Prosecutions under the Water Industry Act 1991 in respect of sewerage offences[62] may not, without the written consent of the Attorney-General, be taken by any person other than a "party aggrieved",[63] a sewerage undertaker, or a body whose function it is to enforce the provisions in question.[64] Where a body corporate is guilty of an offence under the Water Industry Act 1991 or the Water Resources Act 1991, and the offence is proved to have been committed with the consent or connivance of, or to be attributable to any neglect on the part of, any director, manager, secretary or other similar officer of the body corporate or any person who was purporting to act in such a capacity, then he, as well as the body corporate, can be prosecuted for the offence.[65] Where the affairs of a body corporate are managed by its members, this applies in relation to the acts and defaults of a member in connection with his functions of management as if he were a director.[66] In the case of prosecutions under the "water pollution provisions"[67] of the Water Resources Act 1991, where the commission of an offence by any person is due to the act or default of some other person, the latter person may be prosecuted whether or not proceedings are taken against the former.[68]

APPEALS AND APPLICATIONS TO THE COURT

Various sections of the 1936 Act provide for a person aggrieved to appeal to the local Magistrates' Court against a notice or other requirement under the Act. In many cases where the 1936 Act empowers a local authority to serve a notice requiring action to be taken, it is also provided that the provisions of Part XII of the Act shall apply thereto,[69] and in that event a right of appeal is

---

[62] i.e. offences under the "relevant sewerage provisions": see *ante*, p.237.
[63] See *ante*, p.240.
[64] Water Industry Act 1991, s.211.
[65] *Ibid.*, s.210(1); Water Resources Act 1991, s.217(1).
[66] *Ibid.*, ss.210(2), 217(2).
[67] i.e. the 1991 Act, Part III (ss.82-104); ss.161, 190, 202, 203 and 213(2); Sch. 25, para. 4 and s.211 so far as it relates to byelaws made under para. 4: s.221(1).
[68] Section 217(3).
[69] For example, ss.45 and 50 of the 1936 Act; 1984 Act, s.114.

given by section 290, and a number of grounds of appeal are therein specified.[70] In some cases further special grounds of appeal are provided for in the particular section itself.[71] Also, in a number of cases,[72] the Act may provide for a particular matter or question to be determined, in case of dispute, by a Magistrates' Court. In any such case, the proceedings are commenced by means of a complaint for an order, and the provisions of the Magistrates' Courts Act 1980 will apply to such proceedings.[73] Once an appeal has been lodged against a notice, the local authority cannot withdraw the notice without the consent of the person(s) on whom it was served.[74]

In any case of an appeal, proceedings must be commenced within 21 days of the notice or determination, etc. appealed against,[75] but this time limit does not apply to an application to the court for it to determine a matter;[76] in the latter event the time limit of six months provided for in section 127 of the Magistrates' Courts Act 1980 will be applicable.[77]

Unless the case is one which the parties might have referred to arbitration as an alternative to a reference to the court,[78] there is a right of appeal to the Crown Court from the decision of the Magistrates' Court.[79] However, this right is given only to a "person aggrieved". A local authority may be a "person aggrieved" where a decision adverse to it is given in an area where it is required to perform public duties; it is not necessary

---

70 See also s.102 of the 1984 Act, in similar terms, which applies to notices served under the Act.
71 For example, ss.64(4) and 66(5) of the 1984 Act.
72 For example, s.62(2) of the 1984 Act.
73 Section 103(1)(b).
74 *R. v Cannock Justices, ex p. Astbury* (1972) 70 L.G.R. 609.
75 See e.g. ss.45 and 50 of the 1936 Act incorporating s.290(3), and s.300(2) of that Act and e.g. s.103(2) of the 1984 Act.
76 For example, 1984 Act, s.103(2).
77 *Nalder v Ilford Corporation* [1951] 1 K.B. 822.
78 See e.g. s.21(6) of the 1984 Act; where the matter is determined by arbitration, the Arbitration Act 1950 and the Arbitration Act 1979 will apply to the proceedings: see ss.31(1) and 7(1) thereof respectively.
79 Section 301 of the 1936 Act and s.86 of the 1984 Act.

that a legal burden has been placed on the authority by the adverse decision of the Magistrates' Court.[80] Alternatively, either party may ask the magistrates to state a case for the opinion of the High Court on a point of law[81] and, in the event of their refusing to do so, they may be ordered to state a case by an order of *mandamus*.[82] The Crown Court also may be asked to state a case but, in a non-criminal matter, *mandamus* will not lie against it in the event of refusal.[82]

Where proceedings are taken in the County Court (e.g. for recovery of the authority's expenses as a simple contract debt), an appeal lies to the Court of Appeal.[83]

In any proceedings, a copy of a resolution of the local authority concerned or of the appointment of, or of an authority given to, any officer of the authority, which is certified by the proper officer of the authority, is admissible in evidence.[84]

Powers to appear in legal proceedings (either as plaintiffs or defendants) are given to a local authority by the Local Government Act 1972, which also enable it to authorise one of its officers (or even one of its members) to conduct the proceedings on its behalf, although he may not be of counsel or a solicitor.[85]

CLAIMS FOR COMPENSATION

Under section 278 of the 1936 Act, a local authority must pay "full compensation" to any person who has sustained damage by reason of the exercise by the authority of any of its powers under the 1936 Act or those provisions of the Act of 1961 incorporated therewith.[86] This liability to pay compensation does not, however,

---

[80] *Cook v Southend Borough Council* [1990] 2 Q.B. 1.

[81] Magistrates' Courts Act 1980, s.111.

[82] *R. v Somerset JJ., ex p. Ernest J. Cole & Partners Ltd.* [1950] 1 K.B. 519.

[83] County Courts Act 1984, s.77; County Courts Appeal Order 1991 (S.I. 1991 No. 1877), as amended.

[84] Local Government (Miscellaneous Provisions) Act 1976, s.41.

[85] Local Government Act 1972, ss.222 and 223: and see *ante*, p.236.

[86] Shaw's Form PN57 is appropriate.

apply in the following circumstances:

(a) Where the claimant himself has been in default.[87]

(b) In respect of action which the authority is under a duty to undertake, as distinct from a power. This is, however, to be construed strictly, and compensation is payable, for example, in respect of damage caused in the exercise of a power which is itself ancillary to a duty.

(c) The right to claim under the section lies only where no action for damages can be brought.[88] Thus, where a sewer was laid through the claimant's land in a negligent manner, thereby causing special damage, it was held that he had an action against the authority responsible, and that his remedy did not lie under the statute.[89]

Any dispute as to the amount of compensation payable under this section is to be determined by arbitration,[90] unless the claim does not exceed £50, in which event the matter may, on the application of either party, be referred to the local Magistrates' Court.[91] Similar provision is made under the Building Act 1984,[92] and in respect of damage caused by a sewerage undertaker in the exercise of powers under the relevant sewerage provisions.[93] Rights to compensation may also arise under certain provisions of the Water Industry Act 1991.[94]

---

[87] Section 278(1): see *Hobbs v Winchester Corporation* [1910] 2 K.B. 471; *Place v Rawtenstall Corporation* (1916) 86 L.J.K.B. 90.

[88] But no claim will lie in respect of acts lawful under the ordinary law apart from the statute: see e.g. *Hall v Bristol Corporation* (1876) L.R. 2 C.P. 322.

[89] *Brine v G.W. Rlwy. Co.* (1862) 2 B.&S. 402; *Clothier v Webster* (1862) 6 L.T. 461.

[90] As prescribed by s.303, below.

[91] Section 278(2).

[92] Section 106.

[93] Water Industry Act 1991, Sch. 12, para. 4, as amended by the Competition and Service (Utilities) Act 1992, Sch. 2, paras. 30, 31. As to the "relevant sewerage provisions", see *ante*, p.237.

[94] See pp.75, 80-81 and 106, *ante*.

ARBITRATIONS

As a general rule arbitrations, whether under the 1936 or the 1984 Act, will be conducted before a single arbitrator appointed by agreement between the parties or, in default of agreement, by the Secretary of State.[95] By contrast, claims in respect of the depreciation of a value of an interest in land as a result of the exercise of powers to carry out pipe-laying works, or other loss or damage, fall to be determined by the Lands Tribunal because the amount of the compensation for depreciation is to be determined in accordance with the principles contained in the Land Compensation Act 1961.

APPLICATIONS TO THE SECRETARY OF STATE: LOCAL AUTHORITIES

Under section 322(2) of the 1936 Act,[96] if the Secretary of State is satisfied that a local authority has failed to discharge its functions under the Act in any case where it ought to have done so,[97] the Secretary of State may make an order declaring the authority to be in default, and directing it to discharge its functions.[98] If, within the specified time limit, the authority fails to comply with the Secretary of State's order, he may enforce the order by way of *mandamus* or otherwise, or he may instead make an order transferring the functions to himself.[99]

---

[95] 1936 Act, s.303; 1984 Act, s.111; any such arbitration will be subject to the Arbitration Act 1950 (Part I with certain exceptions) and to the Arbitration Act 1979; s.31(1) of the 1950 Act and s.7(1) of the 1979 Act.

[96] As amended by the Local Government (Miscellaneous Provisions) 1976 Act, ss.27(3)(5)(7), 81(1), Sch. 2 and by the Public Health (Control of Disease) Act 1984, s.78 and Sch. 3. There is no longer express provision for any person to complain to the Minister about the default or for him to hold a local inquiry before exercising his default powers.

[97] See e.g. s.45 of the 1936 Act, *ante* p.219.

[98] The same default powers apply to local authorities in respect of their functions under the Building Act 1984; 1984 Act, s.116: see *ante*, Chapter 9.

[99] 1936 Act, s.322(3); 1984 Act, s.116(2). Under the similarly worded predecessor to s.322 (s.299 of the 1875 Act) it was more usual to resort to *mandamus* than to the alternative of appointing a person to perform the duty: see *R. v Staines Local Board* (1893) 69 L.T. 714; and see *R. v Worcester Corporation* (1905) 69 J.P. 296.

ENFORCEMENT AND SPECIAL ADMINISTRATION ORDERS UNDER THE 1991 ACT

These are considered in Chapter 1.[100]

OTHER PROCEEDINGS

In addition to proceedings provided for under relevant statutes, a private individual may have other forms of redress against a local authority or sewerage undertaker arising out of the exercise by them of their statutory functions. These may be summarised as follows:

(a) Action for damages. This has already been discussed; the main point is that a sewerage undertaker in the exercise of sewerage functions must not create a nuisance.[101]

(b) Action by the Attorney-General at the relation of a private individual for a declaration and/or an injunction. This may be brought where the authority or undertaker is acting *ultra vires*; the remedy sought is discretionary. Where the claim is based on nuisance, a private individual may be able to sue for an injunction without joining the Attorney-General as a party, in circumstances where it can be shown that the plaintiff has sustained special damage.[102]

(c) Proceedings on an application for judicial review[103] seeking *certiorari*, prohibition, an injunction or a declaration, where it can be shown the authority or undertaker has erred in law or has acted unfairly to the prejudice of the applicant, or *mandamus* to require it to perform a statutory duty. Cases where these will lie in the present context are exceptional, but they may arise.

---

[100] See pp.17-21, *ante*.
[101] 1991 Act, s.117(6).
[102] See e.g. *Cook v Bath Corporation* (1868) L.R. 6 Eq. 177 (a highway case).
[103] Under Order 53 of the Rules of the Supreme Court.

RECOVERY OF CHARGES UNDER THE 1991 ACT

Section 142 of the Water Industry Act 1991 confers power upon sewerage undertakers to demand and recover charges fixed pursuant to the Act for the performance of their functions. It is expressly stated by section 142(1)(a) that this power extends to the performance of trade effluent functions.

THE MEANING OF "OWNER"

In many cases under the relevant statutory provisions action falls to be taken by the local authority or sewerage undertaker against the "owner" of the premises concerned. It is, therefore, of importance to appreciate the meaning of this expression as used in the Acts of 1936, 1984 and 1991.

By section 343(1) of the 1936 Act, "owner" is defined as meaning "the person for the time being receiving the rackrent of the premises in connection with which the word is used, whether on his own account or as agent or trustee[104] for any other person, or who would so receive the same if those premises were let at a rackrent." The corresponding similar provisions of the 1984 and 1991 Acts are, respectively, sections 126 and 219(1). "Rackrent" is defined in the section 383 to mean, in relation to any property, "a rent which is not less than two-thirds of the rent at which the property might reasonably be expected to let from year to year, free from all usual tenant's rates and taxes, . . . and deducting therefrom the probable average annual cost of the repairs, insurance and other expenses (if any) necessary to maintain the same in a state to command such rent."[105]

These definitions have been the subject of much case law, which

---

[104] The right to recover expenses incurred by an authority against such an "owner" is strictly limited: see note 43 on p.239.

[105] This is to be computed with reference to conditions at the commencement of the lease: *Borthwick-Norton v Collier* [1950] 2 K.B. 594. "Rackrent" is not defined in s.219(1) of the 1991 Act: see further Recommendation No. 18 of the Law Commission's *Report on the Consolidation of the Legislation relating to Water* (Cm. 1483, 1991).

it is not the province of this book to discuss;[106] but the commonest case causing difficulty is where the property is occupied by a tenant who holds from an intermediate lessor. As a general rule (says Lumley[107]) where there are intermediate lessors, and the rent received by each is the same, the person ultimately receiving the rent is the owner, but where a lessor receives from his lessee more rent than he pays, he is the owner within the definition.

A rent collector or a trustee acting on behalf of the owner in the true sense may be an "owner" within the definition, but the amount that may be recoverable from such an "owner" is limited to what he actually receives,[108] and a mere receiver who can do no more than pay money into the owner's bank account on his behalf, is not an owner within the definition.[109]

In those cases where the section empowers a notice to be served on the owner *or* the occupier[110] of named premises, the authority should exercise care in choosing the most appropriate person in the circumstances, in the light of the information available to it; if the person so chosen considers it would have been equitable for the other party to have been served, this may give him grounds for an appeal to the Magistrates' Court under section 290(3)(f) of the 1936 Act.

---

[106] See e.g. *Lumley's Public Health*, 12th edn., Vol. 3, p.2875 *et seq.*
[107] Vol. 3, p.2875, and cases there cited, especially *Cook v Montagu* (1872) L.R. 7 Q.B. 418, and *Walford v Hackney Board of Works* (1894) 43 W.R. 110.
[108] Section 294 of the 1936 Act. See also s.110 of the 1984 Act, and ss.107(5), 109(3) and 160(2) of the 1991 Act, applying (*inter alia*) s.294 of the 1936 Act.
[109] *Bottomley v Harrison* [1952] 1 All E.R. 369.
[110] As, for example, in certain cases under s.290(3)(f) of the 1936 Act; s.102(1)(f) of the 1984 Act.

APPENDIX

Urban Waste Water Treatment Directive – Implementation Requirements

The following table is reproduced from *Discharge Consent and Compliance: The NRA's Approach to Control of Discharges to Water* (H.M.S.O., 1994 – *Crown Copyright*)

Urban Waste Water Treatment Directive – Implementation Requirements

STW Size	Sensitive Areas			Normal Areas			Less Sensitive Areas	
Population Equivalent	Freshwaters	Estuarine Waters	Coastal Waters	Freshwaters	Estuarine Waters	Coastal Waters	Estuarine Waters	Coastal Waters
	All Areas Identified by end 1993						All Areas Identified by end 1993	
>15,000	Collection Systems by end 1998 Extra Treatment by end 1998	Collection Systems by end 1998 Extra Treatment by end 1998		Collection Systems by end 2000 Secondary Treatment by end 2000	Collection Systems by end 2000 Secondary Treatment by end 2000			Collection Systems by end 2000 Primary Treatment by end 2000
10-15,000	Collection Systems by end 1998 Extra Treatment by end 1998	Collection Systems by end 1998 Extra Treatment by end 1998		Collection Systems by end 2005 Secondary Treatment by end 2005	Collection Systems by end 2005 Secondary Treatment by end 2005			Collection Systems by end 2005 Primary Treatment by end 2005
2-10,000	Collection Systems by end 2005 Secondary Treatment by end 2005	Collection Systems by end 2005 Secondary Treatment by end 2005		Collection Systems by end 2005 Secondary Treatment by end 2005	Collection Systems by end 2005 Secondary Treatment by end 2005		Collection Systems Primary Treatment by end 2005	
<10,000			Appropriate Treatment by end 2005			Appropriate Treatment by end 2005		Appropriate Treatment by end 2005
<2,000	Appropriate Treatment by end 2005			Appropriate Treatment by end 2005			Appropriate Treatment by end 2005	

Sensitive and Less Sensitive Areas to be reviewed at least every four years.
Implementation Programme Reports to be made to the Commission every two years.

[shaded] Category does not apply.

INDEX

255